India Retold

India Retold

Dialogues with Independent Documentary Filmmakers in India

Edited by
Rajesh James and Sathyaraj Venkatesan

BLOOMSBURY ACADEMIC
NEW YORK • LONDON • OXFORD • NEW DELHI • SYDNEY

BLOOMSBURY ACADEMIC
Bloomsbury Publishing Inc
1385 Broadway, New York, NY 10018, USA
50 Bedford Square, London, WC1B 3DP, UK
29 Earlsfort Terrace, Dublin 2, Ireland

BLOOMSBURY, BLOOMSBURY ACADEMIC and the Diana logo are
trademarks of Bloomsbury Publishing Plc

First published in the United States of America 2021
This paperback edition published 2023

Cover design: Namkwan Cho and Eleanor Rose
Cover image: Still from *Tales from Our Childhood* (2018), Director: Mukul Haloi

Library of Congress Cataloging-in-Publication Data

Names: James, Rajesh, author. | Venkatesan, Sathyaraj, author.
Title: India retold: dialogues with independent documentary filmmakers in India /
Rajesh James and Sathyaraj Venkatesan.
Description: New York: Bloomsbury Academic, 2021. | Includes bibliographical
references and index.
Identifiers: LCCN 2021004872 (print) | LCCN 2021004873 (ebook) |
ISBN 9781501352676 (hardback) | ISBN 9781501352683 (ebook) |
ISBN 9781501352690 (pdf)
Subjects: LCSH: Documentary films–India–History and criticism. | Documentary films–
Production and direction–India. | Independent films–India–History and criticism. |
Motion picture producers and directors–India–Interviews.
Classification: LCC PN1995.9.D6 J36 2021 (print) | LCC PN1995.9.D6 (ebook) |
DDC 070.1/80954–dc23
LC record available at https://lccn.loc.gov/2021004872
LC ebook record available at https://lccn.loc.gov/2021004873

ISBN: HB: 978-1-5013-5267-6
PB: 978-1-5013-8015-0
ePDF: 978-1-5013-5269-0
eBook: 978-1-5013-5268-3

Typeset by Deanta Global Publishing Services, Chennai, India

To find out more about our authors and books visit www.bloomsbury.com and
sign up for our newsletters.

Dedicated to tiny tots

Naythan James

~~~~

Taran Sathyaraj

Contents

Acknowledgments

A project of this magnitude would not have been possible without the care of many near and dear ones. First, we would like to express our deepest appreciation to all the interviewed documentary filmmakers who responded to our requests, emails, and long phone calls with patience and thoughtfulness. They have been generous with their time and ideas without which the book would have been impossible. Our special thanks to Gopal Menon, who helped us to network with many filmmakers interviewed in this project. He has been a pillar of support since the beginning of this massive and urgent project. We owe a deep sense of gratitude to Anand Patwardhan, Deepa Dhanraj, Amar Kanwar, Sanjay Kak, and Nishtha Jain, whose keen interest in the project has been a source of immense inspiration. Sincere thanks to Aparna Sharma, Department of World Arts and Cultures, University of California, Los Angeles, for her unstinting support and for readily accepting to write a foreword for the book. Her insightful foreword has made this book richer. Thanks also to Laura Mulvey of Birkbeck, University of London, and Ravi Vasudevan of CSDS, Delhi, for their keen interest in the project and for being generous interlocutors. We are profoundly grateful to the reviewers for their thoughtful critiques and valuable suggestions: Giulia Battaglia of Université Sorbonne Nouvelle (Paris 3), Ashvin Immanuel Devasundaram of Queens Mary, University of London, and Gurumurthy Neelakantan of IIT Kanpur. Thanks to Shweta Kishore of RMIT University for readily sharing her book on independent documentary filmmakers and for generously commenting on an early draft of the book. Thanks are also due to K. P. Jayasankar and Anjali Monteiro, Tata Institute of Social Sciences, Mumbai, for their incisive feedback and expertise. The book, no doubt, is much better with their constructive comments. Big thanks to Katie Gallof and Erin Duffy, the editorial team at Bloomsbury, New York, for professional guidance and for sensing the relevance of our project. Without them, the manuscript would never see the light of the day.

Rajesh James
Sathyaraj Venkatesan

This book is a result of collaborative thinking. As an experiment in coauthorship, this book wouldn't have been possible without Sathyaraj Venkatesan, the "Il migilor fabbro." Since I met him at the University of London in 2013, he has been my true mentor and inspiration. I would have been very less a researcher and an individual if I hadn't met him. I still fondly remember the long walk and the lunch we shared on the banks of the River Thames. Since then our camaraderie has deepened and benefited with conversation and encouragement. Thank you SAT for your patience, constant phone calls, surprise visits, brotherly advice, and visionary guidance.

My appreciation is also due to my colleagues at the Sacred Heart College, Thevara, Ernakulam. I thank Fr. Prasant Palakkappillil for facilitating my research interests. I am also grateful to Dr. Tom C. Thomas, my creative muse, for being my constant inspiration. Hadn't it been for him, I would have been lesser. Many thanks to Biju V. V., Librarian, Sacred Heart College, for helping me get hold of some neoteric secondary resources. My students in the Sacred Heart College, Thevara, have been a great source of motivation for my research and filmmaking. I thank them for constantly challenging me and for keeping me motivated.

I am indebted to my teacher Dr. Prathiba Valappil, who instilled in me an aptitude of research and the "true" meaning of compassion. I am also thankful to all my teachers at the University of Calicut and St. Joseph's college, Devagiri, for their guidance. I must also thank Kerala State Chalachitra Academy, International Documentary and Short Film Festival of Kerala (IDSFFK), and Sajeesh N. P. for their help during the process of the book. IDSFFK has been an amazing venue for me as a documentary filmmaker. I am also grateful to Dr. Jyotika Cheema, my best friend, for her continuous motivation. Gina Petropoulou, Sophia Pouloupati, and Peloponnisos International Documentary Festival deserve special thanks.

Much love to my family for their unconditional support and forbearance. I am indebted to my parents, A. C. James and Annamma James, and my siblings (Ancy James, Bincy James, and James E. J.), whose many sacrifices made me realize this book. I am grateful to my wife, Meril Sara Kurian, for her love and care, for all the late nights and early mornings, and for keeping me sane over the past few years. Thank you for being there with me through all my travails and impatience. I am also thankful to my parents-in-laws, Kurian Alex and T. K. Lissy, for their love and care. Thank you, Alex Varghese Kurian, for being steadfast and supportive over the years. I wish to thank my friends James V. George, Ebin P. J., Sanu Varghese, and Ignatius Abraham for all the surprises, freaks, and everyday camaraderie. This book is dedicated to my family, friends, and students who stood by me since its conception.

Rajesh James,
Kochi

Some moments in life are dramatic. I met Rajesh James in a film studies conference at the University of London in 2013. The resonances set in motion about Indian independent documentaries in 2013 soon developed into a productive dialogue and a mutual willingness to turn into a book project. What you hold in your hands is then a result of seven years of labor, seven years of collaborative thinking, and seven years of mutual respect and love. Thanks to Rajesh James for accommodating me in his dream project and for his faith in my professional credentials. I am sure the book has mentored and made me a better scholar.

My salutes to all the documentary filmmakers interviewed here. Thanks to Gopal Menon for his unwavering and steadfast support ever since we started the project. I am grateful to Katie Gallof and Erin Duffy, the editorial team at Bloomsbury, for their support and guidance throughout. I have profited immensely from the members of the graphic medicine group; their energy is infectious and inimitable. My special thanks to Larry Churchill of the University of Vanderbilt for his limitless professional support. Most of all, thanks to Gurumurthy Neelakantan, who taught me the art of writing and interpretation. Special thanks to my faculty colleagues in the Department of Humanities and Social Sciences at the National Institute of Technology, Trichy.

I am grateful to Pavithra Sathyaraj, Taran Sathyaraj, and my mother for being a source of joy in my life. Your love has made this otherwise-daunting journey enjoyable.

Sathyaraj Venkatesan,
National Institute of Technology, Trichy

Foreword

Images make imaginations possible. Composed and received by the eyes, images are seldom without a voice. And voice is not noise.

Voice is shaped by history; it carries character, and it offers a perspective, *a way of seeing* and making sense of the world. In a deeply mediated world where technologies have advanced the resolutions and ease with which images can be made and shared, images have correspondingly become less reliable. Their ability to offer knowledge, to push us in rethinking the worlds we inhabit and the narratives we live by, is increasingly in danger of misuse and outright abuse. The crisis around images is not about media technologies. It is about the hands and minds that design, market, operate, and influence the uses of audiovisual technologies.

Regimes of power that can turn the spread of zoonotic viruses into self-congratulating pageantry, to whom *there is no such thing as society* (RIP welfare state!),[1] and who are incognizant and unapologetic about the deepening metabolic rift on our planet, co-opt images to promote skewed narratives and rationalizations of things. Susan Sontag, while pointing to a capitalist society's need for images, had preempted this escalating crisis when she said:

> It [a capitalist society] needs to furnish vast amounts of entertainment in order to stimulate buying and anaesthetise the injuries of class, race, and sex. And it needs to gather unlimited amounts of information, the better to exploit the natural resources, increase productivity, keep order, make war, give jobs to bureaucrats. The camera's twin capacities, to subjectivize reality and to objectify it, ideally serve these needs and strengthen them. (Sontag 1977: 178)[2]

Against the growing current that co-opts audiovisual technologies for short-sighted, ahistorical, and ill-informed agendas lie some practices that contest the colonization of media and the messages/ideologies they perpetuate. Documentary films in India have persistently questioned the state and its numerous apparatuses for their actions and understandings for shaping an "ideal" community, with a stable history. Documentary films have chronicled the many ways by which the Indian state and its arms exercise power to perpetuate disempowerment, dispossession, alienation, violence, and outright destruction of whole ways of knowing and being.

Documentary films in India align with the voices of those whom the powers-that-be seek to overlook, suppress, silence, and erase. Indian documentary cinema's own voice is thus of dissent, of questioning, reason, facts, poetry, passion, compassion, and a sense of shared humanity that resides in a living relationship with the earth. This voice is far from noise. And, it is not uniform. Indian documentaries are characterized by disparate and competing methods and aesthetics through which hegemonic and normative ideals and agendas get critiqued.

India Retold: Dialogues with Independent Documentary Filmmakers in India is a first-of-its-kind compilation of interviews with practicing filmmakers. The interviews in this volume introduce the motivations and thinking of filmmakers. The interviewees share the environments in which they grew, how they came to documentary making, how this practice enables them to explore and understand social life, and how their films are premised on an imagination for an India of the future. They share the often risk-ridden and precarious conditions in which they work, always with limited financial, social, and emotional support. The interviews bring out the filmmakers' commitments to documenting lived experiences, memories, traumas, and the understandings of ordinary people—the many millions whose ordinariness is the inverse of the glitter and spectacle that circulate both within and outside India to tout her economic miracles and emergence as a player in the global arena.

Documentary media has been produced in India since the early days of cinema. Documentary education has, however, been quite limited in the country. Largely confined to the specialized higher education sector, documentary films are sparsely integrated into curricula say at the high-school level or in university programs other than those related to cinema. Scarcity in funding and infrastructure for making, exhibiting, and distributing documentary films leads to less-than-ideal, on occasions ad hoc, circulation of documentaries within India's numerous public spheres. A few interviewees in this volume raise that oftentimes filmmakers have to actively devise platforms for sharing their work with audiences and that they also undertake promotion and sales of their films. For a long time, the field of documentary media suffered an absence of dedicated scholarship on the subject. A number of volumes have been written in recent years that historicize and contextualize the production of documentary films in India, elucidating how documentary media historicizes, contests, and investigates popular information and narratives about the sociopolitical and historical currents that have punctuated the course of Indian society since independence in 1947.[3] *India Retold* adds to this growing body of scholarship.

The interviews in this volume emphasize documentary making as a process of witnessing and recording history in which the perspectives of both those who exercise power and those upon whom it gets exercised are placed alongside one another. This exposes documentary viewers to agendas and rationalizations for which they may have limited or no access through the state-funded or privately owned media that populates India's social terrain. Independent documentary cinema in India is a serious, sustained, and intellectually rigorous practice that positions us to consider how we think and live in diversity; how justice is a right, not a fight; and how knowledge is a pursuit removed from the mechanics and machinations of the capitalist market system. The wider work documentary cinema performs in India is less about negotiating polarized or conflictual standpoints and more about upholding the values of belonging to a common humanity and planet.

Numerous scholars of documentary and independent cinema in India have recognized the Emergency of 1975 as a formative moment when documentary cinema assumed a decisive voice, independent of propagandist nationalism. Since then Indian documentary's voice has assumed disparate and competing articulations because media technologies and peoples' struggles have all undergone recognizable alterations and proliferations. *India Retold* maps this journey by including different generations of filmmakers. As the generations change, so does the approach and understanding toward documentary. Hence, in this book we learn from filmmakers who use the medium to study pan-Indian phenomena alongside those who speak from deeply situated social-geographies and lived experiences.

As more and more filmmakers from India's social and geographical peripheries take to the documentary medium, difficult work lies ahead for fully grasping the many ways through which hegemonic power expresses itself. Deeper, often challenging dialogues will be needed that both expose and inform about the operations of power. *India Retold* embodies the kinds of conversations in which media-makers must participate to deepen the presence of this vital medium in India's public spheres. The voice and imagination of independent documentary is perhaps one of the few antidotes to our hypermediated worlds where perspectives are polarized, knowledge ever more compromised, and imaginations rather frozen.

Aparna Sharma
University of California, Los Angeles

Notes

1 Margaret Thatcher's famous quote from an interview with *Woman's Own*, 1987.
2 Susan Sontag, *On Photography* (NYC: Picador, 1977).
3 Many of these texts are included in the reading list at the end of this volume.

Introduction

India Retold: Dialogues with Independent Documentary Filmmakers in India is an attempt to situate and historicize the engagement of independent documentary filmmakers (1970–2020) with the postcolonial India and its discourses with a focus on their independent documentary practices. Structured as an interview collection, the book examines how these documentary filmmakers, though not a homogeneous category, practice their independence through their ideology, their filmmaking praxis, their engagement with the everyday, and their formal experiments. As a sparsely studied filmmakers, the book through meticulously tracing wide-ranging historical transitions (marked by communal conflicts and the forces of globalization) not only details the ways in which independent filmmakers in India address the questions of postcolonial nation and its modernist projects but also explores the idiosyncratic views of these filmmakers which are characterized by a definitive departure from the logic of commercial films or state-sponsored documentary films. More important in many ways, these documentary filmmakers expose incongruences in national institutions and programs, embrace the voice of the underrepresented, and, thus, imagine an alternative vision of the nation.

Before offering a brief overview of the history of independent documentary film in India, it would be instructive to define the much-contested term "independence," the criteria of selection, and the interview methodology. Although definitions are arbitrary markers, independent documentary refers to a body of unique cultural, artistic, and issue-based films that emerged during or after the Emergency in India[1] in the 1970s. While the authors acknowledge that there were a limited number of independent documentaries produced before Indian independence, as Giulia Battaglia argues,[2] and a few others produced under the aegis of the Films Division of India, the focus of this book is to situate and trace the contemporary and current independent documentary practices and filmmakers in India. The present book argues that there was a veritable turn in the practice of independence in the 1970s and in subsequent years. These filmmakers illustrate a new sense of "independence" in the way they produced and exhibited films and engaged the postcolonial state, state censorship, jingoistic nationalism, aggressive imperialism, and mindless modernity. More specifically, these filmmakers, who emerged during or after the Emergency in India, purposely undermined the hegemonic and propagandist language of the state-sponsored documentary films, and, instead, constituted nonhierarchical, counterhegemonic, and alternative sites through their (innovative) documentary practices. Being independent also implies that these filmmakers maintain their independent vision by engaging in what Shweta Kishore calls "deprofessionalisation" and "deinstitutionalisation" (rejection of the hierarchical structures in filmmaking) (Kishore 2018: 96), thus allowing an autonomous context in which the filmmakers' vision and political critiques develop through structural innovations and experiments. Again, distancing themselves from the market economics, which Kishore calls "decapitalisation" (minimization of market control in the production/exhibition process) (Kishore 2018: 96), these filmmakers mostly arrange private fundraising through various reliable means such as crowdfunding.[3] The objective of this book is to trace, explore, and engage with such filmmakers who, though they defy any easy classification, unsettle the conventional understanding of the relationship between individuals and the state apparatuses by deploying critical aesthetics and medium-specific affordances. In doing so, these documentary filmmakers retell India through constructing competing cultural narratives, alternative geopolitical imaginaries, and desirable futures.

Thirty filmmakers are interviewed, and the following parameters are used to identify them: articulate a distinct aesthetic; offer an alternative view about the state; public engagement and resultant social awareness/movement; address pressing social problems that impinge Indian society; unfunded by the state; creative engagement with the genre of documentary filmmaking, storytelling, and stylistic novelties; and underexplored and understudied but relevant documentary makers. Further, the filmmakers are also chosen on the basis of their accessibility and our subjective assessment of the importance of filmmakers' contribution based on our field experience and on the previously published research studies. Broadly put, these documentarians have a critical vision that resists normalized, naturalized, institutionalized ways of seeing as they try to foreground the marginalized, subaltern, and underrepresented voices and issues.

Given the geopolitical, ethnographic, linguistic, and ideological diversities of India, the book covers expansive Indian documentary terrain—from the established to the emerging independent documentary filmmakers across India under five thematic clusters, namely nationalism, gender/LGBTQIA, caste, nature, and region. Although filmmakers have worked on crosscutting themes, they are classified in one or the other thematic clusters based on the dominant themes of their films. Every filmmaker defies easy classification. Thus, although the individual filmmakers within each cluster vary in terms of ideology, practice, and aesthetics, they take a position vis-à-vis a particular theme (gender, caste, sexuality, among others). Clustering also helps the readers to map interrelationality, to tacitly build robust dialogues among the documentary filmmakers and to make analytical comparisons between and among the documentary filmmakers. Though less known, the work of emerging documentary filmmakers who ideologically and aesthetically redefine extant colonial, religious, and sociocultural ideologies are also included in this volume. Corporate filmmakers, commercial filmmakers, and state-funded propaganda documentary filmmakers are not considered under the purview of the book. Similarly, documentary filmmakers who produce educational films, adventure films, and conventional historical films are also not taken into consideration. Again, those filmmakers who made significant films but have retired or ceased producing documentaries over a period of time are not included. Finally, given the plethora of independent documentary films produced in India, there is always a risk of being selective. However, exercising choice (based on the aforementioned parameters) is necessary to delve deeper into the films of the chosen documentary filmmakers than would have been possible in an encyclopedic or fleeting engagement with a greater number of documentary filmmakers. Perhaps, a second volume in this series would consider the rest but equally prominent filmmakers.

Except for some sections, most parts of the interview during the last three years of the execution of the project are the result of a face-to-face/one-on-one interview, which was also audio-recorded. The recorded materials were later transcribed word by word and sent to the interviewed for their approval. Some sections of the interview are also carried out through email and telephone owing to Kashmir lockdown and Corona pandemic. The questions were formulated not only through continued qualitative conversations with the interviewed but also through involved watching of their documentaries. The questions to the interviewers are framed in such a way that they bring out filmmakers' ideological preferences, their understandings of independence, their aesthetic practices, and their empirical circumstances such as ethnographic specificities and geopolitical realities. The interviews are copy-edited for clarity and precision. Given the dearth of quality interviews and little theoretical engagement with documentary as a genre, this book would not only fill in the gap in scholarship but also serve as an authentic guide for interested readers and for documentary filmmakers.

Documentary Films in Colonial India

The history of documentary films in India begins with the actuality footage by the first film entrepreneur in India, Harishchandra Sakharam Bhatvadekar[4] (1868–1958), who filmed a wrestling match (*The Wrestlers*)[5] and a man training monkeys (*The Man and His Monkeys*[6]). During the first decades of the twentieth century, many actuality films (also called topicals) such as "Durbar Films of 1903[7] and 1911[8]" were produced, and they gained wide currency in other parts of India, including Calcutta and South India, through travelling exhibitions. Significantly during this time, a young photographer from Calcutta, Hiralal Sen, shot sequences of political agitation and anti-partition marches in Bengal (1905). When Indian freedom movement gained momentum, many filmmakers shot boycott protests, the burning of foreign goods and events connected to Mahatma Gandhi such as the Dandi March[9] (1930). Put together, all these films served as the early prototypes of contemporary documentary films in India.

As the production of actuality films declined in the 1930s, newsreels became an influential documentary form of the period. Realizing the significance and marketability of filming specific themes/institutions, many production companies such as the British Movietone News and Wadia Movietone started making newsreels mostly imported from America. In fact, fearing the critical influence of these films on the people of the colony, the colonial government set up the Film Advisory Board (hereafter FAB), later replaced by the Information Films of India (hereafter IFI), with a mandate to produce and distribute Indian versions of wartime newsreels regularly. Although films produced during this phase were predominantly intended to highlight Britain's efforts in the Second World War and to gain people's support, J. B. H. Wadia (Chairman of the FAB) generously supported "pure documentaries" such as *Women of India* and *Industrial India*, among others (Biren Sharma 2018: 43). However, with the legislation of the Defence of India Act (1943),[10] which mandated compulsory exhibition of state-produced films for exhibitors, the colonial administration could regulate the production, distribution, and exhibition of documentary films in India more than ever.

Films Division Documentary Films

A few months after Indian independence in 1947, a new organization, modelled on IFI, called the Film Unit of the Ministry of Information and Broadcasting, was formed. Later renamed as the Films Division (hereafter FD) in 1948, it was established to disseminate the developmental agenda of the new India. Although the primary purpose of the FD documentaries was to "educate" Indians, in subsequent years, FD used documentary form as a tool to reorganize the nation and build a collective sense of citizenship. In its efforts to cultivate a "normative imagining of nationhood" (Vasudevan 2001: 62), FD patronized themes like public hygiene, family planning, and government-sponsored agricultural schemes at the expense of more urgent issues like poverty, illiteracy, and communalism. These films also uncritically supported state's developmental projects like construction of large dams, irrigation systems, railways, and ports. In short, utilizing documentary as an instrument to "unite India against a common enemy—underdevelopment" (Sutoris 2016: 4), FD over a period of time became an integral part of the state's "nationalist hagiography" (Vasudevan 2001: 62). Within a span of twenty years, the FD produced 2,700 films. These films were exhibited on compulsion in more than 6,000 cinema screens and 20 million cinemagoers were forced to watch them (Kak 2018: 20). Since it was legally mandatory to screen these FD newsreels in cinema halls before every commercial film, the word "documentary" itself generated an aversion among the audience.

Although the FD was "a gigantic failure in generating any noteworthy freshness or vibrancy in documentary film making in India" (Gangar 1987: 35), documentary commentators such as Battaglia, Peter Sutoris, and Srirupa Roy identify a stream of FD films that practiced independence. According to these film scholars, it was Jehangir Bhownagary who, in his capacity as the deputy chief producer of the Films Division (1954–7) and later as the chief adviser (Films) to the Ministry of Information and Broadcasting (1965–7), democratized the FD in that he inspired filmmakers to express themselves and even encouraged producers who were not part of the FD to produce independent films. *Khajuraho* (1956), directed by Mohan N. Wadhwani, and Jehangir Bhownagary's own *Radha and Krishna* (1957) are representative "independent films" of the period. In his second term, Jehangir Bhownagary undertook new projects which were bold and pioneering in content and style. T. A. Abraham and K. S. Chari's *Face to Face* (1967) was produced during this time; it used a direct cinema method in which the camera and the microphone were taken to the street. It is perhaps for the first time in the history of FD films, as Biren Sharma reminds, that an unmediated voice of the people had been heard (2018: 51). S. N. S Sastry's *I Am Twenty* (1967) and *And I Make Short Films* (1968) are early examples of experimentation in documentary practices in India in that they unsettled collectivity and homogeneity implied in FD films.

Filmmakers like P. V. Pathy and S. Sukhdev, who were producers in the Films Division in the late 1960s, also experimented with the documentary form and, in the process, uncovered the limitations of the propaganda films. In deftly utilizing "a mélange of diverse images" (Chadha 2014: 43), these filmmakers presented an inconsonant portrait of India. Sukhdev's films—for instance, *And Miles to Go* (1965), *After the Eclipse* (1967), *India '67* (1968), and *Nine Months to Freedom* (1972)—can be treated as prototypes of independent documentary films that critiqued the conception and vision of the nation-state as presented in the FD films. In particular, his investigative and socially conscious documentaries melded visual aesthetics and the functional power of activism. In a related but different way, P. V. Pathy also offered an eloquent critique of the blatant propagandist agenda of FD films. Both P. V. Pathy and S. Sukhdev, in a sense, are forerunners of the "agitprop" films (protest documentaries) of modern times.

Although filmmakers like P. V. Pathy, Mani Kaul, and S. Sukhdev expressed their individual vision within the institutionalized framework of the FD, their creative advances were at once regulated and deemed as excessive. Explaining the reason for the emergence of such progressive documentary films, Ritika Kaushik observes that it was Sukhdev's friendship with Indira Gandhi that helped him produce a radical film like *India '67*,[11] which was initially stalled by the Censor Board[12] (2017: 116). Predictably, Sukhdev even went so far as to advocate the repressive measures of Indira Gandhi during the Emergency (1975–7), which makes him one of the most polarizing figures in the history of documentary films in India. Irrespective of the "considerable sense" of independence shown by these filmmakers, they were very much part of nation-building enterprise. Put differently, although these filmmakers cultivated their individual style of filmmaking as envisioned by Jehangir Bhownagary, they nonetheless reiterated the dominant Nehruvian discourse of the nation and its development agenda.

Post-Emergency Documentary Films

In spite of the hegemonization of documentary practices under the aegis of the FD, as argued before, the 1970s witnessed the production of an assortment of documentary films outside the patronage of the Films Division. A new generation of documentary filmmakers like Anand Patwardhan, Tapan Bose, and Suhasini Mulay, among others, produced a filmography covering issues such as state-sponsored violence, poverty, homelessness, and injustice, among others. These films critiqued and contested the dominant political economy and the majoritarian discourses of nationhood, thereby foregrounding the marginalized and subaltern voices. What distinguished them from the generation of independent filmmakers who came before them was their dissociation from agents of power, including the state, on the one hand, and their critical outlook toward government and its developmental projects that aggressively marginalized/displaced people and destroyed environments. Although these filmmakers are different in terms of content, form, and their target audience, what binds them is the political critique and subversion, thus laying the ground for oppositional, alternative, and innovative documentary filmmaking practices. Accordingly, documentary film produced during this period marked a definitive point of departure from the itineraries of state propaganda and paternalism, thus inaugurating a new phase in the history of documentary films in India. More important in many ways, this period witnessed the production of politically conscious and privately financed documentary films as opposed to the organized structure of the production and exhibition of documentary films by either the state-regulated or commercial firms. Furthermore, these documentary filmmakers, through their innovative, radical, and unorthodox ways, systematically challenged the hegemonic discourses of the state-funded films (often esoteric, pedagogical, ethnographic, and stereotypical) and, in turn, created a new spectatorial position of solidarity between the filmmaker and the spectators that questioned the official transcripts of dominant discourses which forced spectators to act on the issues discussed in the films.

Examining the reasons for the emergence of independent documentary films in the 1970s as opposed to the mechanical and "mindless" state-funded films, Jayasankar and Monteiro identify the resistance movements of Jayaprakash Narayan[13] and the Railwaymen's strike[14] (2016: 18), among others. Of course, the immediate reason for the emergence of such "provocative" and political documentaries was the declaration of the state of Emergency, which repressively curbed people's political and democratic rights. Since the Emergency had a direct influence on freedom of expression, the constitutional possibility of the right to dissent was suppressed between 1975 and 1977. For another, the Films Division of India considerably deteriorated as the agency of the state during this period. Besides such sociopolitical factors, the introduction of lightweight 16 mm camera (instead of the heavy 35 mm camera) and the commencement of cheaper printing labs ensured an increased production of independent films.

Though there were instances of experiments with independence in the history of documentary films in India, as argued before, it was Anand Patwardhan who pioneered a "new turn" in independent documentary filmmaking in the 1970s. Practicing a "self-avowedly polemical" style (Jayasankar and Monteiro 2016: 21), his oeuvre unwaveringly critiqued the discourses of government, the state's mindless developmental and neoliberal projects, and upended the extant visual grammar, semiotics, and distribution of documentary films in India. For instance, *Waves of Revolution* (1974), shot in 16 mm camera during the Emergency, is now considered "the first true independent political documentary" (Fischer 2009: 42) in the history of documentary films in India,[15] in terms of both the issues it addresses (such as state-sponsored violence, injustice, and poverty) and the way it is filmed (guerrilla filmmaking), edited (improvised editing) and exhibited (underground exhibition). In his later films, Patwardhan also exposed the crypto capitalist designs of the state and coercive and disciplining statecraft. In addition to the strident critique of the state and its mindless development policies, dowries, caste oppression, and women's subordination also bothered him. In essence, his films echoed the concerns of those people who appeared on the screen as individuals rather than as a filmed subject. Like Anand, the films of Goutam Ghose, Utpalendu Chakraborty, and Tapan Bose during the late 1970s undermined the dominant aesthetics and themes of documentary films of the period. Films like *Hungry Autumn* (1974) by Ghose, *Mukti Chai* (trans. *A Cry for Freedom*) (1977) by Utpalendu Chakraborty, and *An Indian Story* (1981) by Tapan Bose, among other films, addressed hunger and violence against women, *Dalits*,[16] and *Adivasis*.[17] They took cameras to the people, rejecting the long-shot and mid-shot techniques of the FD films. Unlike S. Sukhdev, P. V. Pathy, and S. N. S. Sastry, these filmmakers completely distanced themselves from the allegiance of the state and its funding agencies, and made films that captured the critical voices of the period from the perspective of the citizen subjects. Moreover, the lack of infrastructure for screening a 16 mm film forced these filmmakers to arrange private screenings and mobilize an audience through alternative networks. Such efforts toward alternative screenings and the dissemination of documentary films can be seen as one of the early experiments in independent screenings beyond the patronized and commercial spaces. In fact, such a strategy gained a new momentum after the censorship crisis in the state-run film festival (MIFF) in 2004.[18]

During the 1980s, India also witnessed an unprecedented mobilization of women across the country, partly triggered by the Supreme Court verdict on the Mathura rape case in 1979,[19] which brought to the fore the issues of rape, violence, and dowry. Women reacted against such violence both politically and artistically (in the form of street theater, songs, posters, and photographs) not only through questioning the dominant patriarchal norms of family and the state but also through foregrounding the agency and the rights of women. Such interventions were deftly filmed by women documentary filmmakers like Deepa Dhanraj as a way to counter the absence of women in the existing archives, which can be treated as the early attempts at documentary filmmaking[20] among women. The Yugantar collective was formed during this period under the leadership of Deepa Dhanraj, along with Abha Bhaiya, Meera Rao, and Navroze Contractor, with an intention to make "committed documentary" (Waugh xiii) of women's political struggles. Along with other feminist collectives such as *Saheli* (New Delhi) and *Stree Shakti Sanghatana* (Hyderabad), Yugantar explored the lived experiences of women victims, creating a new political consciousness beyond academic radicalism. These films explored the lived experiences and multiple tensions of women in response to the Emergency and the Mathura rape case. As early attempts at participatory filmmaking, these women filmmakers screened their films at a grass-roots level and re-edited their films, if required, based on post-screening discussions with the audience. Unlike the FD films where no filmed subject spoke, these filmmakers foregrounded women's agency, thereby inaugurating a paradigmatic shift in Indian documentary films. Yugantar's *Tobacco Embers* (1982) and Meera Dewan's *Gift of Love* (1983) are typical examples of this feminist/womenist turn in documentary films in India. These filmmakers, while wrestling with the masculine sensitivity and approach of earlier documentaries also, as Jayasankar and Monteiro remind us, foregrounded "the specificity of women's struggle within the context of the larger class struggle" (2016: 22). Along with such radical reformulation in terms of both content and style, significant material changes (such as the introduction of portable video technology in 1982) also impacted the production of independent documentary films. More important in many ways, the advent of portable video technology substantially reduced the cost of filmmaking and the efforts of production and postproduction (such as editing) and even helped to circumvent the bureaucratic film production and distribution (Kak 2018: 23).

Post–Babri Masjid Documentary Films

The period after the Emergency saw the rise of religious and cultural fundamentalism in India, leading to a new disjunctive relation among people and places based on religion, caste, and regional politics. As a culmination, as it were, Babri Masjid[21] was demolished by Hindu fundamentalists on December 6, 1992, which led to a consequential enmity and violence between the extremist Hindus and Muslims. Against such a sociopolitical condition, many independent documentary filmmakers examined the proliferation of the Hindu-Muslim divide, the anatomy of hate politics, and communal violence across India. In effect, communalism became "a running theme" (Chakravarti 2018: 77) in the documentary films produced in this period. For instance, Deepa Dhanraj's *Kya Hua Is Shehar Ko?* (trans. *What Happened to This City?*) (1986) documented the rise of Hindu nationalist politics, which continues to have an impact in contemporary India. However, it was Anand Patwardhan's *Ram Ke Naam* (trans. *In the Name of God*) (1992), now seen as a significant example of an interventionist documentary in the 1990s, that recorded the events leading to the demolition of Babri Masjid in 1992. By critically engaging the idea of an oppressive nation-state and its apparatus which invests in the praxis of nationalist jingoism, neoliberal policies, religious and cultural fundamentalisms, and Dalit oppressions, filmmakers like Deepa Dhanraj, Anand Patwardhan, Madhusree Dutta, and Lalit Vachani,[22] by resorting to different aesthetics of filmmaking (such as the reflexive or the essay style), address the ideologies and everyday programs of right-wing groups as they also explore the social psychology of a fundamentalist. While resisting and exposing the xenophobic aspects of cultural nationalism and religiously inspired violence, these documentaries function as repositories of social and cultural memories which are intentionally erased from the public sphere.

Interestingly, in the 1990s, documentary films produced by women filmmakers took a "self-reflexivity" turn, which implied a new aesthetic of the mediated nature of filmmaking. Although several agitprop[23] films were made during this time, feminist and women-centered documentaries of this phase also witnessed dramatic enactment of the filmed subjects. These films were conscious about the relationship between filmmaker/filmed, filmmaking process, and film as an artistic product. By focusing on individual women's lives—either that of the filmmaker or that of the filmed subjects—these films explored how patriarchal structures constructed female subjectivity and unmasked many guises of male domination. Reena Mohan's critically acclaimed *Kamalabai* (1992), for instance, is at once a reflexive examination of the life of Kamalabai (one of the first actresses in Indian cinema) and the subjectivity of the filmmaker herself, each complicating the other. In a similar way, illustrating, as it were, the personal is political, Vasudha Joshi's *For Maya* (1997) explores personal accounts of women across generations in what was conventionally considered as the "unpolitical space of the home" (Chakravarti 2018: 77). Put differently, the idea of objectivity which was so central to the public/political discourse is displaced in these films; instead, performativity, memory/recollection, disruptive narrative flow, and competing speaker positions are utilized to explore multiple (emotional) truths.

Changes in the paradigm of development with the introduction of New Economic Policy (NEP) in the 1990s, which in turn engendered new sociopolitical and economic discourses in India, also found their place in documentaries during this period. Broadly, the 1990s Indian economy, shedding its socialist inclination, underwent radical transformation toward a liberal economy. Leaving behind the idea of the welfare state, the government started privatizing all its service sectors, like education and health. Responding to these newer sites of contestations, particularly in three major economic sectors, namely agriculture, industry, and services, documentary filmmakers exposed the callous capitalist ideology behind the economic and sociopolitical programs of the state and corporate companies. In the process, they offered alternative vision, like the need for sustainable development that takes into account the Adivasis, Dalits, and other marginalized sections of society countering corporate discourses of development, economic growth, and labor which favor capital at the cost of the environment and the vulnerable. Moving away from the ideology of the educational/wildlife films produced by the Films Division of India, independent documentary filmmakers in the 1990s also explored the impact of human interventions and its destructive influences on nature. Grounded in a nonpuritanical view of nature, filmmakers like Sanjay Kak, Shriprakash, Meghnath, Biju Toppo, and K. P. Sasi, among others, examined the complex interactions of ecologies and societies in their films. Films like *Buddha Weeps in Jadugoda* (1999), *Words on Water* (2002), and *Development Flows from the Barrel of the Gun* (2003) problematized the development discourses of the state that critically affect nature by showing the dire impact of ruthless commercial development on local populations and farmers in particular. The concerns of these films were the long-term and seemingly invisible social and environmental injustices and violence, like environmental pollution, radiation, and deforestation. For instance, Shriprakash, in his films, depicted the impact of mining and the unhealthy disposal of carcinogenic waste and countered the development policies and corporate friendliness of the governments by depicting how the local population is affected by radiation and pollution from industries, and the eventual forced displacement of the local population.

Also, during this time, social hegemonies of the caste system became a significant thematic concern and point of investigation for the documentary filmmakers. Although caste was central to the power relations in India, it had never been a serious concern in documentary films[24] until the 1990s. Films like *Lesser Humans* (1998) by Stalin and *Pee* (2003) by Amudhan R. P. explored in depth how a low caste remains stigmatized and exploited in the Indian context. Almost in an activist vein, these films documented the powerful testimony of those people who fought against the caste system and questioned the middle-class complacency of denying the reality that untouchability existed in India. For instance, Amudhan's *Pee* is a striking rendition of the lives of Dalits who are forced to undertake manual scavenging owing to their lower-caste identity. Though geographically situated in the interior spaces of India, the film demands for greater public attention beyond its regionalist context. While these films critiqued the despicable institution of caste and vindicated the emergence of a radical new Dalit politics in India, they also exposed how the state functions as a tool in the hands of a few in promulgating caste-based discriminations. The arrival of digital (easy and affordable) technology, by the end of the decade, revolutionized independent filmmaking in India. Consequently, many filmmakers from nonmetropolitan places also produced a substantial number of documentary films. By the turn of the millennium, Adivasis and the rural population (*Development Flows from the Barrel of the Gun* by Meghnath/Biju Toppo), human rights violation, voices from the margins (*YCP 1997* by Monteiro/ Jayasankar), gender sensitivity, masculinity, and sexual desires (*When Four Friends Meet* by Rahul Roy) became definitive and urgent concerns of independent documentary filmmakers, thereby exposing fissures and contradictions in the discourses of the state. For instance, Monteiro and Jayasankar in their films addressed a wide range of social and cultural issues that unearth the subjugated knowledge of the marginalized experiences. Grounded in academic background, their films are unique voices that critically integrate ethics, politics, and poetics and weave together multiple perspectives as a means to counter the hegemonic voices of the nation-state.

Post-millennial Documentary Films

As a highpoint in contemporary independent documentary filmmaking, the Gujarat riots of 2002 (communal violence and deadly riots between the Hindus and Muslims across the western state of Gujarat) triggered a series of documentary films. Many independent filmmakers have responded to this incident—for instance, Gopal Menon's *Hey Ram: Genocide in the Land of Gandhi* (2002), Shubhradeep Chakravorty's *Godhra Tak: The Terror Trail* (2003), and Rakesh Sharma's *Final Solution* (2004). Using the testimonies of people who were critically affected by the riot alongside those who propagated the riot, these films explored the nature of religion-inspired violence in Gujarat. These films are very significant in the history of documentary films not only because they were subversive, acrid and oppositional but also because they laid bare political extremism, state-sponsored violence, and the anatomy of hate politics.

Along with these interventionist documentary films, the filmmakers of this period also continued with the experimentation of documentary form, foregrounding the subjectivity of the filmmaker as well as the medium. Amar Kanwar, as a representative filmmaker of this school of documentary filmmaking, followed an open-ended approach. Kanwar's films can be approached as an affective and subjective take on the collective psyche—that is, his films engage with the social space by inserting the self in relation to the other. Unlike the early documentary films, Kanwar's films like *A Night of Prophecy* (2002) and *The Lightning Testimonies* (2007) are self-reflexive in that they negotiate the passage of time by foregrounding the constructedness of the medium. In a similar way, filmmakers such as Pankaj Rishi Kumar, Paromita Vohra, Saba Dewan, Nishtha Jain, Pushpa Rawat, R. V. Ramani, and Surabhi Sharma also explored the meaning of "political" through reframing dominant notions of verisimilitude and objective styles in documentary films. In particular, Vohra, through mixing fiction and nonfiction, the serious and the frivolous, the kitsch and the sublime, introduced a creative aesthetic which disentangled the exclusive definitions of the political in documentary films. With the advent of LGBTQIA rights movements in India, this decade also witnessed filmmakers such as Shohni Gosh, Debalia Majumdar, and Sridhar Rangayan, who through their films addressed nonbinary sexual desires and sexual practices. They used documentary as a platform to raise public consciousness on LGBTQIA issues (institutional subjugation and stigmatization) and envisioned it as a space to celebrate gender plurality and inclusion. Thus, their films at once would complement the existing women/ feminist issues and effectively expand the body of knowledge about LGBTQIA issues.

Documentary films during this period also witnessed the representation of local geographies, ethnographic issues, and the complex exchanges between different regions and the Indian state. In particular, filmmakers like Iffat Fatima (Kashmir), Bilal A. Jan (Kashmir), Hoabam Paban Kumar (Manipur), Stanzin Dorjai (Ladakh), Raja Shabir Khan (Kashmir), Supriyo Sen (West Bengal), Mukul Haloi (Assam), Divya Bharathi (Tamil Nadu), Kasturi Basu (West Bengal), and many others, through their situatedness and through the deft use of their cultural memories, ethnicity, and identity, addressed the heterogeneity of their regions. In doing so, these filmmakers not only discovered India in its plurality and sophistication but also redefined the grand narratives of nationalism, homogeneity, and development. For instance, Iffat Fatima, distancing herself from the popular and touristic representations of Kashmir, reinstated Kashmiri (women) subjectivities in the context of Kashmir insurgency.[25] Similarly, Mukul Haloi in *Tales from Our Childhood* (2017) persuasively evokes Assam (a northeastern Indian state) and its violent past through long shots, conversations with his family members, and his personal memories. In a different way, Stanzin Dorjai, through his critically acclaimed films like *The Shepherdess of the Glaciers* (2016) and *Growing up in Ladakh* (2017), poetically explores the drama, adventure, and thrill of growing up and living in Ladakh (one of the highest mountainous regions in the world). Put together, these filmmakers question the hegemonic voice of the nation-state, and, in doing so, they avoid the dangers of a single story about India. Along these lines, Surabhi Sharma identifies two other dominant models of contemporary documentary films in India: the character-driven narrative documentary and the essay documentary. While character-driven documentary films, to paraphrase Sharma, narrate individual cases of resilience—for example *Gulabi Gang* (2012)—the essay form, through reflection and analysis, examines a contemporary conflict. Films like *Red Ant Dream* (2013), *Muzaffarnagar Baaqi Hai* (2015), *Reason* (2018), and *We Have Not Come Here to Die* (2018) belong to the latter category. Drawing strength from "the ideology of the movements" (Surabhi Sharma 2018: 75) in which they are contextualized such as Dalit politics in the context of Rohith Vemula's suicide in *We Have Not Come Here to Die*, the essay documentary analytically registers contemporary events.

Although multiple modes, as discussed earlier, are utilized to address public and social issues, contemporary filmmakers are yet to resolve the moot question of how to comprehensively foreground the voices of their subjects who are different in terms of caste, class, and gender. With technological advances, shifting ideological boundaries, and aesthetic taste, the practice of independent documentary films is more polyphonic and ideologically complex than ever before. In a period where "professional filmmaker" is no longer required to produce images of the private/public spaces, documentary filmmaking will remain a challenge. Having said that, in an era characterized by authoritarian state, democratic struggles, neoliberalism, media regulations, environmental hazards, and the onslaught of multinational digital platforms (such as Netflix and Amazon), there is more necessity for documentary as a practice and as an artifact than ever before. Put boldly, independent documentary films are and shall remain a window to India's diversity and the untold stories of its people.

Notes

1 The Emergency refers to an order issued by Prime Minister Indira Gandhi which suspended elections and curbed people's civil liberties for a period of twenty-one months from 1975 to 1977.

2 Moving beyond the conventional reading of documentary practices in India, Battaglia in *Documentary Film in India: An Anthropological History* (2018), from an anthropological perspective, argues that independent documentary filmmaking was in vogue and thriving even during the colonial era under the aegis of the Films Division of India.

3 Many scholars such as Jayasankar and Monteiro (2016: 4) and Shweta Kishore (2018: 79) have argued that mere association with the nongovernmental organizations (NGOs) will not disqualify filmmakers from the definition of independence, unless that association ideologically or institutionally determine and shape a filmmaker's aesthetic practices/critical perspectives.

4 The name Bhatvadekar is also spelled as Bhatwadekar.

5 P. K. Nair, in his "A National Cinema Takes Root in a Colonial Regime: Early Cinema in India," identifies *The Wrestlers* as an early example of an actuality film. *The Wrestlers* is a factual film by Bhatvadekar showing the fight between two wrestlers named Pundalik Dada and Krishna Nhavi (2017: 207–20).

6 The film is also titled as *A Man and His Monkeys, Man and Monkey, The Man and The Monkey* by different documentary commentators.

7 Durbar Films of 1903 refers to the actuality films shot during the mass assembly and celebrations held in Delhi, popularly called "Delhi Durbar of 1903," which marked the coronation of Edward VII as the emperor of India.

8 Durbar Films of 1911 refers to the actuality films shot during the mass assembly and celebrations that happened in Delhi. "The Delhi Durbar of 1911" commemorated the coronation of King George V as the emperor of India.

9 Dandi March is a nonviolent protest march led by Mahatma Gandhi from his ashram in Sabarmati (Gujarat) to Dandi (a coastal place in Gujarat) between March 12 and April 6, 1930, to protest against the repressive salt tax imposed by the colonial British government.

10 Defence of India Act (1943) is a legislation that made it mandatory for film exhibitors in India to screen government-approved films in every cinema hall in the country to secure an audience (Aparna Sharma 2015: 244).

11 Kaushik, in "'Sun in the Belly': Film Practice at Films Division of India 1965–1975," argues that "[i]t was Bhownagary who decided that Sukhdev produce *India '67* for the upcoming Montreal Expo' 67 (1967)" (2017: 116). Commenting on the origins of the film, Sukhdev explains the mandate thus: "the Films Division was making a documentary for the Montreal Film Festival. They asked me to make it" (Mohan 1984: 42).

12 The Censor Board is a Government of India–controlled certifying and rating agency. The objective of the Censor Board, as the website states, is to regulate "the public exhibition of films under the provisions of the Cinematograph Act 1952." In recent times, the Censor Board was renamed as the Central Board of Film Certification (CBFC).

13 Jayaprakash Narayan is an Indian independence activist, theorist, and political leader. He is remembered for leading the mid-1970s opposition against Prime Minister Indira Gandhi.

14 The Great Railwaymen strike was the biggest strike in the history of Indian railways in 1974.

15 Commenting on the emergence of independent political documentary films in India, John Fischer in his "Oppression: Indian Independent Political Documentaries and the Ongoing Struggle for Viewership" contends that the independent documentary movement was "born in 1975 during the Emergency era, a period in which President Fakhruddin Ali Ahmed, under the guidance of Prime Minister Indira Gandhi, suspended constitutional civil liberties and oversaw the imprisonment and deaths of many innocent civilians" (2009: 42).

16 Dalit refers to a person belonging to the lowest caste within a caste-based social system.

17 Adivasi refers to a member of any of the aboriginal tribal groups living in India.

18 Mumbai International Film Festival (MIFF) is the largest biennial film festival organized by the Films Division of the Ministry of Information and Broadcasting. MIFF (2004) insisted on a censor certificate to screen the films in the film festival.

Several documentary filmmakers voiced against state censorship and intervention. To counter this, a collective and a parallel festival named *Vikalp* (trans. *Films for Freedom*) was formed in 2004.

19 Mathura rape case refers to an incident of custodial rape of a young tribal girl named Mathura on March 26, 1972. In an unusual verdict, the Supreme Court of India acquitted the accused in 1979, which in turn fueled several protest movements across India.

20 Elaborating various reasons for the emergence of feminist documentary films, Madhumeeta Sinha in "Witness to Violence: Documentary Cinema and the Women's Movement in India" identifies the following: publication of a report named "Towards Equality: Report of the Committee on the Status of Women in India" (1974), the UN's declaration in 1975 as International Women's Year, the availability of NGO funds and the emergence of an alternative audience (365–73).

21 Babri Masjid was a mosque in Ayodhya, Uttar Pradesh, which was demolished by a Hindu mob on December 6, 1992.

22 Lalit Vachani's *The Boy in the Branch* (1993), while critiquing the ideology of right-wing fundamentalists, also analytically journeys into the psychological disposition of the ideologues of the Rashtriya Swayamsevak Sangh (RSS).

23 Agitprop refers to propaganda films or films made in support of a cause.

24 Although Loksen Lalvani's Films Division of India–supported *They Call Me Chamar* (1980) addressed the contentious question of caste, it was filmed from the perspective of a dominant-caste man showing his troubles after marrying a lower-caste woman. *Chamar* is one of the untouchable communities in India.

25 Kashmir Insurgency refers to a series of conflicts between various Kashmiri separatists who demand local autonomy and the Government of India.

1

Decoding Ideology

Nationalism, Communalism, and Its Critiques

The intentional homogenization of national identity irrespective of India's diversity led to a violent reorganization of people and places based on religion, caste, region, and language. The demolition of the Babri Masjid on December 6, 1992, was a critical highpoint of sorts that culminated in the growing tension between the Hindus and other religious minorities including Muslims. In a way, it communalized India on religious lines leading to a reimagining of India as a Hindu nation. Events similar in magnitude such as the Gujarat riots (2002) and Muzaffarnagar riots (2013) further deepened the crisis. Against such a background, communalism, hate-pogroms, and fundamentalism became a recurrent theme in documentary films produced especially after the 1980s. Unlike the commercial cinema which underplayed sensitive themes such as communalism and religious fundamentalism or the Films Division (FD) films which made ultra-nationalistic films, many independent documentary filmmakers such as Anand Patwardhan, Amar Kanwar, Rakesh Sharma, Gopal Menon, Nakul Singh Sawhney, and Kasturi Basu, through resorting to different aesthetic styles (such as observational, interactive, essay, and self-reflexive style) of filmmaking, probed the anatomy of hate politics and communal violence. Furthermore, these filmmakers, for instance Tapan Bose, boldly expose systemic violence, human rights violations, and the fundamentalist ideologies that shape contemporary India. In critically examining the nation-state and its apparatus which invests on the praxis of jingoism, religious, and cultural fundamentalism, these filmmakers also uncover the inner workings of the ideologies and everyday programs of the authoritarian state that fuel hatred and fear. In doing so, their documentaries function as repositories of social and cultural memories that get consciously erased by the influential forces and institutionalized history. The following interviews throw light on the workings of communalism, divisive politics, production of religious alterities, and extremist ideologies in contemporary India.

Anand Patwardhan

Figure 1 Image Credit: Rajesh James.

Deemed as the father of independent documentary films in India, Anand Patwardhan is a distinguished voice in postcolonial Indian cinema. Born in Bombay in 1950, he received a scholarship for a BA program at Brandeis University, USA. During that period, he was imprisoned twice for anti–Vietnam War protests and also worked for six months as a volunteer with the Cesar Chavez-led United Farmworkers Union (UFW). He returned to India to work in Kishore Bharati, a voluntary rural development and education project in Madhya Pradesh,[1] and later joined the Bihar Movement,[2] which eventually led to the declaration of Emergency in 1975. Having made his first documentary *Waves of Revolution* in this period, he had to smuggle it abroad in parts during the Emergency. Anand was able to get a teaching assistantship to do his master's in arts from McGill University, Canada, where he put his film back together to screen as part of the anti-Emergency movement. Partly inspired by the New Latin American cinema, his films since the 1970s have concentrated on sociopolitical and human rights issues in India, including the rise of religious sectarianism. *Waves of Revolution* and *Prisoners of Conscience*, his early documentaries on the Emergency (from 1975 to 1977) paved the way for the introduction of the independent political documentary films in India. His films boldly explore religious fundamentalism (*Ram Ke Naam*) and sectarian violence and caste-based discriminations

(*Jai Bhim Comrade*). As a self-proclaimed secular rationalist, he is one of the fiercest critics of *Hindutva* ideology and its attendant practices in India. In a career spreading over four decades, he has produced several documentary films including *Father, Son and Holy War*, which was adjudged as one of the fifty most memorable international documentaries of all time by Dox. As an opponent of religious extremism, his films are uncompromising cinematic critiques of an oppressive nation-state and its jingoistic policies. They challenge the sectarian violence, caste-based discrimination, and patriarchal determinism that plague contemporary India in the guise of "nationalism."

Selected Filmography

Reason (2018)
Jai Bhim Comrade (2012)
War and Peace (2002)
A Narmada Diary (1995)
Father, Son and Holy War (trans. Pitra, Putra aur Dharmayuddha) (1995)
Ram Ke Naam (trans. In the Name of God) (1992)
In Memory of Friends (1990)
Hamara Shahar (trans. Bombay Our City) (1985)
Prisoners of Conscience (1978)
Waves of Revolution (1974)

What made you a documentary filmmaker? How did your love for the documentary medium begin?

I did my BA in English at Bombay University in 1970. Then I got a scholarship to do another BA in sociology at Brandeis University, USA. I returned to India in 1972 and worked for a village project for a few years in Madhya Pradesh, mainly doing social and educational work. But the pace of work was very slow, and I was getting frustrated. At that moment the Bihar Movement had begun. It was a nonviolent student movement, which turned into a mass movement against corruption and other social evils like dowry and caste. I went there to see what was happening and got involved in it. As a part of the movement, I was asked to take photographs on a particular day (November 4, 1974) when the police were expected to use violence to curb a mass demonstration. I went to Delhi to borrow a camera but instead of a still camera I found a friend Rajiv Jain who had a Super 8 camera. The two of us came back with his Super 8 camera and my 8 mm camera that had belonged to my late grandfather. With this low-grade equipment, we filmed that day's demonstration, which was pretty violent. And then, I thought I could do something more with it, because Super 8 was a format where you shoot on reversal film, not on a negative. That is, every time you project the film, it gets scratched, or breaks, or you could lose it altogether. So we blew it up to 16 mm. As I didn't have money, we projected it onto a screen and refilmed it with a 16 mm camera. The projector and camera were not in perfect sync so we got a strobe-like effect but it looked dramatic. Then I invited another friend, Pradeep Krishen, to join me as he had just bought a second-hand, three-turret Bell & Howell 16 mm camera. You needed to actually hand-crank it, to shoot for less than one minute at a time. So, with that equipment, we went back and filmed in Bihar. None of the sound was synchronized. We had a cassette tape recorder to record voice at the same time, but it was never accurately matched. The film stock itself was outdated, old color footage that Shyam Benegal[3] was going to throw away but someone told us that it may still work as black and white. So, there were all these technical problems when *Waves of Revolution* was made. By the time the film was completed, the Emergency was declared, and most of the people I had filmed were in jail. We couldn't show the film openly because of the fear of ending up in jail but held a few clandestine screenings for friends. I then cut one print of the thirty-minute film into four smaller segments and smuggled these out through friends going abroad. A few months later I reached Montreal, Canada, where I got a teaching assistantship at the McGill University to pursue an MA degree. I then put the segments together and we showed it at various universities abroad as a protest against the Emergency. When the Emergency ended in 1977, I came back to India. I found that all political prisoners had not yet been released, though the Janata Party had come to power saying that they would release all prisoners. So, I continued making a film on the condition of prisoners, during, before, and after the Emergency. That became *Prisoners of Conscience*. Over time, I eventually ended up becoming a filmmaker, although it was not my original plan.

What is the process of your documentary practice?

That is quite vague. Take, for instance, the films I ended up doing about communal violence. They started from the general fact that communal feelings were being cynically manipulated by political forces. More and more in the mid-

1980s, we saw examples of communal riots. I wanted to intervene, but didn't know how. When the Khalistan movement began, I was looking for a way to intervene, especially after the 1984 anti-Sikh massacre. As many as 3,000 Sikhs were killed on the streets of Delhi after the assassination of Indira Gandhi.[4] I went to the camps where refugees from Sikh families were camped in front of the Rashtrapati Bhavan[5] in the Boat Club. Those days, people could go and demonstrate there; now you can't. I interviewed some of the widows and mothers who had lost their loved ones. I still didn't know what to do next, as it was a very depressing moment to see the horrific incidents that had happened. People were already forgetting it, pretending it hadn't happened. I wanted to go to Punjab[6] to do something useful, to fight the polarization that was taking place there. I finally got my opportunity when I met a group of Hindus and Sikhs who were carrying forward the message of communal harmony as spoken and written by the legendary martyr of India's freedom struggle, Bhagat Singh.[7] They were carrying this message going from village to village in Punjab. I followed them. Typically, I end up doing my research while on the job. I don't usually first research something and then decide to make a film. I start making a film instinctively and then study the subject more in depth. So, I read about Bhagat Singh's writings and was amazed at this person. At the age of twenty-three, Bhagat Singh had already done enormous reading. His handwritten diary shows that he had read everything from Wordsworth, Mark Twain, Gandhiji, Tagore, Marx, Engels, and others. His diary had quotations from all he had read while in

Still 1 Anand Patwardhan during the filming of *Waves of Revolution*. Image Credit: Raghu Rai.

prison. From prison he also wrote a booklet, *Why I Am an Atheist?* That became a kind of backbone for the film—Bhagat Singh's message at a time of communal violence between Hindus and Sikhs. The structure and storyline and everything emerged from the process, and was not prethought.

I never have a script; I don't know exactly what I am doing while I am doing it. I have my own camera and am on call. I follow my intuition, and there are plenty of things I shoot that don't end up in any film. They become a kind of a personal archive. But eventually, when I am following a particular issue related to a particular subject, after a while I start seeing the patterns in what I have shot, by watching it again and again and seeing how some aspects interconnect. The film structure then evolves from the editing process.

War and Peace *is about the trajectory of a nation that achieved Independence through non-violent means to a country that is strengthened by nuclear weapons? Do you think it's only people's security and interests that is behind such a shift? Why do you think the Gandhian notion of nonviolence is still valid?*

Nuclear weapons have made not just India but the whole world insecure. Today, the world is once again on the brink with a mad Korean and a mad American both with their fingers on the button. *War and Peace* like all my films was not scripted but emerged from what I observed over four years, shooting in four countries. Of course, my own influences, which are a free-flowing mixture of Gandhi, Ambedkar, and Marx, impact what and how I film, but the outcome is not predictable even to me. As the editing went on (this is where the film takes on structure), I realized the need for a first-person narrative to bring disparate parts together. As I traced India journey from non-violence to nuclear nationalism, Gandhi's assassination was the perfect place to begin. In September 2001, I was going to end the film with a scene of memorial peace lamps going down the Hiroshima River. Then the attack on the twin towers of the World Trade Centre took place and the crazy American "revenge" bombing of Iraq began. Could nonviolence have been appropriate even after 9/11? Again, I found my answer in Gandhi's words. So, Gandhi became the two bookends of the film.

Father, Son and Holy War *is an examination of the post–Babri Masjid sectarian/religious violence. The second half of the film called "Hero Pharmacy" is a hilarious take on Indian machismo. Elaborate on the choice of the title? Do you*

think the patriarchal values ingrained in Indian psyche are behind communal violence?

The two parts of *Father, Son and Holy War* were titled "Trial by Fire" and "Hero Pharmacy." "Trial by Fire" looked at what our religious patriarchal system has done to women, exploring both the concept of Sati among Hindus and of Talaq among Muslims. It also examined the effects of communal riots, especially on women. The second part "Hero Pharmacy" looked at how patriarchy has socialized men into equating sexuality with violence and machismo. In fact, if you study war and communal violence anywhere in the world, you will see this same connection. Men's fragile self-image and feelings of sexual inadequacy make them vulnerable to charlatans peddling aphrodisiacs, be they the mendicant on the street or the politician on the podium exhorting his followers to prove their manhood against "the other."

Jai Bhim Comrade *was your response to Dr. B. R. Ambedkar and his politics. Can you explain the philosophy and the vision behind the film?*

The title came very naturally. Before I started showing the film to people, when they had only heard the title, some people in the Dalit community got angry. This was because they thought I was calling Dr. Ambedkar a Communist, as in Comrade Ambedkar, as Bhim is a loving short form for Bhimrao Ambedkar. There is a friction between the Communist ideology and the ideology of Dr. Ambedkar and many Ambedkarites. Some people exaggerate the difference between the two. In reality, the title of my film doesn't refer to Dr. Ambedkar; it is actually about Comrade Vilas Ghogre, the person I knew who had earlier sung in my film *Bombay Our City*. I mean, he didn't sing in my film; he was not a musician that I hired. We were working together against the slum demolitions, and I recorded some of the songs he sang. One song of his runs through the whole of *Bombay Our City*. Later, when the Ramabai firing occurred in Mumbai in 1997,[8] ten Dalits were shot dead by the police because they had been protesting on the streets against the desecration of an Ambedkar statue. Somebody had put a garland of footwear on the Ambedkar statue, and people came out of their colony onto the streets to protest. They were just sitting and blocking the road nonviolently. The police arrived and shot ten people dead on the spot. They even fired into the colony. They killed people who had nothing to do with that minor protest. Vilas Ghogre, who lived in the neighborhood, visited the spot and became so depressed that four days later he hung himself in his own hut. I was shocked. He was a Dalit

Ambedkarite who had become a Marxist. I couldn't understand why he would commit suicide because he was a revolutionary whose music I had recorded over a long period many years ago. He was full of optimism and courage, not one to take his own life. Trying to understand this took me further into his story and his music, and I ended up recording a lot of other musicians who were using poetry and the music of protest within the Dalit community. So, it became a film about music and resistance as well as about the police firing and its aftermath.

As a documentary filmmaker, what is the responsibility you feel toward your subjects? How do you deal with ethics when you edit certain footage? When you are working with people, you have so much responsibility and how do you deal with that?

There is no formula. Film theory talks of "self-reflexivity" and it is fashionable to show yourself filming, so people understand the concept of subjectivity. You can always pretend that you are ethical through this or that device but I think ethics is deeper than that. Ethics is the way you understand the world and react to it. If your reasons for making a film have integrity, it will also end with integrity. When it is like that, you will not relax after the film is made; you will make sure that the film is used, and make sure that the film is shown to people whom the film is about. Through such interaction, you can gauge if your film is indeed in some way useful. Otherwise, you may merely be robbing people of their image and selling this as an exotic product. That sense of responsibility is not something one can teach; it has to come from inside. It will inform how you make your films and it will inform how you show them.

You've been constantly stopped and constantly told by the state that you can't show your films. You've fought against the state but you've also been highly awarded. Why is the state so important? And, why do you always have to fight to have your films screened?

I am not a revolutionary who believes in the armed overthrow of the state. I am fighting a constitutional battle. We have a good Constitution that gives us a lot of weapons to fight for social and economic justice. I am trying to do that. All my films are well within the spirit of the Indian Constitution. When the state violates this spirit, I have the full right to oppose this. If and when the state gives me an award, they are not doing me a favor. If I fight in court and get my films on Doordarshan,[9] they are not doing me a favor. They are supposed to do that. If a film has won a National Award, they should be showing it on a national TV. We always argue in court that when the government gives me a National Award, it cannot then say that the film mustn't be shown on Doordarshan. That means they are saying that some elite jury in a festival can watch the film but the public cannot. We have won all these battles. These battles have been constitutional battles, and I am not the first person to fight them. People like K. A. Abbas[10] has done it long before me. My lawyers and I used judgments that already existed that said that freedom of expression is important in our Constitution, as is the right of the public to information. If we live in a democracy, we have to have freedom of expression. And let's face it, even if a Left government came to power, I could still be fighting the same battles for the freedom of expression.

Bombay Our City *was a shocking portrait of the sufferings of people who were displaced in the name of development. In fact, you were marching with the protesters supporting the displaced? Do you think such activism is essential for a documentary filmmaker? And how do you respond to the anger of a woman for filming their perils?*

We reached Bandra (in Bombay) just after a slum had been demolished and people had temporarily moved onto a nearby footpath with their meager belongings. The anger and frustration of the woman I interviewed was palpable. For her, we photographers were mere parasites who could do nothing to help. While it felt bad to be branded, I knew that what she was saying was true. I kept filming despite my own discomfort. In retrospect, it is one of the most powerful moments in the film. It confronts those of us who record other peoples' misery as voyeurs. Similarly, when the film is later screened for an audience, the charge of voyeurism confronts the audience. In a sense, it forces both filmmaker and audience to confront voyeurism. What are we going to do about what we see?

In fact, after the film *Bombay Our City* was made, we screened it in slums all over the city, including in the slum where the angry slum dweller had confronted me. She loved the film and saw it many times. Later I joined a group of slum dwellers who had been displaced after a new demolition on an indefinite hunger strike to get relocated on a new plot of land. After the famous film actress Shabana Azmi[11] (who had recently seen *Bombay Our City*) joined our hunger strike, we became front-page news and within five days the government conceded to our demands and relocated the slum dweller in Goregaon. It was a minor but significant victory.

How each individual reacts is his or her own prerogative. Activism is a part of my process. I may have begun a film from the impulse of activism but my involvement cannot end when the filmmaking ends. I have to justify my act of filmmaking to myself by exploring how best the film can be useful as a palpable instrument of change.

Over these years, how have things changed in your filmmaking? Do you feel that you are more reflective now or is there something that has changed in your filmmaking?

I think that is for others to judge because I don't perceive the change very clearly. That change is probably happening very slowly; it is not dramatic. The technology has changed. I started out with 8 mm and moved to 16 mm film from the 1970s to 1995. Celluloid film was more expensive and cumbersome but, as a result, you shot much less and with greater planning. After 1995 I switched to video, first Hi 8, then VHS, then mini DV tape and now digital HD. This was cheaper and easier than celluloid but I ended up shooting huge amounts. So, your workload actually increases. You have to watch so much more material than before and you're never fully satisfied, because you can always tweak it. The film is never settled. In the old days, once you cut the negative, the film became sacrosanct as recutting it would be messy. Now you shoot a lot and hope that somewhere you hit the target. But in the old days, you had to be very careful because you did not want to waste any footage. I actually ended up becoming a cameraman for that reason. When I was relying on a camera person to shoot, a lot of footage went to waste because sometimes the cameraperson would shoot what I did not want. So, I started shooting myself to control the economics. Later, I started enjoying the eye contact in an interview where I was the camera person because the person is looking directly into my camera, and not off to the side. One disadvantage though is that when you are both the cameraperson and the editor, it narrows down the element of surprise by reducing the possibilities of happy accidents. To get the best of both worlds, I sometimes shoot myself but also have another cameraperson to shoot alongside. When that person is someone you know very well, like it was with Ranjan Palit in *Bombay Our City* or Simantini Dhuri in some of my later films, it opens up greater possibilities.

Notes

1 Madhya Pradesh is a Central Indian state.

2 Led by Jayaprakash Narayan, the Bihar Movement (in the Indian state of Bihar) is a political movement against the corruption of the then ruling state government. The movement later became a national movement against the Indira Gandhi-led government.

3 Shyam Benegal is a distinguished Indian filmmaker who is known for his films like *Ankur* (trans. *The Seedling*) (1974) and *Nishant* (trans. *Night's End*) (1975).

4 Indira Gandhi was the first female prime minister of India.

5 Located in New Delhi, Rashtrapati Bhavan is the official residence of the president of India.

6 Punjab is an Indian state that shares borders with Pakistan.

7 Bhagat Singh was a revolutionary freedom fighter of the Indian independence movement. He was executed on March 23, 1931, by the British in India.

8 The Ramabai firing refers to the unprovoked firing of police officers on Dalit residents at the Ramabai Ambedkar Nagar colony in Mumbai on July 11, 1997.

9 Doordarshan is the official television channel of the Government of India.

10 K. A. Abbas is an Indian filmmaker and screenwriter from India. As one of the pioneers of neo-realist cinema, he is known for his films like *Dharti Ke Lal* (trans. *Children of the Earth*) (1946) and *Pardesi* (trans. *Journey Beyond Three Seas*) (1957).

11 Shabana Azmi is an Indian film and theater actress known for her roles in films like *Ankur* (trans. *The Seedling*) (1974) and *Khandhar* (trans. *The Ruins*) (1984).

Tapan Bose

Figure 2 Image Courtesy: Tapan Bose.

Known as a human rights activist and an interventionist writer, Tapan Kumar Bose is an independent documentary filmmaker from West Bengal,[1] who is currently settled in New Delhi. He began his documentary filmmaking in 1971 as an assistant to S. Sukhdev, a renowned documentary filmmaker. Bose is now regarded as a pioneering voice in the independent documentary film movement in India. A national and international award-winning filmmaker, his films majorly defend human and democratic rights. His film *An Indian Story* is now considered as an early example of independent political documentary in India. Issues like human rights violations (*An Indian Story*), Khalistan movement (*Behind the Barricades*), and Adivasi[2] rights (*The Expendable People*) are major thematic concerns of his films. He is the founder of Pakistan-India Peoples' Forum for Peace and Democracy in 1994 and the president of Other Media, New Delhi. He has been an active member of Citizen's Initiative on Kashmir since 1990. In 2017, he returned his national award as a mark of protest against the failures of the ruling government.

Selected Filmography

The Expendable People (2016)
Behind the Barricades (1993)

Bhopal: Beyond Genocide (1986)
An Indian Story (1981)

You are one of the forerunners of the independent documentary filmmaking movement in India. At what point in your life did you identify yourselves as a documentary filmmaker?

I have always loved films. I would see them all: Hollywood, Bengali films, Bombay films. My transition from a voracious viewer of all kinds of films to a more discerning film viewer happened when I came to Delhi in the early 1960s. During those days, the Soviet, German and the French cultural centers held regular film screenings. I became a regular visitor to these screenings. The immediate reason could be when I saw a long documentary called *India '67*,[3] an almost hour-long film without comments and music. The camera of the film had travelled all over the country, capturing in most intimate detail the diversity of the people, the terrain and lifestyles. It presented a picture of a country which, unlike fiction films, made me feel that I was seeing real India. It is after watching this film that I felt I should also make a film on something which is thus far not discussed in commercial and popular films.

Your filmmaking career started with the Films Division and your association with S. Sukhdev. How do you look back at those years? What moved you away from the kind of films made by the Films Division and become an independent filmmaker? And how specifically did the Emergency impact you as a filmmaker?

It is because of Sukhdev that I became a filmmaker. It is he who initiated me into filmmaking. He asked me to work with him in the film *Nine Months to Freedom* (1972). He told me thus: "help me make this film and I will make you a filmmaker." That sealed my future. I gave up my job and left for Calcutta the very next day. I never looked back after that. But after completing *Nine Months to Freedom*, I had a series of differences with him. In order to survive, S. Sukhdev returned to making advertising films that sold soap and soup. It was a strange shift for me as I moved from idealism to crass commercialism. The only good part was that they paid well. As a part of S. Sukhdev's production company, I also began to work on films for the Films Division during that time. Whenever the Films Division called for projects, I submitted proposals. It brought me in direct contact with the officials of FD who assigned films to outside producers. I soon realized that the FD documentaries had nothing to do with the people and their problems but were interested only in projecting the "success" of government's programs and schemes.

In 1973, FD assigned us to make a film on food crisis. I was happy to work on the film because I believed in the need for state control of trade in food grains. When I presented the script to the "subject experts" of the film, to my utter surprise, they told me that I should not go into all those details about farmers being cheated and people going hungry. I told Sukhdev that I was not interested in the film anymore. He told me, "Don't give up. Let us do the film. We will slip in our perspective where we can." With diffidence, I stayed with the film. The film became a mere propaganda film for Indira Gandhi's *Garibi Hatao*[4] agricultural policies. I was determined to make different kinds of films after my difference of opinion with Sukhdev and with the policies of the FD. But the experience of making *Nine Months to Freedom* deterred me from venturing into another independent film. I was married and was a father of a baby girl then. At home, I would agonize about wasting my time doing propaganda films. I must record that Maya, my wife, was more courageous. She kept encouraging me to strike out on my own. In June 1974, when the Railway Men's Federation gave a call for an all-India strike in support of their demand for higher wages, I. K. Gujral[5] called Sukhdev to make a series of documentaries that explain why the strike was bad for the country. He agreed to make these films. Since it was clear that the films would propagate the government's point of view without giving the workers a chance to explain their position, I left S. Sukhdev. I respected him as a teacher but no longer supported his politics. I think the Emergency had made my politics clear and my sense of documentary films.

Your first documentary is called An Indian Story. It was on the blinding of undertrial prisoners in Bhagalpur.[6] From the propaganda films of FD, how did you come to this film which is a severe critique of the establishment?

In 1981, in Bihar's Bhagalpur district, about thirty-seven undertrial prisoners, mostly belonging to lower castes and poor families, were blinded by using acid. Although everybody was agonized, Jagannath Mishra, then chief minister of Bihar, asserted that the blinding had "social sanction." The police force of Bihar justified this barbarism on the ground that it brought down the crime rate and ensured the safety of the people of Bhagalpur. We met some of the victims in Delhi outside the Supreme Court of India, where they had come seeking justice. I was frightened by the sight of their mutilated eyes. It was scary to realize that the police could indulge in such acts of barbarism and get away with it in the name of controlling "crime." Since the Emergency, civil rights and democratic rights are under pressure. Dissent was being criminalized. Anti-Naxalite operations had added "encounter" to the lexicon of policing in India. This was a coverup for extrajudicial killings. The blinding of undertrial prisoners in Bhagalpur and backing of this by the business community and sections of the press posed a serious question about the nature of democracy and the future of fundamental rights of the poor.

I spent several days listening to them, asking questions about their life in Bhagalpur, the kind of work they did and about their families. After recording their interviews, we went to Bhagalpur. It was clear that we had to be very careful of the police. We were told by Gajendra Singh, the deputy inspector general of police, Bhagalpur Range, that the chief judicial magistrate, S. K. Sinha, was too liberal in granting bail to criminals. We were told that criminals roamed about freely intimidating witnesses so that the police were unable to prove the cases against them. Under these circumstances, the police had no option but to blind these criminals. It was clear that the police enjoyed the support of the ruling elite. In my mind's eye, there emerged a film which would put all these in a context.

While travelling we came across a village called Nawada Bazar. It was inhabited mainly by the lower-caste people. During the 1970s, a social activist Rajkishore along with the villagers built a dam and a reservoir there as a solution to the water crisis faced by them. Instead of congratulating the villagers for building a dam, the district officials were angry with what had happened. They accused the people of Nawada Bazar of encroaching on government land, building an unsafe dam, and spreading anti-state propaganda. The village was told to disband the people's committee which was managing the dam. When people refused, hundreds of armed police descended on the village, beating up and arresting the people. The police dynamited the dam, destroying it totally, and dug up the road. Nawada Bazar was declared a Naxalite village. We recorded the story sitting in the main *chaupal* (an open meeting place in a village) of the village, surrounded by people. In the group was an old man wearing round glasses. Through the lenses I could see his eyes still asking why the government destroyed their village. The old man's face with the silent question gave us the idea of the film. The film not only tells the story of blinding but also foregrounds the instances of ruthless exploitation of the peasantry by the dominant caste landlords who

Still 2 A still from the film *An Indian Story*. Image Courtesy: Tapan Bose.

enjoy the maximum share of sociopolitical and economic resources of the state. It also shows the ugly nexus between the landlords, the politicians, bureaucrats, and the police.

Beyond Genocide *was first of its kind documentary on Bhopal Gas* **Tragedy.**[7] *As the title suggests, do you think it was genocide with larger implications than a tragedy? Don't you think it was risky to take such a position since there was an involvement of state and corporates?*

It took me almost a year and a half to complete this film. I could do this because I was also a part of the movement. In fact, there are two versions of this film. One is the longer version of about one and half hours, and it is called *Neerasha Ke Andher Mai* (trans. *Inside the Frustration*) and the other one is *Beyond Genocide*. This is the kind of film which I always dreamt to make. The focus of the film is people and their effort to get justice for the kind of tragedy they suffered. It's not much about the incident of the gas leak but what was happening inside the factory. As a filmmaker, I always believe that film visuals should speak. With that in mind, we shot whatever we could shoot. We tried to expose the lies behind it by exploring the real situations. We could explore the carcinogenic effect of this manmade disaster. We reached the poisoned city on the third day after the gas leakage. We worked with the victims' community and decided to tell the story which the official media could never tell. The film questioned everything, including the official press conference where "the Government had already made up its mind that MIC [*methyl isocyanate* gas] would not have any long-term effects." The film ends with an image of the back of a baby gasping for breath. She was a little girl Zaina, who died when she was eighteen days old. This image even haunts me now. It was clear from the autopsy report that she was poisoned in her mother's womb. The film exposed the criminal negligence of the multinational company and the inadequacy of the Indian laws. It also established the criminal nexus between the multinational company and Indian politicians/bureaucrats.

Behind the Barricades *presents Khalistan*[8] *movement in Punjab. There is a risk when you make a film on separatist movements. Your point of view may generate fury either from the state or from the separatists. How difficult it was to make a film on such a complex topic without compromising your point of view?*

It was in 1989 that I completed *Behind the Barricade*. It begins with still shots of the massacre of the Sikhs after the assassination of Indira Gandhi by her two Sikh bodyguards. Holding an entire community responsible for the actions of two of its members and branding them as anti-nationals created a situation of a war within the country. The organized killings of the Sikhs all over the country and states complicity forced thousands of Sikhs to return to Punjab. The Khalistan militancy, which was on the wane, revived thus. Rajiv Gandhi's government dealt with the militancy with brute force. There was no attempt to dialogue or to heal the wounds inflicted on the Sikh community. Punjab was put under the rule of the central government and the Parliament of India enacted a law suspending sections of the Fundamental Rights guaranteed by the Constitution. My film, while foregrounds the visuals of the acts of state repression, also traces the development of Sikh political consciousness or what may be called the Sikh identity politics over a period of six decades from the 1930s. It juxtaposed the present-day repression with the past experiences of repression through rare historic old paintings preserved in the Golden Temple museum,[9] interviews with Sikh militants, moderate and radical leaders, Sikh army officers, and common people.

Your films like The Expendable People *and* Jharkhand *are a fervent appeal for justice for the Adivasis. Why do you think such indigenous stories should be filmed? As an outsider, how do you position yourself in the film?*

My last two films, *The Expendable People* and *Jharkhand*, focus on the lives of indigenous communities in Jharkhand (a state in East India). *Jharkhand* was meant to be part of a trilogy, but the other two films could not be completed because we ran out of money. The film attempts to examine the social and economic dilemmas of the Adivasis. It also seeks to document how the Adivasis lost control over the forests which sustained them. I made *Expendable People* a few years later using archival footage and interviews with the legendary anthropologist Christoph von Fürer-Haimendorf[10] and Adivasi activists from the 1980s and 1990s. Some of these Adivasis activists were killed by the Indian security forces for their opposition to commercial forestry projects. The film spans the continuing struggle of the Adivasis for their right to life and dignity against British colonialists and, now, as citizens of India, against their own government and democratic institutions. The film also focuses on a moment of hope. Although the government brought in the Forest Rights Act (2006) to right the "historical wrongs," it only betrayed its own promise. Although this has been done from an anthropological point of view, I have never tried to speak for the community in the film. I knew that I am an outsider and my approach was just to witness the events that happened. I was very conscious that I should not once again victimize them through the film. It has been framed in such a way that Adivasis speak for themselves.

Notes

1   West Bengal is a state in East India.
2   *Adivasi* is a collective term that refers to the tribal population in India.
3   *India '67* (1968) is a documentary film directed by S. Sukhdev to commemorate twenty years of India's freedom. It was produced by the Films Division of India.
4   *Garibi Hatao* (trans. Remove Poverty) was a slogan used by Indira Gandhi during her parliamentary election campaign in 1971.
5   Inder Kumar Gujral was the minister of Information and Broadcasting during the Emergency in 1975. He later served as the twelfth prime minister of India.
6   Bhagalpur is a district in Bihar, a state in East India.
7   Considered as one of the worst industrial disasters in India, Bhopal Gas tragedy refers to a toxic chemical gas leak incident at the Union Carbide India Limited pesticide plant in Bhopal (a city in the state of Madhya Pradesh) in December 1984.
8   The Khalistan movement refers to the demand for an independent state by Sikhs in the Punjab region of the Indian subcontinent.
9   Golden Temple museum is in the Golden Temple, located in the city of Amritsar (Punjab).
10 Christoph von Fürer-Haimendorf was an Austrian ethnologist and a professor at the SOAS at London.

Amar Kanwar

Figure 3 Image Credit: Monica Tiwary.

Based in New Delhi, Amar Kanwar is an artist whose oeuvre varies from documentary films through art exhibitions to installations. Although he works with documentary and archival images, his use of cinematic methods such as editing, narration, cross-referencing, among others, have pushed the documentary medium beyond its definitions, regular motives, and claims of realism. Integrating testimonies, silent images, and poetry, his films register issues such as territorial conflicts (*A Season Outside*), sexual violence (*The Lightning Testimonies*), and ecological aggressions (*The Scene of Crime*). Moving between abstract yet choreographed images and innovative narratives, his films often engage the intersectional and multidimensional aspects of an issue at hand. Although his films are affective and experimental narratives, which involve and interpret various occurrences of his times and beyond from multiple points of view and in different artistic formats, they, intriguingly, express strong political content.

Selected filmography

Such a Morning (2017)
The Sovereign Forest (2011)
The Lightning Testimonies (2007)

Somewhere in May (2005)
A Night of Prophecy (2002)
The Many Faces of Madness (2000)
A Season Outside (1997)
Marubhumi (1996)

When did your love for documentary filmmaking start? Was it an accidental turn or a calculated entry? Share your early exposure and influences that shaped you as a filmmaker?

There are many influences. Filmmaking was totally accidental. I had no intentions or dreams or even basic understanding of filmmaking. Often everything seems to happen by chance. Getting admission into the Department of History of the Ramjas College at University of Delhi was perhaps the most significant. Ramjas was quite a violent place; it had a very strong presence of gangs of men from the youth wings of the BJP and Congress. It was a practice ground, a stepping-stone before breaking into national politics. There was muscle and money power on show, and physical violence, thrashings, and knife incidents occurred every now and then. I don't think I went to the college canteen till almost the middle of my second year because it wasn't safe. I was fortunate not just to move into this kind of troubled space but to also join a history department that had several exceptional teachers. It was informed, innovative, sincere, passionate, and engaging teaching and opened many windows and ways of thinking. If I had gone to another college or even to another department, most likely the trajectory of my life would have been very different. Three years later, in 1984, when the Sikh massacres began in Delhi, the teachers in the history department felt it was necessary to respond. Informally the department shut down, and everyone tried to help in any way possible. I had just seen the priest of my neighborhood *Gurudwara* (a place of worship for Sikhs) being thrashed in the street and shops of Sikhs being burnt in my local market in the presence of the police as the other shop owners were watching on. In a few days, I joined the citizens groups managing relief and spent the next few months in relief camps as a volunteer, helping, listening, doing anything that I could. This grew into campaigns for justice later. More than 3,000 people were killed in three to four days in my city in broad daylight, and the system stood by and allowed it to happen. This single fact was enough to alter one's mind and life path.

In a month, the Bhopal gas leak happened. Again, there were people who responded in many ways and I joined that as well. These events were very disturbing; I saw that those responsible for the Bhopal disaster and the anti-Sikh massacre were being protected by the government. Most of the victims in Bhopal happened to be Muslims living in the poorer part of the city where the gas had leaked. Both events had a strange resonance. The public and the political system pretended, accepted, rationalized, justified, protected, and moved on.

After that I didn't feel like staying on forever inside the university. I wanted any course anywhere that was a bit open and without torturous systems of evaluation. Again by chance, I heard about the course at the Mass Communication Research Centre at Jamia Millia University in Delhi. I applied and somehow got in and learned to make film. All of this seemed to come together. Later I felt documentaries were a way to express, bear witness, argue, and respond to all that was happening around me. I didn't question it much at that time.

A year after the course was over and after making a couple of films, I quit the profession feeling that it was not the right thing to do. Filming others was not comfortable; it was also too expensive, and there seemed to be too many basic contradictions. Again by chance, a new initiative was developing, and I joined even before it formally came together as the People Science Institute. But mainly what matters is that I left making films, for good, as I thought then. I left the city too, and became the only researcher in a project on occupational health of coal miners. The next two to three years were spent mainly in the coal mining regions of Central India, almost always on my own, very unsure of what I was doing but still talking to coal miners and their families and learning from those who had conceived the project. These few years taught me in many ways what this country was all about. In late 1991, I began filming in Dalli-Rajhara in Chhattisgarh. I started on the day after Shankar Guha Niyogi was assassinated. I was to come earlier but I didn't own a camera or any financial resources to film. The experience of the weeks after the murder and of the people's movement there has also never left me. All of this impacts every film I made later.

Unlike your early films, **A Season Outside** *experiments with the form. There is a deliberate presence of the filmmaker available in the form of voice-over, juxtapositions or cross-references. Could you explain your creative choices? How do you revisit the film both in terms of the content and form after twenty years of its making?*

You have three questions actually and I will try to answer briefly because the real answer to this is a pretty long conversation. I made the film about twenty years ago, in 1997–8; it's still very fresh in my mind. I had made several films before but for various reasons I had felt like I was again at the end of the road. It was not possible to survive economically making films the way I wanted, and it was too difficult to make films the way others wanted. So, when the possibility of this film came along I was quite sure that this would be perhaps my last film.

So I tried to make it exactly like I wanted, trust my feelings rather than what was expected or what I ought to have done. I felt that there was something terribly wrong with the way I was working, making films had become too convoluted, and forcing images, people, and opinions into a presentable, acceptable jigsaw was a bit torturous. I had decided to do many things: make a list of what I didn't want and why; and, make a list of what I would like to try why, and then test it out and see how that evolves. In brief and indicatively: I was tired of the "predetermined correct line" and the going out and getting and presenting the reality jigsaw that followed. I was also tired of the reactions to this form, which seemed to be creating another series of templates like for instance, of doing away with the perception of an obvious point of view, reducing the presence of the maker and making it seem as if the audience and the subject were getting closer, be a fly on the wall, tell a human interest story, follow the festival matrix of charming ironic intriguing untold under belly, underdog story, or the dramatic inspirational struggle or the structured entertaining captivating narrative arc woven deftly and almost invisibly into the unfolding of seemingly organic real events, and so on and so on. I was tired and uncomfortable with my own high skill at manipulating interviews so that I got the right words in the most efficient manner for the greatest of impacts in the least duration so that it would not become tedious to listen. I was also tired of seeking appreciation from one paradigm or the other. I was curious to see the difference in the images, the eye and nature of intuition that arose, and if I researched a location or if didn't. I wanted to cook long, slowly and see what emerged. I wanted to make like I think. Could I think aloud and still tell and share? Can I go from my mother to the tree outside to the past and return to the present and still be coherent and relevant? Does the audience have to understand everything I say? Can I say something for one and another thing for another? Is reality only what you can see and tell? Is the inner self also part of understanding our social reality? Can I speak about the contradictions and vulnerabilities that exist within political struggles? Can I relate to the self without being narcissistic and yet be political? Can my own vulnerabilities, confusions, and search become real and part of the film? Are fantasies more real and closer to the truth than fact and data? If so, then what

Still 3 A still from the film *A Season Outside*. Image Courtesy: Amar Kanwar.

is the language that could tell the reality of fantasy? Can these two languages intersect seamlessly? Can there be layers and layers so that every viewing, telling reveals more and more? Can I present a point of view without needing for you to agree to it?

These were some of the questions that led to the making of *A Season Outside*. Interrogating intent also shapes content and perhaps therefore organically creating a form. Ever since then I have added a few more questions to the list and perhaps I am making the same film over and over again, trying various ways and routes to comprehend the violence of our inner and outer selves.

As a sequel to **A Season Outside,** **A Night of the Prophecy** *engages with violence in a broader sense of the word. It travels throughout India and seeks to address the fault lines of caste, nationalism, labor, and self-determination using poems and songs. What is the vision behind the film?*

I had travelled extensively throughout India for a few years with *A Season Outside* screening to various kinds of rural and urban audiences, with lengthy post-screening interactions and discussions. Just prior to the making of *A Night of Prophecy*, again I was travelling almost continuously for about three years, to very different regions, researching and filming. I had a sense of extreme churning, despair, and remarkable resilience in these journeys. I also felt exhausted by a kind of super articulation all around, those who could speak were speaking skillfully and continuously but it seemed like no one was really listening or understanding each other. I also wanted to entangle the discussions from within *A Season Outside* with another set of experiences and questions. Was listening, dialogue, and comprehension really possible? At another level, in another way perhaps? What were the many ways in which people expressed their sorrow, strength, and histories? I had read Prakash Jadhav's poem "Under the Dadar Bridge." The poem was stunning and reminded me of my own attenuations. I had felt then that any alternative politics in India must be able to comprehend many realities in varied and deeper ways. It must also be able to understand the past and have a sense of the future. There was also a need to find a way to break out of ideological camps and find a way to relate to the human condition. These were just thoughts that, for instance, led to the following hypothesis [only for myself]: Is it possible for multiple and deeper comprehensions to occur through a poem? Is it possible to understand the passage of time through poetry? And if you could do that, for one special moment, then would it be possible to predict and see the future? The search for possible answers to these questions became the film.

The Lightning Testimonies *is available both as a documentary film and as an installation. So is* **The Sovereign Forest.** *Again, some of your films from a puritan point of view are less documentaries and more of installations. What is the rationale and philosophy that guides you in such experimentations?*

The same that guides most of my experimentation: curiosity, inadequacy, searching for more meanings, trying to understand, and express in varied ways. For instance, the installation form of *The Lightning Testimonies* presents the possibility of seeing several events in simultaneity, at times designed, at times random and temporarily destroying the chronological understanding. The possibility of seeing new interconnections may suddenly emerge or you could make your own personal narrative. Gujarat 2002 could intersect with Nagaland 1952 and Khairlanji 2006 and Punjab 1947. Flashbacks and flashforward could be experienced together. Sexual assault by a victorious mob could be seen in parallel with sexual assault by a defeated mob. How to understand the large-scale sexual violence and abductions of 1947 and the mass rapes of 1971 during the Bangladesh liberation struggle? Testimonies are also fluid, changing, and expressing themselves in varied ways often outside the spoken and written word. How does one sense those narratives? Many known accepted meanings may fade away when one is freed from chronological conclusions, and new comprehensions could become possible. The installation even switches from multiple narratives into a single narrative but then spoken in a language that you don't know and yet you understand, in some other deeper way. A certain way of looking may create a certain kind of comprehension that may create a certain kind of compassion.

Nothing is static, pure, greater, or lesser. One set of inadequacies creates a set of dilemmas that in turn creates another set of experimentation. In *The Torn First Pages*, the many dimensions of the Burmese democracy movement seemed impossible to reduce into a single narrative, so I began with four short films, each of them operating on different rhythms of time, trying to find varied routes of understanding and commenting as well. There was no client, funder, commission, or deadline. I felt the need to respond as I understood more.

I made a little bit more. These films were shown in various ways for a few years: in a foyer of a club, in university large open-air night screenings, in a village *maidan* on a small television, in the Nobel Museum in Norway, on a ship in the cargo hold-turned-stage, and so on. Eventually, it also grew into a multiple projection installation with three parts, the second part presenting a spectrum of archival time, and the third becoming an experience of multiple time. It was another way to try and present a sense of the very complex multiethnic democracy movement in Burma, and the experience and memory of several decades of resistance and of living in exile.

In *The Sovereign Forest*, sometimes a central film like *The Scene of Crime* creates the possibility of new meanings and raises important questions such as How to understand crime? Is legally permissible evidence adequate to understand the extent and nature of a crime? Can "poetry" be presented as "evidence" in a criminal or political trial? What is the validity of this evidence? Adding evidence in multiple forms around this film slowly grew into the larger installation *The Sovereign Forest*. Intersecting vocabularies and forms about a recurring crime may reopen forgotten senses. Eventually *The Sovereign Forest* became a fluid expanding installation attempting to initiate a creative response to our understanding of crime, politics, human rights, and ecology. The validity of poetry as evidence in a trial, the discourse on seeing, on compassion, justice, and the determination of the self—all came together in a constellation of films, texts, books, photographs, seeds, and processes. Installations like *The Sovereign Forest* also allow and create possibilities of multidisciplinary collaborations and other voices to come in and make newer meanings, experiences, and understandings. So, as it develops there are different rationales for each work.

There is the dual project of archiving history and archiving life in every documentary film. Documentary films in a sense are available museums of time. But, in the case of installation, once you dismantle the fitting and furnishing, we rarely get a chance to experience your work. So how do you preserve the installation for the generations to come?

I have made more than perhaps fifty films by now for various modes of disseminations, maybe a couple of dozen for television, screened in a few hundred film festivals, distributed thousands of DVDs and VHS tapes, and also made about three to four moving image–based installations. Work that resonates with people and has some meaning for others tends to survive. If not, it disappears. Sometimes the installations have different versions to enable showing in different contexts; sometimes a part of the installation can be shown on its own as films. So some parts and versions have different lives. Installations are also about being able to engage with audiences in a city, through the entire day, every day, over a long duration of time. People return to the work again, bring more people; get students, open varied kinds of relationships and processes with the work. I have presented one installation in India, in a self-rented warehouse for almost five years, continuously open to the public and accompanied with a sustained audience interaction process. Again, another installation was presented in a busy modern shopping mall in another city for seven months. There are more such illustrations. All of these have taken years of preparation with detailed and widespread audience engagement and educational programs in collaboration with and hosted by local activist and cultural groups and organizations. I don't think there is much to worry about the preservation of these installations. Perhaps, in the years to come, there will be a few public institutions who will ensure that these installations will find a permanent home and keep showing them for future generations.

Independent documentary filmmakers in India are usually praised for turning filmmaking into a more democratic space by reducing the distance between the filmmaker, the filmed and the viewers. Your documentary films, on the other hand, are to a certain extent esoteric. Do you consider your documentary as elitist?

I learned quite early that there are several notions about the "public" and what is suitable or not, for them. I had thought then that perhaps it's better to go and show something, interact, listen to people, and check it out for myself. I soon learned that the first person was quite different from the second. Sometimes the first one was quite different from even himself or herself at various moments. Very soon you also realize that everyone is thinking in varied ways at varied points in time for varied reasons due to varied experiences. Further, people living by the river remember in a certain way; others living on the top of a hill may recall and tell in an entirely different way.

Reflection, introspection, abstraction, experimentation, flexibility, hybridity, fusion, innovation, speculation, philosophical explorations, metaphysical inquiries, complex space and time transformations and interconnections, and so on are not only the terrain of elites or highly educated or rich people. If you look at the many older, big and small, traditions of dance, music, language, and poetry in India, you can easily find, both in the form and content, deep complexity, stunning beauty, grace, and elegance, and the most incredible distillation of meaning and thought. And all these understood and related to, over and over again by the so-called common folk. If you compare this with the documentary film form of expression, exploration, meaning making, and telling, then it often doesn't come close to the fluidity and sophistication of these narrative forms.

Rakesh Sharma

Figure 4 Image Courtesy: Rakesh Sharma.

Rakesh Sharma embarked on his filmmaking career with Shyam Benegal, a versatile Indian filmmaker, as an assistant director of a TV series *Bharat Ek Khoj* (trans. *The Discovery of India*). This was followed by a three-year stint in documentary filmmaking, working on BBC projects as well as coproducing/codirecting international projects including *Ringmasters* (1990) and *Democracy in Crisis* (1992). Although Sharma advanced to broadcasting in 1993–4, he returned to independent documentary filmmaking nearly a decade later. As a filmmaker, he is known for his political critiques of the extant practices of democracy and abuse of human rights in India. Through the deft use of images and spontaneous interviews, Sharma's films not only expose weaknesses of political processes, governance, and ideologies but also bring to the fore the paradoxes and the systemic violence plaguing modern India. For instance, his first documentary, *Aftershocks—The Rough Guide to Democracy*, explores the impact of globalization of economy and the corporatization of democracy in India. Through visual narration of the life of the displaced villagers, Sharma sheds light on how a welfare state succumbs to corporate diktats in the name of development. His best-known film, *Final Solution*, graphically depicts the trauma and violence inflicted on Muslims during the 2002 Gujarat riots. His soon-to-be-completed project, *Final Solution Revisited*, filmed over ten years, is a sequel that explores the long-term effects and aftermath of the Gujarat carnage on the community, society, and polity at large.

Selected Filmography

Final Solution Revisited (in progress)
Final Solution (2004)
Aftershocks—The Rough Guide to Democracy (2002)

Your first independent documentary, Aftershocks—A Rough Guide to Democracy, is about the corporatization of democracy. How did you come to that project?

Aftershocks was never even meant to be a film. I was in Kutch, which had been devastated by the January 2001 earthquake,[1] as a Greenpeace volunteer installing solar panels in villages which were still without electricity. The story is exactly as it unfolded in the film. While documenting the solar panel installation on video, I stumbled upon a mining company's team, conducting a strange survey, not of the devastation but of people, their possessions, livestock and trees, and so on. I found that the villagers were being denied earthquake compensation as a bid to pressurize them to cooperate with the government-owned GMDC (Gujarat Mineral Development Corporation), which saw the earthquake as a chance to rush through its long-pending land acquisition. The mining company officials, like vultures, were preying on tragedy. They were forcing the villagers to accept whatever rehabilitation package they were offering to them. Authorities even warned them to leave: "we will give you money to build you a brand-new village. Because it's a lignite rich belt, you have to vacate and leave now, or else you'll get nothing." Ironically, all this bullying and coercion was being done as per the law by the officials from the Land Revenue department working in tandem with GMDC officials. That is, through following the due processes like organizing village *panchayat*[2] meetings and putting formal resolutions to vote.

Another dimension that caught my attention was the fact that GMDC adopted two different approaches in both these villages: conciliatory with the upper-caste *Rajput* Durbars of Umarsar[3] and antagonistic with the lower-caste nomadic *Rabaris* of Julrai.[4] Initially, I saw *Aftershocks* only as an advocacy video: an intervention to get the illegally withheld money released to the villagers of Julrai and Umarsar.[5] But then the entire sequence of events began to unfold rapidly. Eventually, it turned into a film that explores the globalization of the economy and the corporatization of democracy. To my surprise, *Aftershocks* won the Best Documentary award at its international premiere in Europe, and got invited to over 120 film festivals worldwide. What was meant to be a small advocacy video shot on a handheld MiniDV Palmcorder took a life of its own!

Who is the target audience of your films? What do you hope your audience gets away after seeing your documentaries?

When I was filming *Final Solution*, these were the questions in my mind: "Why am I making this film?" and "Who am I doing it for?" After a quick initial trip, I even stayed away from Gujarat for five months till I was clear about these questions. I had little interest in speaking to the hardcore fundamentalists (can't reason or argue with faith) or secularists (why preach to the choir?), but only to the vast majority of in-between folks. I wanted to hold up the film as a mirror and ask them: Is this what you support? Do you endorse such barbaric and targeted violence in your name? I hoped that a large number of my audience would shrink back in horror with a resounding "no." I wanted to pierce the shield of apathy, ignorance, silence, and even mild approval with these images.

This, in turn, dictated the tone, tenor, structure, and style of the film. Unlike *Aftershocks*, I do not narrate *Final Solution* in the first person. There is, in fact, no commentary, narration, or voice-over in the film. It is a series of intertwined stories that add up to a meta-narrative of our times and of our polity. Through personal stories of riot-survivors, the film exposes the patterns of preplanned violence that points to far larger designs than were immediately obvious. I interspersed the film throughout with incendiary speeches by the local *pracharak* activists[6] and by the state's top political leadership during the *Gaurav Yatra*.[7] It juxtaposed the interviews of the riot-accused and their families with the condemnation of revenge and retribution by the families of *karsevaks*[8] who were killed in a fire in the S-6 compartment of the Sabarmati Express at Godhra.[9] I have interwoven all these with the Gujarat election campaign of 2002 that catapulted a virtually unknown Narendra Modi into the national political arena.

My cameras act as eyewitnesses by bringing the stories directly from the ground and leaving the audience to form their own opinions and judgments. I used only primary and first-hand material. Interviews with activists, commentators, or experts were not included. In the whole film, you won't hear even once words like "communal" or "fascist" or any other such jargonized words that ceased to have any meaning beyond the rhetoric. Again, I haven't deliberately used even the usual cathartic note of hope at the end (such as the candlelight vigil or the we-shall-overcome moment). I showed what I saw and experienced with the hope that the film will shock the gut and agitate the mind of my viewer. I hoped that both the head and the heart of the viewers would respond with the same sense of urgency that I felt.

How did you come to documentary filmmaking? What prompted you to make a film like* Final Solution, *which obviously had many political consequences?

I come from a family that suffered during the Partition of India. I had grown up hearing stories and anecdotes about the tremendous upheaval caused in my maternal grandmother's family. From being "landed gentry" in Pakistan, they turned paupers overnight in 1947, barely escaping to India in time. Since I was the oldest grandchild who frequently escorted my grandmother, often on chaperon duty, to sundry reunions within the "partition community," I was privy to their incidental narratives of grief, loss, tragedy, and mayhem.

There were always many literary magazines and books at home. Thanks to my father, a writer of short stories, who held a day job as a banker. By the age of eight or nine, I was familiar with writers such as Premchand.[10] It was Manto[11] who gave me a broader understanding of the fragmented narratives, traces of bitterness, and the occasional outburst of visceral hate that I heard from my family and many others I met during the community reunions.

After the 1984 anti-Sikh riots in Delhi,[12] I volunteered for relief work and wrote journalistic pieces. During the 1992–3 Bombay riots,[13] I took a break from my documentary filmmaking and ran a relief camp in the worst-affected suburb of Jogeshwar as a full-timer for eight months. In all those months, I couldn't bring myself to shoot even still pictures, let alone record videos. So, in 2002, when I travelled to Gujarat, a film was the last thing on my mind. I thought I might volunteer for quasi-legal relief work such as processing compensation claims, registering police FIRs (First Information Report) and coordinating with lawyers and so on. But, when I reached, I could see a pseudo-narrative being peddled there: the ongoing violence was a spontaneous reaction to what had happened in Godhra. Everything was being swept under the carpet. A month after the riots, when I was travelling in the *bastis* (ghettos), I could see that FIRs were being either fabricated or manipulated. That's when I felt that I need to go beyond being a mere relief worker/volunteer. I understood that my best "intervention" would be to ensure an unimpeachable counter-narrative that ensures justice by using all my skills, abilities, and talents as a filmmaker.

It is by sheer coincidence that I started shooting Final *Solution* on October 2, 2002, the day of Mahatma Gandhi's birth anniversary. I was detained at the end of the first day's filming because mine was the only two "private" cameras accompanying Chief Minister Modi's cavalcade to the hinterland whistle-stops during his *Gaurav Yatra* (Pride Parade) campaign. I could sense that my arbitrary detention and on-the-spot interrogation were nothing but an attempt of intimidation and harassment. It sparked a fire in me. How dare anyone stop me from filming on the streets of my own country! The credit for my making the film should go to the Modi government and its police. Had I not been arrested, I would have given up the documentary after a month of shooting. Because the kind of people we were interacting with and the horrific stories we were listening to were taking a tremendous toll on me. This episode motivated me and kept me focused. I wasn't going to let anyone intimidate me into silence, not in my own country. I, in fact, resumed filming the *Gaurav Yatra* itself the very next morning! At its premiere at the Berlin International Film Festival, *Final Solution* won the Golden Bear for Best Debut (then known as Wolfgang Staudte Award). I didn't even know that my film was in competition (with over 100 narrative feature films) or that documentaries were even considered for this award. The jury, headed by Catherine Breillat, created history and made *Final Solution* the first and only documentary so far to get this award.

In Final Solution, *you resort to a child's point of view to probe the intensity of violence that happened in Gujarat riots. Can you comment on the form and the process of making* Final Solution?

I wished to hold a mirror and ask a question: "Is this the India that we want to leave behind for our children?" Instead of speculating with my audience in post-screening sessions, I wanted to show them how the children and their minds are being poisoned. At some point, I realized that my biggest challenge was to break and get past the barriers inside people's mind. Remember: this was the first fully televised riot on TV played out in our living rooms. Most people either felt that they already knew the necessary facts about the riot or held fairly definitive opinions about it. The first hurdle was to break past that and draw them into the universe of stories I was telling. Some have criticized me saying that "I am repetitive." But it is a very deliberate choice. I am repetitive only because I wish to appear relentless. I want to give the audience the fact that this happened right across the state in a coordinated and organized manner. My intention of presenting the story after story and the pattern after pattern was to make the factual basis of the film absolutely impeccable and irrefutable.

I believe Gujarat government even held meetings after the film got serious press attention following its early international recognitions. Apparently, various legal options were discussed, including the suggestion that the documentary posed a threat of obstruction to justice since it mostly showed stories that were part of actual *sub judice* cases. But then I had anticipated and structured my material with such potential legal obstacles in mind. For instance, there were official denials about the death toll as well as the nature and the extent of violence. So, I focused only on primary eyewitnesses, in story after story, from different parts of the state. No social commentators or journalists or politicians who make allegations or utter hearsay were included in the film.

There's a nuance about hearsay that people often miss. You must understand that the most riot survivors, huddled together in relief camps, repeatedly hear each other's stories being narrated to journalists, activists, government officials, or cops. After repeated hearings, some elements of these stories became their own in that they faced similar, if not the same, set of horrors. I came across such powerful accounts, only to realize that the person had "heard" the story, not witnessed it personally. I either did not shoot or discarded all such filmed material.

Just to give you an example, the most horrific story that came to symbolize the carnage was that of Kausar Bano of Naroda Patiya,[14] whose belly was apparently slashed and the fetus therein impaled on a sword. Obviously, I could not verify the story in any way through government or police sources. Key eyewitnesses were either in hiding or too terrified to speak on camera. Dozens claimed they had "heard" definitive accounts. I broke in my head for weeks and then a simple question popped up in my head. I asked a surviving family member, "Where did you finally take the body for burial?" and he said, "XYZ graveyard." The next morning, I was in the graveyard talking to the attendants who had buried the bodies. These were eyewitnesses who had washed, clothed, and handled the

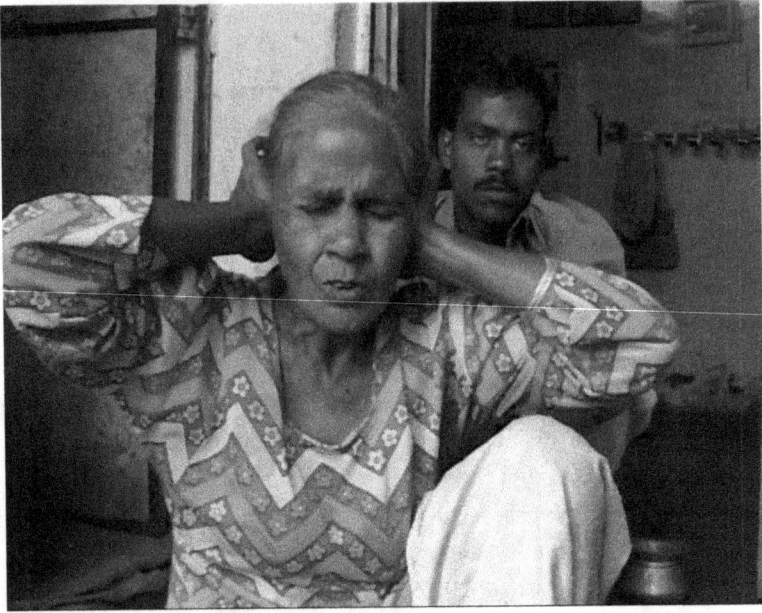

Still 4 A still from the film *Final Solution*. Image Courtesy: Rakesh Sharma.

bodies. So, when they said, "We buried the babies too, and cut their umbilical cord," it became indisputable as a direct eyewitness account of sorts.

How arduous and emotionally demanding is the experience of revisiting Gujarat riots once again in your forthcoming work, **Final Solution Revisited?**

In many ways, it was tougher to return many years later. In 2002, in the immediacy of the aftermath, the sheer scale and nature of violence has totally numbed me. But five or ten years later, the tragedies seemed starker and weathered by time. Most personal or family universes had either been destroyed or altered forever. While some people had moved on, made peace with "God's will," or "compromised" with the perpetrators, the others clung fervently to their hope for justice. What helped this time was the fact that I had an ongoing relationship with people I filmed in *Final Solution*. I kept in touch with most of them over the next ten years. Not only did they continue to share their own trials and tribulations but, in some cases, they persuaded other people to speak to me.

The most challenging part of the follow-up filming was my new focus on the Hindutva foot soldiers who formed the rioting mobs and those who were now under trial. They were facing charges of looting, arson, destruction of property, and so on. As I filmed them or their families, in a sense, I began to see them as victims too. Curiously, an overwhelming number of the convicts and those who are undertrials seemed to be from among the worst oppressed sections, namely Dalits, OBCs (Other Backward Castes), and tribals. A caste survey, by Gujarat *Jati Nirmoolan Samiti* (the Society for the Eradication of Caste), of nearly 1,500 detainees lodged in Sabarmati Jail (Ahmedabad) revealed that over 1,400 were Dalits and OBCs! They were recruited and used to unleash mayhem, and then cynically discarded, and left to rot in jails.

Another set of people I focused on, for instance, were the families of the Godhra tragedy, in whose name the Hindutva cadre had unleashed violence and continued to justify "vengeance." Of the dozen families I met, almost everyone felt angry and used. Several insisted on record that they were neither karsevaks nor Hindutva activists of any kind and that their tragedies had been used for political gains, while they had been abandoned and left to fend for themselves soon after the 2002 elections were over. *Final Solution Revisited*, thus, explores the many gray shades of truths and realities, especially the ambiguities and ambivalences that were impossible to probe in the immediate aftermath of the riot.

Notes

1 Earthquake refers to the earthquake that happened in the Indian state of Gujarat on January 26, 2001.
2 Village panchayat is the village-level self-governance system in India.
3 Rajput Durbars of Umarsar refers to the people who belong to the Rajput clan hailing from Umarsar village in Gujarat.
4 Rabaris of Julrai refers to the ethnic community who hail from the village of Julrai in Gujarat.
5 Julrai and Umarsar are villages located in the Kachchh district of Gujarat.
6 *Pracharak* is a full-time worker of Hindu nationalist organization, Rashtriya Swayamsevak Sangh (RSS).
7 *Gaurav Yatra* (trans. Pride Parade), similar to a road show, is a political campaign organized to consolidate public opinion.
8 *Karsevaks* is a term used to refer to religious volunteers.
9 The Sabarmati Express fire at Godhra refers to the burning of Sabarmati Express at Godhra in Gujarat on February 27, 2002.
10 Munshi Premchand was a legendary Hindi writer.

11 Manto was an Indian writer in Urdu language who migrated to Pakistan after the Partition of India.

12 The 1984 anti-Sikh riots in Delhi refers to a series of violent attack and killings of Sikhs in India in response to the murder of Indira Gandhi, India's then prime minister, who was assassinated by her Sikh bodyguards.

13 Bombay riots (1992–3) refers to the communal riots in Mumbai between December 1992 and January 1993 that resulted in the death of many people.

14 Kausar Bano of Naroda Patiya was a pregnant woman who was killed during the riots of Gujarat in 2002.

Gopal Menon

Figure 5 Image Courtesy: Gopal Menon.

Gopal Menon is an independent documentary filmmaker known for his people-oriented and activist documentary films. Born in Kerala,[1] he started his career producing an ecological documentary on Nilgiris biosphere (refers to a range of mountains spread across the South Indian states of Tamil Nadu, Karnataka, and Kerala). He was part of the People's Union for Civil Liberties (PUCL), a human rights body which worked on defending the rights of all members of society. His films primarily focus on religious fundamentalism, human rights, and nationality questions among others. For instance, his first feature-length film, *Naga Story: The Other Side of Silence*, documents Naga's struggle for self-determination and the subsequent human rights violations in the northeastern region of the Indian subcontinent. While *PAPA 2* concerns with the enforced disappearances in Kashmir in the 1990s, his critically acclaimed documentary *Hey Ram: Genocide in the Land of Gandhi* deals with the Gujarat riots in 2002. As the first filmmaker who made a film on Gujarat riots within the first three weeks of the riots, the film records the testimonies of the victims. In making visible the anguish and helplessness of the subjects of the riot, *Hey Ram* is a bold attempt that explores hate politics, communal riots, and right-wing fundamentalism. Known for his guerrilla filmmaking techniques, he usually films at the conflict zones very often getting hurt and arrested by the authorities. As a strong critique of extreme conservative right-wing movement in India that usually thrives outside the mainstream political debate, his films by far are the most vociferous against religious hatred and human rights violations.

Selected Filmography

The Broken Camera (2020)
The Unholy War—Part 2: In Search of Justice (2014)
The Unholy War—Part 1: In the Name of Development (2014)
Killing Fields of Muzaffarnagar (2014)
Let the Butterflies Fly (2012)
Naga Story: The Other Side of Silence (2003)
Resilient Rhythms (2002)
Hey Ram: Genocide in the Land of Gandhi (2002)
PAPA 2 (2002)

Born in a remote village in the South Indian state of Kerala, how do you look back at your journey as a documentary filmmaker? What drew you to the world of documentaries?

I started making documentaries when I was nineteen years old as a part of the protest against the destruction of Nilgiris biosphere in Kerala. With the help of environmentalists like Professor Shobhindran (my college teacher), I produced this film. I also got incredible support from my father figure in the early days, Dr. Ramakrishnan Palat. I was also helped by my father who gave me money and arranged a cameraman to produce the film. After my graduation, I wished to join a film institute; but, my parents, especially my mother, were dead against the idea. Instead, I was sent to a management institute in Coimbatore called PSG College of Technology. I was not at all interested in the course. During this period, I met C. R. Bijoy, a well-known Forest Rights and Civil Rights activist who was also part of People's Union for Civil Liberties (PUCL).[2] With the help of Bijoy, I joined Other Media Communications, a company that was created to support people's organization and movements by finding space for them in the mainstream media. At that time, Tapan Bose, a well-known documentary filmmaker who was vocal about the human rights violations in Kashmir valley, introduced me to some people who wanted to make a film on human rights violations in the Kashmir valley. These friends asked me if I could make a film on the human rights violations in Kashmir with the high-8 footage. I made a seven-minute film called *The Wounded Valley*. I still remember the opening shot of the film very vividly. The camera pans from the ground to a group of women mourning a death. As the camera zooms in, you see a mother wailing with her son on her lap and then she removes the shirt of the seven-year boy to see a single bullet mark on his neck. This small film reinforced my belief in the power of the documentary medium and I soon came to a conclusion to what Ritwik Ghatak[3] once said: "I am making films for my people; Art means war." Later, the director of Other Media Communication, Deenadayalan, suggested me to do a film on the Naga movement in the northeastern parts of India. I immediately agreed and embarked on my journey as a documentary filmmaker.

The Naga Story: The Other Side of Silence *is a sixty-minute film on the history of the Naga people which took almost five years to complete. It is the first of its kind in its treatment of the Naga struggles for identity and self-determination. How challenging was it to make a film in a geopolitically sensitive and conflict zone?*

As someone who belongs to Kerala, a South Indian state, I didn't have any idea of Northeast India. It was Deenadayalan[4] who introduced me to the world of Nagas.[5] I met a group of Naga students belonging to the Naga Students Federation,[6] and they told me many unbelievable stories of human rights violations that Nagas had to face in their ancestral lands from the Indian state. In 1998, Naga people's movement for human rights celebrated their twentieth anniversary. I was one of the invitees. I went there with a camera. Then the UN commissioner for human rights was Julian Berger. He was expected to inaugurate the meet. But he was denied a visa. So, it was inaugurated by Deenadayalan. After the meeting, I stayed back in the Naga areas. They were quite apprehensive to give me their food in the beginning, as they thought that I won't eat their food, like most of the Indians. But later they understood that I am less prejudiced than a North Indian. Culturally, Nagas are closer to the people of Southeast Asia and not South Asia. They are uninhibited in their choice of food. They relish a wide range of delicacies from insects, dogs, pork, and beef. So, when I started eating happily whatever they offered me, they began to consider me as one of them. I came to know from them that thousands had been killed in the Naga hills ever since they launched the first War of Independence against the Indian state in the 1950s, which was called the Battle of Kohima.[7] I also understood that the Naga movement was the oldest nationality movement in the Northeast. Then I made several trips to Naga ancestral lands that speared across the four states: Nagaland, Manipur, Assam, and Arunachal Pradesh. To my utter dismay, there was very little written documentation about their history and struggles. They were fiercely independent tribes till the late 1800s. Even the East India Company[8] couldn't defeat them nor could the missionaries "civilize" or convert them. But the American Baptists somehow succeeded in converting them to Christianity. So, we had to really go to the remotest places to understand their original culture. Since it is a highly militarized place, we had to travel with human rights activists who belonged to that area. Sometimes, we were stopped and taken into the military camps. During the last schedule of a one-month shoot, I went with a cameraman, Rajeev Ravi, and my editor, B. Ajithkumar. We shot in a church where porn films were screened by the Indian army. A young girl in the village was raped. After shooting the church which showed it close proximity to the military camp, we decided to shoot the interview with the rape victim whom I had met before. I proceeded to do the interview. Rajiv and Ajith stayed back in the village as she was comfortable only to talk to me. When I returned, I saw that both of them were surrounded by the Indian army. They threatened us and forced us to delete a lot of footage. But we managed to smuggle some footage without their knowledge. Otherwise, this film wouldn't have happened.

PAPA 2 *was on the enforced disappearances and notorious interrogation center in Kashmir. How critical is the situation of disappearances in Kashmir? And why did you title your film as* **PAPA 2?**

PAPA 2 was the biggest interrogation center in Kashmir run by the Central Reserve Police Force (CRPF) of India. Most of the people who were taken away from Kashmir were brought to PAPA 2. Some people who came out of PAPA 2 told me that it was like concentration camps. There is a man whom I met, who lost his eyesight because of the persistent use of light while torturing him. I have also met people who have been incapacitated because of torture. In fact, most of the people who are taken to PAPA 2 ended up dead. More than 8,000 people have been missing since 1989 and enforced disappearances are still continuing there. They have ended up either in jail or in the Dal Lake (a major lake in Srinagar). When the Dal Lake cleaning campaign took place, a lot of skeletons and skulls were dug out. There were also many other interrogation centers like PAPA 1 and Hotel 4. PAPA 2 is a bungalow located in Srinagar, and, later on, it was named as Fairview Castle and housed top bureaucrats and politicians. Since most of the people I interviewed for the film were taken temporarily or lodged in PAPA 2, I named the film so. I encountered scary moments during the shooting of the film. I was travelling with the chairperson of the Association of Parents of Disappeared Persons,[9] Parveena Ahanger, whose son had also disappeared. In the place called Anantnag I saw pro-Indian militants roaming around the

Still 5 A still from the film *The Broken Camera*. Image Courtesy: Gopal Menon.

streets brandishing their sophisticated weapons. Although Parveena asked me not to shoot, I got out of the car and started shooting. Immediately, they picked and took me to a military camp. They interrogated me for eight hours and let me off since they felt that I was a curious onlooker with a camera. When I came back to the vehicle, I found that Parveena was waiting for me there. I think the situation is not so different in Kashmir even now. Anyone can be interrogated in Kashmir at any time.

Resilient Rhythms, Marching Towards Freedom, and Of Inhuman Bondage *have addressed Dalit issues. You belong to a dominant caste. What is your take on the question of representing the vulnerable and representing Dalits?*

It would be obnoxious to think that I represent the community I make films about (including Dalits, indigenous people, religious minorities, or sexual minorities). It is another matter that I deeply identify with the causes and struggle of these people. Even though I believe in class struggle, I do think that identity politics is very vital to strengthen the struggles of the marginalized against systemic racism, discrimination, dispossession, and struggles for equality and justice. I do agree that I have the social capital of being born into a dominant caste family. Caste, class, gender, and education are all part of the privileges one has. But I have used this social capital to work with these oppressed and downtrodden people. From an early age, my political lenience and cultural inclinations have always been with the oppressed. Within my family, I have witnessed some members practicing untouchability toward the tribals who were workers in my father's farm. But my father's worldview has always been socialist and very inclusive in nature. Maybe he inherited such a sensibility from his totally uneducated mother who used to cook, eat with the tribals, and work for their rights particularly when untouchability was quite rampant in Kerala. She even distributed most of her land to them. One of my editors said I should change my name to Dalit X. If I were to do so, I would have to change my name according to the identity of every single film I make. It has always been my endeavor to make films which I hope can strengthen the struggles of the oppressed for emancipation and liberation. When I started filming *Resilient Rhythms*, I travelled extensively throughout the country documenting Dalit realities and how they were oppressed culturally, politically, and economically. Such an experience really opened my eyes to the issues and resolved my commitment to continue working and making more films highlighting various facets of Dalit life. At best, I am just an amplifier and a comrade in arms using the social capital and skills for the service of the oppressed and the marginal. As a filmmaker, my attempt is to break the shackles of hegemony. So, judge me based on my twenty years of work and not based on my name.

Hey Ram: Genocide in the Land of Gandhi *was on post-Godhra violence. How disquieting was making a film about Gujarat riots of 2002? And how did you go about conducting on-the-ground interviews with the victims?*

The situation was very bad when I started my shooting. There was violence everywhere and thousands were kept in refugee camps. I was told that in one of the worst-affected areas there were a lot of dead bodies dumped into a well. It was the beginning of the shoot and I had a long beard. As soon as I reached the spot, I stamped on something like shit and, to my horror, I realized that it was a burnt human flesh. The people around the place started shouting and running toward me as if I am a Muslim and, in fear, I ran and escaped in my friend's bike. The next thing I did before resuming the shoot was to shave my beard. I came across many terrible stories in Gujarat. There was a nineteen-year-old boy named Junaid, who told me that twenty-nine members of his family were killed. He even said, "I want to retaliate against this. I will blast bombs." During my shoot, I met an old Muslim man. He had blood on his body and shirt. He told me that his little grandson was burned alive. I saw a Muslim woman who said she was gang-raped. I met a series of people like this and I interviewed them. It was a very traumatic experience; I could not sleep even after making the film. While editing, I saw this material again and it was very dehumanizing. I could not have made this film but for the solid support of my ex-wife Sandhya Rao, who stood like a rock along with me when the producers were initially hesitant to complete the film. She even got her father to buy us an editing machine. She was a trained filmmaker. Importantly, she just didn't give me emotional support but also contributed heavily in the production of not just this film but also the Naga film, Dalit film, and others. *Hey Ram* was released on March 23, 2002, and the riots went on till the first week of May.

The Killing Fields of Muzaffarnagar *was on Muzaffarnagar riots. As a documentary filmmaker who has done films on riots such as in Gujarat, how is Muzaffarnagar riot different from other riots?*

The violence that happened in Muzaffarnagar had a different dimension than Gujarat riots. Although it was organized, it was not a genocide, even though many Muslims were killed here as well. Compared to Gujarat, the number of Muslims killed were very less (about 170–200). In Muzaffarnagar, even though the state was complicit, it was not a state-sponsored pogrom. In terms of the scale of violence, you cannot compare them. What happened in Gujarat was completely one-sided. I treat it as a genocide. More than 1,000 Muslims were killed in a span of three days in the streets of Ahmedabad alone. More than 800 people have disappeared. Places of worship like mosques, *masjids* (a place of prostration), and *dargahs*[10] were destroyed. The 500-year-old dargah was destroyed using bulldozers of Ahmedabad Municipal Corporation. Overnight, masjids were demolished and, in its place, temples were built. Women and children were attacked and made special targets of organized violence. A nine-month-old pregnant woman's, Kausar Bano, stomach was cut open. They pulled out the fetus and put it in fire. That's the height of human cruelty. In that sense it is more than a riot. Another reason why I consider Gujarat riots as a genocide is because the properties of Muslims worth hundreds of crores were destroyed over three days in Ahmedabad Municipal Corporation. Since Ahmedabad has a history of riots, many Muslim-owned shops had Hindu names like Krishna Agencies. They had a clear idea which shop belonged to Muslims and Hindus. Only the Muslim shops were attacked. Even Hindu women participated in the act of violence.

There is a criticism against a few independent documentary filmmakers including you that they rarely treat documentary as an aesthetic medium. What is your response?

Content is primary but form is not secondary. I try to synchronize both content and aesthetics in my films. For me, a fine blend of both is important to deal with a story most effectively. PAPA 2 revolves around Parveena Ahanger and is presented in an international broadcast format. Of all my films, *The Naga Story* (which almost took five years to make) used narration to tell a large canvas story in an hour. *Resilient Rhythms* used graphics and songs as narrative technique. This was an experiment at that time. But many people were of the opinion that a traditional narrative text would have increased the reach of the film. *Hey Ram*, my most watched film, was completed in fourteen days. It was basically a collation of hard-hitting interviews told in a straightforward way, resembling a news documentary. It was hugely successful in that it allowed the audience to know the extent of the carnage. I have done most of my films on a shoestring budget. This is the case with most of the Indian documentary films. So, most of the time, I double up as a cameraman, sound recordist, and editor and use stock music. But many times, because of the urgency to tell a story (typically suppressed by the mainstream media, state, and market forces), I have ventured out to do films all by myself. Should I worry about aesthetics? I also believe that films should ideally have intellectual depth, academic vigor, and vibrant aesthetics. But in this era of post-truth, films which are timely in terms of journalism are also important to bring out the political exigencies happening in India.

Notes

1 Kerala is a South Indian state.
2 People's Union for Civil Liberties (PUCL) is one of the largest human rights organizations in India that works for the civil liberties and human rights of the people. It was established under the aegis of Jayaprakash Narayan in 1976.
3 Ritwik Ghatak is a prominent filmmaker from West Bengal. He is known for his social realist films like *Meghe Dhaka Tara* (trans. *The Cloud-Capped Star*) (1960) and *Subarnarekha* (trans. *The Golden Line*) (1965).
4 Deenadayalan was an Indian human rights activist.
5 Nagas are the tribal population who live in the state of Nagaland, Manipur, and Arunachal Pradesh in India.
6 Naga Students Federation is a student's organization of Nagas who live in Delhi.
7 The Battle of Kohima refers to the war that was fought between Japan and the British empire in India during the Second World War around Kohima in the Northeast Indian region.

8 The East India Company was a trading company during the British empire in India.
9 Association of Parents of Disappeared Persons is a human rights organization that provides support to the family members of the missing persons in Kashmir. Parveena Ahangar is the founder of the organization.
10 Dargah is usually a shrine/tomb of a venerable religious person.

Nakul Singh Sawhney

Figure 6 Image Courtesy: Nakul Singh Sawhney.

Nakul Singh Sawhney, whose creative and critical oeuvre spans across issues like honor killing, communalism, caste, and gender justice, is an Indian independent documentary filmmaker. An alumnus of the Film and Television Institute of India (FTII) (Pune), he is the founder of a media collective, *Chalchitra* Abhiyaan,[1] which while training the local people to produce videos of their own also addresses local issues that concern marginalized communities. Majority of his films are crowdfunded and are usually exhibited in alternative venues like independent film festivals and universities. His first significant documentary, *Izzatnagari ki Asabhya Betiyan* (trans. *The Immoral Daughters in the Land of Honour*), concerns the resistance of a group of women against honor killings and the diktats of the village authorities called khap.[2] His next film, *Muzaffarnagar Baaqi Hai* (trans. *Muzaffarnagar Eventually*), records the sociopolitical and economic aftermath of Muzaffarnagar communal riots in 2013. *Kairana, After the Headlines*, and *Savitri's Sisters at Azadi Kooch* are his other notable works. Besides documentary, he is also a part of a New Delhi-based amateur theater company, *Jana Natya Manch*. In committing himself intensely to social causes, Sawhney has opened new avenues for documentary filmmakers in India.

Selected Filmography

Savitri's Sisters at Azadi Kooch (2017)

Kairana, After the Headlines (2016)

Muzaffarnagar Baaqi Hai (trans. Muzaffarnagar Eventually) (2015)

Izzatnagari ki Asabhya Betiyan (trans. The Immoral Daughters in the Land of Honour) (2012)

Why and what draws you to a particular subject and documentary form?

Documentary filmmaking is the perfect culmination of so many of my interests. The story telling in documentaries, for instance, is so much more visceral, real, and even interactive. At a very personal level, there is a constant process of questioning, learning, unlearning, and churning within while working on each film. It can be very exhausting but it's also a state of mind that drives me to push myself. It's also so important and fascinating when one sees how documentary films become part of larger movements and how they often throw up many new questions for the audiences. To generate debates is so important. Documentary films can suddenly start living a life of their own and reach the most unexpected quarters. From the conception through the making to the distribution, it's often a beautiful organic process. I can't really explain what draws me to a particular subject. I think it is more of an organic and instinctive call. There are many subjects that one wants to follow. But there is always this one issue or subject that just draws you.

What brought you to the world of independent political documentaries?

I started watching independent documentary films when I was in college. I was immediately drawn by the medium. I watched films on a range of issues and by several filmmakers, from Anand Patwardhan to Rahul Roy and Sanjay Kak. I was instinctively hooked and drawn to the medium. These films had such an impact on me. That was the time when the National Democratic Alliance[3] was in power. News of the Gujarat massacre had reached far and wide and, as young students, many of us were witnessing a kind of cultural and religious policing of that scale for the first time. It was troubling us. As student activists, we even began to screen many documentary films. The kind of debates it generated among students were fascinating. I was so hooked by the form that around that time I was finishing my undergraduate course and I was certain this is what I wanted to do in my life. As someone who has a keen interest in politics, cinema, travelling, meeting new people, and exploring new cultures, documentary filmmaking was a perfect package that catered to all my interests. The first ever independent documentary film I watched was Anand Patwardhan's *Ram Ke Naam*. I then remember watching films by Rahul Roy, Saba Dewan, Sanjay Kak, Lalit Vachani, Paromita Vohra, Deepa Dhanraj, and Rakesh Sharma. All these filmmakers had a deep impact on me. I remember how Gopal Menon's *Hey Ram!* was screened widely. It was perhaps the first major film on Gujarat massacre. Its immediacy made such a lot of difference. That film gave us a sense of the scale of the massacre. While the form of each filmmaker varied immensely, it opened me to the many possibilities of the craft.

Though there is a consistency in the content of your films, you have always played with the form of documentary whether it be in Muzaffarnagar Baaqi Hai *or* Kairana: After the Headlines. *How important is form in your documentary films?*

Form is as important as content. My content determines my form. One flows from another and they share a symbiotic and dialectical relationship. Safdar Hashmi[4] had said that if you want to take theater to the people, then take good theater. Similarly, for documentary films or any other progressive forms of cultural expression, I believe one has to be just as honest with their form as with their content. It's an ever-evolving process. I sometimes look back at many of my previous films and cringe at the way some bits are done! So each film is a learning process even where form and control over the craft are concerned.

Your films have always been non-status-quoist and anti-authoritarian. Have you ever been intimidated for such a critical position?

Yes, I've been threatened, intimidated, and called names. So what? The number of people who're appreciative of my films is far greater. So many more people have stood by my films and even resisted an assault on it. That's what keeps me going. When a right-wing all India students' union violently stopped the screening of *Muzaffarnagar Baaqi Hai* at Kirori Mal College in Delhi University, *Cinema of Resistance*[5] gave a call to hold protest screenings across the country. It was overwhelming. We lost count of the number of people and institutions that reached out to us with a request to screen the film. Student's organizations like ASA[6] and Democratic Student Federation (a left-wing student union) arranged protest screenings just three days after the assault on the film. The times we live in, the assault is but natural, but the resistance that comes from the audience is what is important.

How did you arrive at Muzaffarnagar Baaqi Hai? What compelled you to make such a political film that challenged and exposed the extreme religious forces?

I had visited Muzaffarnagar way back in December 2010 when I was researching my previous film, *Izzatnagari ki Asabhya Betiyaan*. Back then we sensed that the dominant caste identity and gender politics in this region will soon slip into the larger narrative of Hindutva and eventually will play a big role in Indian politics. That's exactly what happened. When we visited western Uttar Pradesh again, roughly a week after the 2013 massacre, it was clear that Modi was becoming the prime minister of India. The violence had polarized Uttar Pradesh enough to ensure a thumping victory for BJP in Uttar Pradesh. The violence in Muzaffarnagar and Shamli districts in the state of Uttar Pradesh had become the most significant turning point for the 2014 general elections in India. Perhaps, it has become the most significant milestone in the growth of Hindutva in independent India. The moment I reached Muzaffarnagar, I instinctively felt that a larger film around this issue needs to be made.

You have used highly personal and affective testimonies of the victims in your work. What did you find after talking to the families in the area when you visited them? Although your film is emotionally charged, your documentary also points to the material and political conditions that led to the systemic problems. What actually happened there?

I guess every riot has its own dynamics and, at the same time, has similarities. What struck us very significantly when we spoke with the affected families was the sense of betrayal they felt at being attacked by the same people they'd lived with for so many years. There was still a sense of disbelief in the riot survivors when we met them for the first time. Imagine a situation where people whom you live with for many years begin to hate you and try to kill you. It was not just the violence that mattered but the psychological shock of realizing the animosity of people whom you lived with for many years.

What is your response to the arguments that your films are a strong critique of Hinduism and also to be called an "Urban Naxal"?

I am sort of used to it now. But I have noticed that these accusations come from people who have preconceived notions and strong ideological positions. So, they've already judged the film before watching it. The fence-sitting audience is always a lot more accepting and receptive to facts and open to engagement. About those who claim the film is not "neutral" and so on, my simple request to them is to counter me or my film with facts. They can't. That's why they physically attack the film and stop screenings.

Kairana: After the Headlines *is a short documentary. It's unlike your other documentary films. You have used voice-over and the film has a mild journalistic flavor to it. Why did you edit your film differently from your earlier films?*

It was a conscious decision to make it like a news feature. The idea was to invert the idea of a news feature, while using that form. That's why we also called it *Kairana, After the Headlines*. We planned it as a news feature that looks beyond the headlines.

Izzatnagari ki Asabhya Betiyaan *concerns honor killing. It's a unique documentary of its kind in terms of its content and form. Trace the beginning of the project.*

There were many reports on the spurt of killings and other crimes in the name of honor. Most of the incidents were in and around Delhi, where I stay. People roughly my age group were being killed or indicted for having "contentious" marriages. One was obviously disturbed and there was curiosity to know more. When we travelled to Haryana for the first time, we were also trying to understand why there was a spurt in such crimes. The one thing that struck us most significantly was the resistance by young women on a whole range of issues concerning their lives. Among them was their decision to marry on their choice. It was an assertion that was challenging caste and patriarchal hierarchies. This led to a kind of caste and patriarchal backlash in the form of *khap* diktats and "honor" killings/"honor" crimes. Nonetheless, the resistance continued. While it was depressing, it was also fascinating and had to be documented.

What is your take on the relevance of documentary form in an age where social media and visual media are strong? What is the objective behind **Chalchitra Abhiyaan** *initiative?*

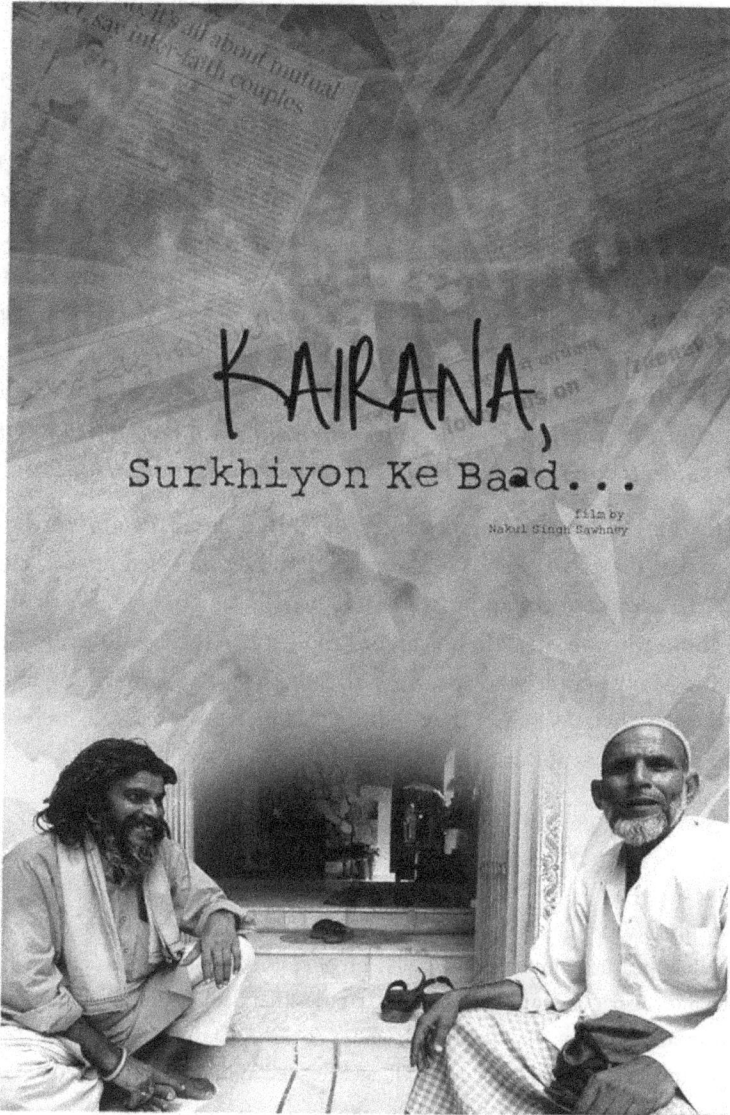

Still 6 Film poster of *Kairana, After the Headlines*. Image Courtesy: Nakul Singh Sawhney.

Social media has opened up avenues for us like never before. Of course, people's retention and concentration have receded. But in *Chalchitra Abhiyaan* we've been able to use social media to invite audiences to the screenings of longer films. I think documentary films have to figure out how to adapt to social media. After the recent mobilizations by the BJP for *Ram Mandir* (temple) in Ayodhya, some people started circulating a video from Anand Patwardhan's *Ram Ke Naam*. The clip went viral. And that motivated a lot of people to watch the entire film. I think social media also opens up avenues like never before. The question is: Can documentary filmmakers adapt to social media and what it requires of us? *Chalchitra Abhiyaan* emerged out of the need to have a progressive media platform that counters the polarizing works of the paid media. This was formed in the context of the Muzaffarnagar and Shamli killings in 2013 which was caused by the circulation of a fake video. We needed to counter such polarizing attempts of local mainstream media by showing people more progressive films and videos.

There is a criticism against your films that your films are left liberal stereotypes. As an activist filmmaker, how do you think your documentaries are going to help the subjects you film? And who are your ideal target audience?

I honestly don't ever have a target audience in mind. After the film is ready, I try to ensure that the viewership is not restricted to the usual "left liberal" circles in metros. The idea is to try and disseminate it as far as possible. We're also very careful about who we speak to on camera and explain the possible ramifications of the film. Many people who speak are already those who are willing to take on the fundamentalists. Whether they "help" the subjects or not, well, it's best if you speak to the subjects about that.

Notes

1　*Chalchitra Abhiyaan* is a film and media collective that brings out documentary films, news features, interviews and live broadcasts that focus on local issues which affect various marginalized communities that usually do not appear in the mainstream medium. Nakul Singh Sawhney spearheads the collective.

2　Khap panchayat is a union of a few villages headed and dominated by males of that village. They exercise quasi-judicial powers.

3　National Democratic Alliance refers to the alliance of right-wing political parties in India led by Bharatiya Janata Party (BJP).

4　Safdar Hashmi was a well-known communist playwright known for his contributions to the Indian street theater.

5　Cinema of Resistance is an organization committed to the screenings of independent political films.

6　Ambedkar Students' Association (ASA) is one of the student's organization in India that represents students from oppressed communities like the Scheduled Castes and the Scheduled Tribes.

Kasturi Basu

Figure 7 Image Courtesy: Kasturi Basu.

Kasturi Basu is an independent documentary filmmaker, film programmer, writer, and journal editor based in Kolkata (India). She is a founder member of People's Film Collective (a political-cultural cinema collective which screens and popularizes documentary films and political cinema among diverse audiences in West Bengal[1]) and Radio Quarantine Kolkata (a community radio launched during the post-Covid lockdown period with an aim to bring social solidarity to social isolation). Additionally, she is a co-editor of *Protirodher Cinema* (trans. *Films of Dissent*), a popular Bangla journal of documentary, films and counterculture, published by the People's Film Collective. She has been an integral part of the organizing and programming team of the Kolkata People's Film Festival (KPFF) since its inception in 2014 and has also worked as an invited film programmer for the ViBGYOR Film Festival in Kerala. She is also a founder member of the People's Study Circle, an independent platform of research and study for activists and academics with an interventionist approach and is active with several people's movements in West Bengal including the ongoing movement to save citizenship that rejects the National Register of Citizens[2] and the Citizenship Amendment Act (NRC-CAA),[3] the gender movement, and the movement to fight housing discrimination and profiling of tenants based on religion and other markers.

Selected Filmography

A Bid for Bengal (2021) codirected with Dwaipayan Banerjee
S.D.: Saroj Dutta and His Times (2018) codirected with Mitali Biswas

S.D.: Saroj Dutta and His Times *narrates the communist movements in India through the life history of a communist poet and a radical journalist, Saroj Dutta. Through the personal narrative, the film segues into the political history of West Bengal. How did you come to this film? And why did you choose to narrate the life of Saroj Dutta?*

Saroj Dutta was brutally murdered in police custody, and his killing disappeared from the official records in 1971. He had become a threat to the state for wielding his only weapon—the pen. In that sense, he is in the league of revolutionary poets and journalists like Victor Jara,[4] Federico Garcia Lorca,[5] or Julius Fucík,[6] who were well-known public intellectuals assassinated for their communist political beliefs. Dutta's story is an intriguing one to tell on many counts. Dutta was a chronicler of his times. So his story also leads naturally into the fascinating story of the Naxalbari rebellion (an armed peasant revolt in 1967 in the Darjeeling district of West Bengal) of which he was an ideologue. Though I was born into the post-Naxalbari generation, we grew up hearing histories and anecdotes about the period as children. What intrigued me most was the absence of documentary footage from this important episode in our history. No documentation or documentaries except a bit from *Louis Malle's Calcutta 1969*[7] exists in the public domain from this period. This is a curious void, if you contrast it with contemporaneous events like the Bangladesh Liberation War,[8] which is richly documented in the medium of film.

So, in the centenary year of Saroj Dutta, we set out to make a film on him. Through the life and times of Dutta, our film unwraps a complex story of the long history of peasant struggles and urban uprising, leading to the Naxalbari rebellion of 1967 and its immediate aftermath. So, it goes beyond a man's life story and becomes one of a historical period, of which Dutta was both a chronicler and an active participant.

As a documentary filmmaker, why is revisiting history important? With the rise of conservative forces in India, left parties are nowhere in the politicalscape in India except in a few states. In such a context, do you think a film like S.D.: Saroj Dutta and His Times *is an effort to counter the hegemonic discourses of the right-wing ideologues?*

It is uncanny that five decades later, almost every substory in the story of Saroj Dutta and Naxalbari resonates with our present. The socialist project of agrarian revolution is still an unfinished business. Revolutionaries are still being incarcerated and brutalized, while the "justice system" watches silently. The debates about ethics in arts and journalism have become more pertinent than ever. The zeitgeist of iconoclasm has now made a spectacular comeback in India with people rediscovering working-class icons and having a critical relook at the classical canon of icons. The Black Lives Matter protests have brought forth this phenomenon worldwide. The youth are revisiting colonialist icons, pulling their statues down with a youthful vitality to iconize a socialist politics which is not blind to the colonial past. In the midst of this, a century-old communist movement in India still remains ideologically fractured and struggling to find direction. And yet, brave battles are being fought from within and without the communist movement with a burning dream of socialism. Isn't it eerie to find such resonances with our present moment? The film does not get dated. History keeps repeating on a spiral path.

Standing at the crossroads, it is imperative for us to take a good look at this and other defining episodes in our history. Within the communist movement, the Naxalbari moment marked a departure from past traditions. Outside the communist movement, it was the first time, when the twenty-year old Indian republic felt serious tremors of mass discontent and disillusionment. I don't think it is escapist to look back at such epochs in our history. Without a good sense of history and how we got here, we cannot understand our present fault lines and cannot strive to change our circumstances.

As for the battle of narratives, history has always been a contested terrain. The centrists have written their dominant history which clashes with people's history as memorialized and remembered by ordinary working people. The right wing, of course, has a century-old extremist project of claiming their own ahistoric imagining of India as a land of the Hindu. What makes *S.D.: Saroj Dutta and His Times* all the more interesting in all of this tussle over history is not just that the film unravels certain forgotten epochs of our history but it also unfolds the debates on historiography. The political debate over iconoclasm depicted in the film is essentially a debate on historiography—over contesting ways of writing and remembering histories. The other important historical element is the internationalism of that era, which the film relives. Where did that internationalism disappear, and how does that affect our struggles? That's a question to ponder!

In the film **S.D.: Saroj Dutta and His Times,** *there are many scenes in which the filmmaker herself is shown. Talking heads who appear in the film are mainly "grand voices" of the yesteryears. The frames have been composed as if they were the meeting place of different generations. Comment on the formalistic innovations and stylistic choices of the film?*

Stylistically, the film does indeed oscillate temporally between the past and the present. All the locations of Kolkata and Naxalbari that you see in the film are spaces where many of the events of yesteryears actually took place. These sites, now stripped of their historical significance, are ordinary parts of our everyday

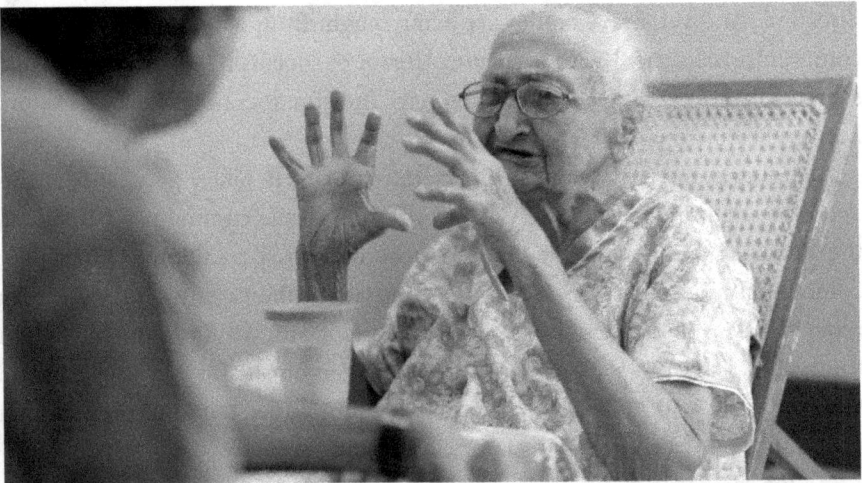

Still 7 A still from the film *S.D.: Saroj Dutta and His Times*. Image Courtesy: Kasturi Basu.

lives in the present. Now that we make a journey in the film to dig out that history, don't those sites change meaning for us and the viewers of the film? Can we continue to view the same street sign, the same house, the same killing fields with our habitual nonchalance any more, or do we see history coming alive, offering up natural frames for a meeting place of generations to talk to each other?

Visually, the film also oscillates in three layers. One layer is the history we uncover through our encounters and interviews. The second layer holds history that was earlier archived through oral, visual, and printed documentation. The third layer crafts a dramatized depiction of the protagonist Dutta as a chronicler of history himself, where we try to evocatively use his poetry and prose pieces to spring to life in the film. We have drawn heavily on archival material, newsreel footage, old radio announcements, archival sound, interviews, revolutionary songs, and Dutta's poems, writings, and translated works in creating the tapestry of the form.

Your films are deeply connected to Indian politics and could be called independent political documentaries in the strict sense of the term. Why do you think that activist/propaganda films are relevant? How important is form in your films?

Form is integral to my films. What is a film without a well thought out form? Form constitutes language of a film. Every film would have to find its own unique language to take the story forward. Devising form is as political as it gets. I think this "form versus content" (as implied for the "arty versus activist" documentary) debate is misplaced and somewhat silly. Propaganda or the agit-prop documentary too has had a rich history of formalistic experiments, that of developing styles and techniques, and finding a suited language for each film. Any committed documentary has had to develop its form—aesthetics, narrative structure, stylistic elements such as the visual and aural texture and editing techniques. Look at the soviet experiments over the decades. Look at the Third Cinema movement in Latin America. Look at contemporary work, from a Michael Moore to a Anand Patwardhan, each developing their own documentary form and aesthetics. Look at the wide-ranging body of newer documentary practice in India.

When there is a disjoint between content and form, it is either lazy or pretentious or failed filmmaking. When I am working on my films, we as a team are constantly thinking of form and content as one whole, dialectically talking to each other. Let's talk about some examples. Situation A: You are unlikely to be telling a story of conflict and war with lavishly pleasing cinematography and mellifluous sound design. So, you must think about form. Situation B: You couldn't be so wedded to your favorite technique at the cost of losing connection with your subject. Let's say you love using the extra-long camera shot, or the static frame, or the nondiegetic sound, or slow cinema, or infrared photography, or the vérité style—each of these powerful cinematic devices in their own right. But can you forget to check if the techniques are adapting well to your film? That would be pretentious or "designer" filmmaking, which does not work for me. We may go "wow!" over techniques after the first watch of such a film, but then very little actually stays with you. So, you must think about form. Situation C: Could you be shooting interviews of ten "talking heads," shoving the microphone in their mouth, simply stitching it up, and claiming your film is political just because those ten people said fiery and correct things into your mic? That would be lazy filmmaking and giving a bad name to the agit-prop genre. So again, you must think about form. Please keep in mind that by giving these examples, I am not suggesting to freeze into certain templates here. If one conceives it consciously (as opposed to lazily), one could even make a powerful documentary using interviews alone. An impactful film can be made with unconventional or conventional forms, in popular or offbeat formats. But the form and content must talk to each other and come together as one whole— whether it is a propaganda film, an observational film, an ethnographic film, an agit-prop film, or a reflexive film.

How would you categorize a film like *Gadi Lohardaga Mail* (Biju Toppo and Meghnath)—simple, unassuming, austere, rooted, sharply political, and, at the same time, joyous and celebratory. Effortlessly brilliant form, isn't it? On the other hand, look at the highly stylized classic documentaries *Kamlabai* (Reena Mohan), *Babulal Bhuiyan ki Kurbani*[9] (Manjira Dutta), *The Other Song* (Saba Dewan), among others. Look at the very recent *Tales from Our Childhood* (Mukul Haloi) set in Assam or *Strangers*[10] (Oskar Zoche) set in Kolkata—are they any less political because they are so stylized? At the end of the day, form and subject have to come together as a whole in a language suited to the particular film. And the audience should be able to emotionally connect to the film, with something to stay with them after they have finished watching. There lies the challenge and joy of filmmaking.

A Bid for Bengal *is on the Hindu right-wing's growth in the state of West Bengal in recent times. The state of West Bengal, which has been known for its liberal democratic values and diversity, has now become a site prone to violence. What compelled you to make this film?*

I won't say that it's a right-wing majoritarian state as yet. Although we have had a history of political violence from the late 1960s, which we showed in our first film, you have to read all "violence" in the political context. Even structural violence is violence, no less. But, we are indeed going through something new that we are not accustomed to. For the last fifty years, West Bengal had been mostly free of communal or religious violence. We have been mostly insulated from the Hindu nationalist politics for most of our history. So, when BJP-RSS started to grow in our state, I was indeed quite startled. In a way, this film is born out of our unease with the changing pattern of our "home." Among the many factors aiding the recent growth of Hindu right-wing politics is the steady growth of the RSS-VHP-led social engineering, which is most often ignored. What led to that growth? In our second film *A Bid for Bengal*, we have tried to find answers to that question which was hovering in our minds.

The year 2004 is significant for the documentary filmmakers in India. Vikalp[11] was formed. In fact, many alternative film festivals were formed after that. But when you look back, many of them have died down. As a filmmaker and as a documentary commentator, what is the relevance and politics of film festivals like the Kolkata People's Film Festival (KPFF)?

It is true that Vikalp has not been as regular as it used to be. Several other alternative festivals have died down as well. But I think regular spaces of documentary screenings have not faced a significant reduction. For example, *Marupakkam* in Tamil Nadu has continued to organize festivals in Chennai and Madurai for twenty-two long years. One reason for these festivals' resilience, which I figured from my chats with Amudhan R. P., is that they never stopped the regular documentary screenings. Also, I would argue that these spaces have impacted how the documentary is screened and appreciated in regular film festivals in a significant way.

Through our praxis we continue to learn that how film is screened—the dialectics between the viewer and the viewed—is as important as what is in the film. From our experience, we have come to value the independent documentary as a potent site for nurturing counterhegemonic ideas, narratives, and languages that, given a chance at a back-and-forth communication between the filmmakers and the wider audiences, can play a significant role in unsettling the dominant consensus—"common sense" in Gramscian terms—on matters of politics and philosophy, aesthetics and art. This informs the politics of the KPFF and other festival spaces like it.

The Kolkata People's Film Festival is such a critical and crucial place for any independent documentary filmmakers in India. Since its inception it has been doing wonders as far as screening of the independent documentary films are concerned. You are one of the persons behind the beginning of such a festival. How did you come to this idea of beginning a festival of this sort? It is almost eight years now. How do you look back at the festival now?

The Kolkata People's Film Festival, or the KPFF, has been on the annual calendar of People's Film Collective since 2014. As such, the idea of a documentary festival sans institutional funding is not something unique. Beginning with the Vikalp in 2004, several small documentary film festivals were happening around the same time. But the KPFF has evolved over the years, and the evolution was a learning curve for us.

The first Kolkata People's Film Festival mostly saw participation of the urban-middle- and lower-middle-class audience with a significant presence of youth and students from schools, colleges and universities. In contrast with our travelling and street screenings, participation of the working class has been far less in the city festivals, except for some specific segments.

Over the years, the People's Film Collective tried to make the KPFF space more and more inclusive and accessible to various sections of the public. We moved the festival venue from an auditorium housed within a university campus to an old theater hall located in the middle of the city. When we outgrew its seating capacity, we moved to another city hall with a seating capacity of more than 800. It was heartening to see more and more film screenings get a houseful audience.

Over the years, we also tried to turn KPFF truly into a platform and meeting point for all committed filmmakers from South Asia. For the first three years, it used to be a curated festival with new and old documentary films from India. From the fourth edition, we opened up the call for entries for filmmakers (from anywhere in the world) working on stories from India and South Asia. We started looking out for recent work, fresh from the oven, so to speak. This hugely broadened the scope for discovering new films and filmmakers. We put in a lot of effort to train members to form a strong programming team. We never outsource our work to external selectors. After eight years, I think we have managed to create a critical mass of audience as well as a much-needed platform to forge long-lasting friendships and bonds with filmmakers who have participated in the KPFF.

We typically screen three to four documentaries from West Bengal in each edition of the KPFF. Over the years, it has been heartening to see that these films are increasingly made by our young filmmakers. Gender and LGBTQIA rights still remain the most common themes in recent times. But that doesn't mean documentaries about other subjects are not being made in our state. Communalism, state repression, critique of the politics of "Development" also find expression in documentaries being made in Bengal.

Our audiences have most often stayed on with us, some offering to volunteer, some becoming regular contributors, and the most committed turning into activists of the Collective. As the audience numbers grow steadily, we no longer have to depend heavily on contributions from our members and extended friend circles, for the regular audiences have chipped in to sustain the rolling costs.

Our annual Bangla journal *Protirodher Cinema* (Films of Resistance) is also published during the KPFF. The work of critical writing on documentary, political cinema, and counterculture in our mother tongue has helped in popularizing documentary cinema among our communities. This has supplemented our screening work, in attracting people's attention and holding their interest to a good degree.

Notes

1 West Bengal is an eastern state of India.
2 The National Register of Citizens refers to the official citizenship register of all Indian citizens. It was first implemented in the North-eastern state of Assam in 2014.
3 Citizenship Amendment Act (CAA) is an act that was passed in the Indian Parliament in 2019 that conferred citizenship to the persecuted minorities except Muslims who came to India from Pakistan, Bangladesh, and Afghanistan before December 2014.
4 Victor Jara was Chilean theater director, poet, and political activist who was killed during the dictatorship of Augusto Pinochet.

5 Federico Garcia Lorca was a Spanish poet who was supposedly killed by the nationalist group during the beginning of the Spanish Civil War.

6 Julius Fucík was a Czechoslovak journalist and a communist party member who was tortured and killed by the Nazis.

7 *Calcutta* (1969) is a French documentary about Calcutta by Louis Malle.

8 Bangladesh Liberation War refers to the revolution in East Pakistan (currently, Bangladesh) on account of the self-determination movement happened during 1971 Bangladesh genocide.

9 *Babulal Bhuiyan ki Kurbani* (trans. *The Sacrifice of Babulal Bhuiya*) is a documentary by Manjira Dutta released in 1987.

10 *Strangers* (2019) is a documentary by Laura Kansy and Oskar Zoche.

11 Vikalp is a collective of documentary filmmakers and a parallel platform for screening films. It started in 2004 as a campaign for freedom of expression and against censorship.

2

The Subversive Eye

Gender and Sexual Identities

Documentary filmmaking in India was predominantly a male-dominated enterprise till the early 1980s. However, feminist movements and the reinterpretation of gender in sociopolitical discourses ushered in a "gender turn" in independent documentary. While documenting women's responses to subjugation and violence, a group of independent filmmakers such as Deepa Dhanraj, Abha Bhaiya, and Meera Rao also foregrounded the agency and rights of women from variegated contexts. Unlike the Films Division-commissioned films and the neutrally observational and journalistic reportages of the earlier documentaries, these independent documentary filmmakers use women's lives as a lens to explore the ideological and political position of the state and to reflect on their own position in the society. Particularly, through contextualizing women's struggle in relation to class, caste, and gender, these documentary filmmakers not only inventively pushed the film form but also brought to relief the political and social issues from women's perspectives. Further, by focusing on individual women's lives—which also takes into account the individual subjectivities of the filmed and filmmaker—a new band of filmmakers such as Reena Mohan, Saba Dewan, and Paromita Vohra, among others, emerged in the 1990s. Put together, these documentary filmmakers through cultivating an aesthetic of multiple modes of reflexivity (such as such as autobiographical, performative, and self-reflexivity) and other innovative documentary forms not only foregrounded the politics of the domestic and the personal but also reclaimed personal histories that were conveniently glossed over by the authoritative and earlier documentary films. Complementing feminist/gender turn in documentary filmmaking, filmmakers such as Rahul Roy, Nishtha Jain, Surabhi Sharma, and Sridhar Rangayan boldly explored different aspects and granular realities of gender, sexuality, and sexual desires. More important in many ways, these filmmakers, drawing on a broad range of documentary practices and themes such as labor, migration, and music, made explicit the emerging meanings of gender and sexualities in diverse Indian contexts and geographies. If, on the one hand, Nishtha Jain, Rahul Roy, and Surabhi Sharma through aesthetic innovations and imaginative playfulness conveyed the nuance and drama of gendered life, then, on the other, Sridhar Rangayan through his activism-informed realism made a plea for sexual tolerance and diversity.

Deepa Dhanraj

Figure 8 Image Courtesy: Kolkata People's Film Festival.

Based in Bangalore, Deepa Dhanraj is a groundbreaking independent documentary filmmaker who has been involved in various women's movements for more than four decades. Her extensive filmography spans issues of women's civil and political rights, women's health and education, and women's labor and domestic conditions. Although Dhanraj started her career as an assistant to Pattabhirama Reddy, a pioneering face in Indian cinema who produced films such as *Samskara* (1970), she soon developed a visual grammar and a political sensibility that shaped all her future artistic productions. Her entry into documentary filmmaking was chiefly motivated by the Emergency of 1975 and its explicit violation of the fundamental rights of the citizens of India. Besides producing critically acclaimed documentaries on several pertinent issues such as communal riots (*Kya Hua Is Shehar Ko?*), fertility control and forced sterilization (*Something Like a War*), corrupt judicial system of male-dominated *Jamaats* or community councils (*Invoking Justice*), and women's alternative courts (*Nari Adalat*), she is also a founding member of *Yugantar*, India's first feminist film collective. Following a participatory and collaborative method in filmmaking, her films not only map the complex human experience of negotiating and living through the exceptional times (such as the Emergency) but also serve as a testament to women's agency.

Selected Filmography

We Have Not Come Here to Die (2018)
Invoking Justice (2011)
The Advocate (2007)
Taking Office (2001)
Nari Adalat (trans. Women's Courts) (2000)
The Legacy of Malthus (1994)
Something Like a War (1991)
Kya Hua Is Shehar Ko? (trans. What Has Happened to This City?) (1986)
Sudesha (1983)

You started your career as a documentary filmmaker in the 1980s. Since then you have been making documentary films and actively involved yourself in many women's movements. How do you look back at your journey as a filmmaker? And what keeps you motivated as a filmmaker?

Rather than being motivated, I am engaged continuously in certain subjects. Sometimes, a film may emerge; but, even if it doesn't, I continue to follow the events and debates around them. I don't mean it in a narrow legal sense rather in the lived reality of law. All our lives are to a large extent embedded in and shaped by its workings. For example, both *Something Like a War* and *The Legacy of Malthus*, look at how official family planning targets can only be achieved by coercion (though coercion cannot be publicly acknowledged). At the same time, a neo-Malthusian consensus has to be built across society. Ironically, the collective good for the nation is achieved by invoking punitive action. *Taking Office*, a 2001 Kannada language video, emerged from a three-year engagement with the elected women Panchayat representatives. It was an attempt to critically look at the substantive effects of 33 percent reservation after the Seventy-Third Constitutional Amendment was passed.

Nari Adalat (trans. *Women's Courts*) portrays a tribal women group's engagement with alternate conflict resolution in cases related to domestic violence, bigamy, and divorce. *Invoking Justice* tracks the Tamil Muslim Women's *Jamaats* (councils). It is a closer look at male-dominated Jamaats and the need to reform a corrupt system which allows men to take refuge in the most extreme interpretation of the Qur'an to justify violence toward women. *We Have Not Come Here to Die* looks at the student movement that arose after the tragic suicide of Rohith Vemula, a PhD research scholar at University of

Hyderabad. His mother, Radhika Vemula, a Dalit Mala woman and a survivor of domestic violence, raised her children in a Mala colony. She insisted that her son's death is caused by caste violence. *The Advocate* is a biography of one of the foremost human rights lawyers in India, K. G. Kannabiran. A firm believer in the Constitution, K. G. Kannabiran in a legal career spanning forty years argued against the impunity of the police in extrajudicial killings and custodial deaths, creating invaluable legal precedents.

It may seem that the films are like new reports. But what I do want to point out is that the films do much more. They map the complex human experience of negotiating and living through different circumstances. What sustains one through each production considering the fact that each one lasts, on an average, fifteen months to two years? It's curiosity. It's an intimate dance, being with people, witnessing, listening, and inviting a conversation. It's this process, from the first encounter through filming to editing, that is addictive that draws one back to making films.

How did you come to filmmaking? How influential was the Emergency as a force in shaping you as a filmmaker? And how did you overcome the challenges you faced as an independent woman documentary filmmaker?

My first memory of watching a film in a cinema theater was *Chaudhavin Ka Chand*[1] (trans. *Full Moon*). I was seven years old. It was in dramatic black and white. When the color sequence was introduced, we all gasped with delight. Although I did not understand the plot of the film, I could *feel* the emotions. It was visceral. The flickering images from the film left me in a daze that lasted for hours. I pestered my mother repeatedly to tell me the story, which she edited judiciously. My passion for cinema started there. Summer holidays in Hyderabad meant afternoon matinee shows. My sister and I would go regularly to the nearest theater where Telugu mythological films were screened. My knowledge and the love of epics, *Ramayana* and *Mahabharata*, came from Telugu cinema. Our favorite film was *Maya Bazaar*[2] (trans. *Market of Illusions*), which we saw many times with wonder.

The first documentary I remember watching was in school. It was a National Film Board of Canada film about spawning salmon. The only fragment that made an impression was the shoals of colorful salmon trying repeatedly to leap up a waterfall. More films on nature followed leaving us with the indelible impression that documentaries were basically like Animal Planet. It wasn't till I left college and started attending film society screenings that the world of "art films," as they were called then, became available. Thanks to the National Film Archives of India.[3] We were able to see many wonderful international films here. Unless one had money to attend the International Film Festival in Delhi, poring over a film catalog was the only option. It's difficult to imagine now in a world of live streaming and torrentz!

After completing a degree in English literature and journalism, I was searching for a job. It so happened that I met Pattabhirama Reddy, who was looking for volunteers to work on his new film, *Chandamarutha* (trans. *Wild Wind*). He had directed *Samskara* (trans. *A Rite for a Dead Man*), an adaption of U. R. Ananthamurthy's acclaimed and controversial novel critiquing Brahmin hypocrisies. In a short time, the Emergency was declared. Pattabhi's wife Snehalata Reddy was arrested and incarcerated at Central Prison, Bangalore.[4] The Emergency was for most of us a brutal political baptism. It's interesting to think of surveillance then and now. While some phones were tapped, most of the surveillance was physical, that is, policemen were in mufti with their tell-tale haircuts and in their brown shoes. Today, the surveillance is invisible. During the Emergency, impunity is no longer theoretical, instead it's in the everyday. It's there in the courts where political prisoners are brought for bail hearings, in prison visits, in rumors of encounter killings and disappearances of students and so on.

Ever since it's not hard to see how impunity reproduces itself in every era. Besides the physical running around that one had to do during this period, it was also a time of reading many small pamphlets and articles written by people living underground. The language and ideas in those pieces impacted me as they were usually drawn from polemical writings across the political spectrum (such as Lohiaites, Socialists, and Trotskyites). In a Freirean sense, one was gaining political education. Once the Emergency officially ended, I worked with M. S. Sathyu[5] on *Bara/Sookha* (trans. *Drought/The Famine*) and C. Chandrashekhar[6] on *Huli Banthu Huli* (trans. *Tiger Has Come*). All these projects were run on a low budget with small crews. This meant that one had to quickly take up the slack in any department. I have to admit that it was a steep learning curve. Retrospectively speaking, it was an uneven film education in terms of both exposure to both films and technical skills.

You are one among the founding members of **Yugantar** *film collective. It has been an inspiration for many other film collectives thereafter. Can you talk about the relevance of such independent film collectives now?*

As soon as the Emergency ended, I joined the autonomous women's movement. It was an exciting time despite the evidence of torture, encounter deaths, and continued incarceration of political prisoners during the post-Emergency period. Members of the movement were a mixed lot. Many young women, left radical, left student groups, and Gandhian groups. Some older women were part of civil liberty groups, mass organizations, and trade unions. Many women were from academics. And then there were scores of women who were taking part in a political activity for the first time.

Daily street protests were the routine. Songs were written and street plays were performed. There was tremendous creativity. Given the fact that Navroze[7] was the only qualified camera person in our group, it was audacious and foolhardy of us to create a film collective. But given our full optimism, it didn't worry us too much. The *Yugantar* collective members were Abha Bhaiya, Meera Rao, Navroze Contractor, and myself. Yugantar made four films: *Molkarin* (trans. *Maid Servant*), on the unionizing of domestic workers in Pune; *Tambaku Chaakila Oob Ali* (trans. *Tobacco Embers*), on the struggles of tobacco workers in Nipani; *Idhi Katha Maatramena* (trans. *Is This Just a Story?*), on the story of marital violence; and, *Sudesha* (1983), a portrait of an activist in the Chipko movement. Except for *Sudesha*, all the films were shot on 16 mm black-and-white ORWO (a German brand) stock. Later, they were dubbed in four languages and the prints were screened widely in four states. We had to craft a film practice that would be participatory in every sense, where the women would decide how they wanted their struggles to be framed, both visually and narratively. Three of these films have been restored at the Arsenal Living Archive project. The challenge now is how to work with this feminist archive in the present. Recently, a screening in Bangalore in 2017 of the struggles of tobacco workers was met with tremendous enthusiasm. Representatives of garment workers' unions and domestic workers' unions were keen to have copies of the film to show to their members. It was thrilling to see that the films still carried the charge of the political moment they came out of.

Something Like a War *critically examines India's family planning program during the Emergency. I would imagine the film thus: a woman filmmaker fighting and resisting against the Emergency issued by a woman ruler (Indira Gandhi). Comment on the use of feminine body (both of the filmmaker and of the filmed) as a battleground for justice in the film.*

The film was completed in 1991. Now that I look back at it, I remember, the energy and excitement of the debates and activism of the women's movement, especially the way they explored women's health as a political site. In Hyderabad,[8] *Stree Shakti Sangatana* disrupted a clinical trial of NET-EN[9] on poor women who were recruited without observing the protocols of informed consent. In fact, *Saheli* and other women's groups filed a writ petition in the Supreme Court[10] against the Union of India, Indian Council of Medical Research (ICMR), Drug Controller General of India (DCGI) demanding a stay on the NET-EN trials. Women's groups in Rajasthan[11] exposed the corrupt practices of turning women away from food-for-work programs unless they agreed to be sterilized. It seemed as if feminists all over the country were acting and creating theories that went totally against the grain of existing frameworks on how government health institutions had configured women's health. It was a heady time, and it was inspiring to be part of it. It was clear that *Something Like a War* has to have a similar political intervention and tell a complex story. Apart from screenings, it was a surprise to watch how the film began to have another life. Transcripts from the film were used in a court case to show that women who were part of Norplant trials were not aware that consent was required. Women activists from India and Canada used it to persuade IDRC,[12] Canada, to stop funding the vaccine trial. It is still used widely in many universities in India and around

Still 8 A still from the film *Something Like a War*. Image Courtesy: Deepa Dhanraj.

the world as a study of the history of the politics of population control, the role of national and international agencies, and women's health and reproductive rights. I have often thought of revisiting the entire field, especially the new reproductive technologies which are now being touted as the latest "fix" to examine the implications for women. I wonder what has changed and what has remained the same. Maybe the time has come for *Something Like a War* redux!

You have made films in both film and digital formats. Share your thoughts about shooting films using film roll (16 mm) format.

Shooting on 16 mm film in the 1980s was not easy. Renting a camera was expensive and an attendant came along with the gear. Obtaining the film stock was equally expensive. And you had to go through many bureaucratic procedures as well. Each reel lasted ten minutes. And we literally shot in a 1:1 ratio. After processing the negative and editing in a studio where you were paying commercial feature film rates, you prayed that they wouldn't scratch the negative. Finally, you had to get a censor certificate and deposit a copy in the lab before they release your print. So, you can imagine the control/regulation and stress at every step of the production. Film reels were heavy, and you had to lug the projector around to screen the films. It wasn't easy when you had to travel to small towns. When I first saw a digital file being put onto a small hard disk, I couldn't control my delight!

What is the creative vision behind We Have Come Here Not to Die? *In the context of recent protests in the universities in India, how do you see this new rise of politics in the campuses against communal forces?*

Rohith Vemula's[13] suicide note was so powerful. I couldn't sleep after reading it. It was completely intuitive. Normally, I never start shooting with no preparation. This time I felt we should just be there on campus. We followed events post his death for almost eighteen months. During the filming, we went to Osmania University (Hyderabad, Telangana) and JNU (New Delhi). In both places, caste discrimination on campuses was widely discussed. It is a very positive development.

How do you find budget for your films? With the emergence of alternative media, online platforms, what do you think about the future of documentary films in India?

Raising funds for documentaries in India is not easy as there is very limited funding. Every film is a challenge. We own basic equipment so we can start filming and then look around for post-production funding. For the last two films, I have managed to raise funds for post-production from NHK,[14] Japan. The spread of 24-7 news channels and the tsunami of images from smart phones/WhatsApp will pose a serious challenge to documentary filmmakers. How will we distinguish our work especially if you are dealing with events in the public realm? On the hopeful note, many young filmmakers are using formats which are more poetic, experimental and cinematic. It is this aesthetic treatment that can set the films apart.

Notes

1　*Chaudhavin Ka Chand* (1961) is a feature film in Hindi language directed by Mohammed Sadiq.

2　*Maya Bazaar* (1957) is a mythological film directed by K. V. Reddy.

3　National Film Archives of India (NFAI) is a media unit that preserves India's cinematic heritage. Founded by P. K. Nair, it is headquartered in Pune, Maharashtra.

4　Bangalore is the capital city of a South Indian state of Karnataka.

5　M. S. Sathyu is a leading filmmaker from India. He is known for his films like *Garam Hava* (trans. *Scorching Winds*) (1973) and *Bara* (trans. *Famine*) (1980).

6　C. Chandrashekhar is a filmmaker in Kannada language. He is best known for his directorial *Dhanalakshmi* (1977) and *Huli Banthu Huli* (1978).

7　Navroze Contractor is a multi-award-winning cinematographer from India.

8　Hyderabad is the capital city of a South Indian state of Telangana.

9　NET-EN, or norethisterone enanthate, is a hormonal contraceptive.

10　The Supreme Court is the apex court of India.

11　Rajasthan is a state in Northwestern India.

12　International Development Research Centre (IDRC) is a Canadian research organization that conducts research and offers solutions for the problems in the developing countries.

13　Rohith Vemula was a young research scholar at the University of Hyderabad. Owing to the casteist pressure, he committed suicide. This resulted in social unrest in various Indian universities and reinvigorated debates on caste.

14　NHK is the national broadcasting corporation of Japan.

Madhusree Dutta

Figure 9 Image Credit: Roshan Jose.

An alumna of the National School of Drama (New Delhi), Madhusree Dutta is a documentary practitioner, curator, producer, and an activist. She is one among the early filmmakers who used video format for making documentary films in India. By extending the meaning of the form of/in documentary, she currently engages in multiple projects like installations, theater, and film curations. Motivated into filmmaking by the Mumbai riots (1992–3)[1] and the Babri Masjid demolition, her work besides concentrating on political issues also engages Indian visual culture and traditions in various forms and formats. Interestingly, she revisits the works of writers/artists (such as Namdeo Dhasal,[2] Narayan Surve,[3] and Faiz Ahmed Faiz[4]) of historical and political significance as a means to reveal and address contemporary politics and religion. Starting with *I Live in Behrampada*, her films address wide-ranging issues such as gender, riots, migration, identity, multiculturalism, and nation. *I Live in Behrampada*, her first documentary, addressed sociopolitical situations post Hindu-Muslim riots in Behrampada. In *Memories of Fear*, she explored the growth of a girl child through different age groups in four parallel narratives. In deconstructing fact-fiction binary in *Scribbles on Akka*, she explores the possibility of using fiction and imagination in documentary films. She is also the cofounder and executive director of *Majlis*, a center for rights discourse and interdisciplinary art projects in Mumbai.

Selected Filmography

7 Islands and a Metro (2006)
Made in India (2002)
Scribbles on Akka (2000)
Memories of Fear (1995)
I Live in Behrampada (1993)

You belong to a generation of filmmakers who started their filmmaking adventures in the 1990s. How did you come to documentary filmmaking?

If we look at documentary films from a puritan perspective, I am not a saint filmmaker. I am an accidental filmmaker. I haven't watched many documentary films before I came to filmmaking. In those days, it was really tough to access documentary films. I worked in the translation of Hindi documentaries to Bangla (language primarily spoken by the Bengalis in South Asia) before I came to make my own films. My filmmaking career began in Bombay when I was wondering what to do as a new migrant there. As I had a theater background, I assisted in some Bollywood fiction films. During that time, a riot happened in Bombay. I wanted to document some of the evidence for any future court case. That's how my first film *I Live in Behrampada* happened. I never thought I would make this film. I had to watch *Hamara Shahar/Bombay, Our City* maybe more than twenty times to get the structure of the documentary. By the time *I Live in Behrampada* was completed, I almost fell in love with the film and could identify a lot of possibilities in the documentary form. All my love for fiction films and theater did not hinder my amusement in documenting evidence, testimonies, and interviews. They all came together in my film. I wanted to break the magic of testimony or the magic of the real because when people watch it, there is a distance. So amateurishly, I started mixing fiction and documentary. That's how my engagement with the form started. I have a very few films to my credit. I also haven't made any films for the past few years. I guess that makes me a retired filmmaker. These days, I no longer limit myself to making documentaries but also involve in the production of films, introducing debutant directors and installing artworks.

Your first documentary is I Live in Behrampada. What prompted you to make the film? How significant is I Live in Behrampada in your career as a documentary practitioner?

I always believe that all creative people basically make only one film in their life. The rest is a continuation of that film. Similarly, a filmmaker makes only one film. As the editions change, the work is modified, given appropriate additions and omissions. I never wanted to be a documentary filmmaker. The sociopolitical contexts were such that I ended up making *I Live in Behrampada*. The success of that film, especially when I received awards and accolades, created in me a genuine interest in documentary filmmaking. I started watching documentaries. When I felt like making one, I made one. As I mentioned earlier, all documentaries are a single book by the same author. It is the inadequacy of the preceding works that persuade the author to correct the mistakes and better his creation. Sometimes you sense that your work has been simple and you're forced to make matters more complex. Fifteen years after *I Live in Behrampada*, I made *7 Islands and a Metro*, where I used quotes from *I Live in Behrampada*. Both these films were exclusively based on Bombay. Back in those times when Hindutva was at its infancy, we thought that we were able to control it. By the mid-2000, we realized that it was too big a fish to hold in our humble nets. *7 Islands and a Metro* is a more complex film that addresses issues of fundamentalism. In such a context, the film upholds relevance. Documentary films, amazingly, have a longer shelf life than other mediums. Perhaps documentary films are of timeless significance. I was quite surprised when I realized that my films that portray a fighting citizen are relatable to people born after the occurrence of these events. Documentary film has its own life, and it works on its own beyond even the ideology and politics of a filmmaker. That's why I find the idea of revisiting and recycling interesting.

Scribbles on Akka, which delves into the world of a thirteenth-century saint poet, Mahadevi Akka, challenges the conventional form of documentary in that it not only mixes fact and fiction but also uses the work of contemporary

artists, writers, and testimonies of commoners. How do you look at this film today? Also, share your views about the uses of imagination and fiction in a documentary form.

It is always a different experience to look back at my film *Scribbles on Akka*. It was a film that embodied the very essence of the late 1990s. It is Babri Masjid demolition that has made me a filmmaker. That time, there was a dichotomy of popular culture and public culture and religion stayed in the middle of it. I come from a classical staunch atheist-leftist background. I made this film a decade after *I Live in Behrampada*. That was a period of feminism and local literature. There was a tendency among people to trace the hidden discourses. I thought of working on Mahadevi Akka. While I was working, no document about her was available. She is a thirteenth-century character. I was not sure whether all stories about her were true or anecdotal. As a documentary filmmaker, I should talk about situations of the twentieth century while doing a film on her. So, I need to work on fiction too. In a nutshell, I talked about the religion of my period based on a poet who is called a saint poet. That was my artistic and political choice. Sometimes *just* evidence is not enough. For me, fiction gives that space to have an imagination while dealing with evidence. I tried to imaginatively deal with the life of a saint poet of the thirteenth century. In retrospect, my approach was right and I can reiterate that evidence cannot give the complete picture of what had occurred.

Still 9 Madhusree Dutta during the shooting of her film *Scribbles on Akka*. Image Credit: R. V. Ramani.

Seven Islands and a Metro is set around imaginary debates between Ismat Chughtai and Saadat Hasan Manto, the two legendary writers who lived in Bombay. Bombay occupies a serious concern in this film. Why have you used Manto and Chugtai? Was it a means to reflect on your own engagement with the multilayered city of Bombay?

Saadat Hasan Manto and Ismat Chughtai are absolutely fictitious characters in the film. Manto died in 1954 and Chughtai in 1992. I bring them back in my film. For placing them in 2006, I quote from their own writings and integrate fiction and documentary. I was imagining what they might think about the state of affairs at that time. They wrote in Urdu and were part of Progressive Writers Movement. That time, the state was after them not because of the political content of their books but under the charge of obscenity. Interestingly, they were also a part of popular culture. They wrote typical Bollywood stuff. They were diehard Bombaities. When partition happened, Manto moved to Pakistan. He wanted to move there because as an Urdu writer he had no space in a secular country. But Chughtai stayed in Bombay till 1992 when death separated her from the city. Surprisingly, she never wrote a single line about Bombay. But she wrote about Lucknow and Delhi. But Manto, who went away to Pakistan, wrote a great deal about Bombay. So, the question is: Who leaves and who stays? What is documentary and what is fiction? The question about migration also excited me. Every time you reach a destination, you are also departing from somewhere. When you leave you arrive. Leaving and arriving is more experiential than physical. I tried to bring out such aspects in the film.

Unlike other riots, Mumbai riots have received less attention among independent documentary filmmakers. As a filmmaker who has made a film on these riots and has thus archived those memories, what are your reflections on Bombay/Mumbai?

Unlike other cities in India, Bombay has a peculiar quality. Bombay never had a single identity. Bombay is Bombay. But it is also Maharashtra. It is never like other cities such as Kochi or Calcutta. Calcutta is a Bengali city and Kochi[5] is a Malayali city. Bombay is not like these cities. It has more than a single spoken language and people with multiple languages and identity. People are always moving to reach their destinations. There is a constant commotion as it is putting up a semblance of a dream city. It is not a financial city too. Bombay stays more as an image. The vision of Bombay in popular culture may have contributed to this process. Bombay is a city of much diversity. In a city like Bombay, which doesn't have a single identity, communalism rarely thrives. Communalism after a certain point will fail here. They don't want it to be suppressed by any caste or religious identity. People are more aspirational here.

Do you think there is a tendency to homogenize the practice of documentary films in India? Is there an assumed meaning in the word "political" in documentary?

One of the greatest Indians to exercise documentary practice is none other than Amitav Ghosh. His novels are documentary novels. He uses archaeology, data, and statistics to compile a fantastic story. Documentary practice is not progressive or regressive in itself. If it is argued that documentary practice and documentary film are the same, it is almost as absurd as visualizing documentary film only as a method of protest. Protests can happen anywhere, for instance in painting, music, or dance. The romantic or conventional documentary defines politics in a confined syntax. I question it. The idea of a documentary is now defined by television. In the 1990s, television robbed the teeth out of conventional documentaries. Every hour they telecast real people. This happens with all the necessary ingredients—argument, opinion, and interview. Everything is present but exactly in the opposite of what a true documentary might do. Real and actual shouldn't be confused together. Real can be entirely different from what is actual. It is a mode of perception that determines the actual, but what is real can be the polar opposite of the former. Documentary is a much wider concept than the present. Something that has been incorporated in documentary making, whether it be state or independent documentaries, is that we don't encourage our audience to participate. They show them what reality and facts are. I look at this skeptically. The audience aren't idiots. It would be audacious to claim that one is morally superior to the other. I don't care whether a thirty-five-year documentary filmmaker is able to buy a big mansion by the age of forty. But I am bothered about the political narrative. I want people to make good use of this medium. From my observations, I have understood that today's documentary films have transcended the screen to other forms. Giving credit to capitalism for being the harbinger of this phenomenon, which deceives the public by making them believe they still possess the power of choice, I recommend that the scope of documentary is extended to accommodate the audience as a partner. About a decade ago, European television found out that documentaries from

India were good products to sell in their countries for its novelty and ability to procure viewership. But such attention pushed documentaries to feature a single character. It is widely acknowledged that European or American audiences are reluctant to read subtitles, and an inclusion of a load of characters apparently makes it difficult for an average American viewer. A single-character documentary is easy to dub, is economical, and can satiate the average foreign spectator. I have nothing against single-character documentaries. But I'm against the "pushing" for such a medium of expression just because of the financial viability. My worry about censorship comes only second due to this frightening constraint of creativity.

Notes

1   Mumbai/Bombay of 1992–3 refers to the communal riots that happened in Mumbai resulting in the death of many people.
2   Namdeo Laxman Dhasal was a poet, writer, and Dalit activist from Maharashtra. He was awarded Padma Shri in 1999.
3   Narayan Gangaram Surve was a Marathi poet from Maharashtra.
4   Faiz Ahmed Faiz was a celebrated Urdu poet and a Marxist writer from Pakistan.
5   Kochi is a city in Kerala, a South Indian state.

Saba Dewan

Figure 10 Image Courtesy: Saba Dewan.

Saba Dewan is an independent documentary filmmaker and a writer based in New Delhi. After completing her graduate studies from the Mass Communication Research Center, Jamia Millia Islamia (New Delhi), she started producing films along with Rahul Roy. Her notable film, *Dharmayuddha*, is one of the early documentaries that described the rise of extreme rightist forces in India. Dewan's films through integrating interviews, archival texts, among others, meticulously record the historical and the political dimensions of the everyday experiences. The major thematic concerns of her films include gender (*Delhi-Mumbai-Delhi*), sexuality (*Naach*), communalism (*Nasoor*), and culture (*The Other Song*). Furthermore, her films like *Khel* (trans. *The Play*), *Barf* (trans. *Snow*), and *Sita's Family* offer socially nuanced reflections on the underdiscussed imaginings of the feminine and also illustrate the emergence of the self in the new Indian documentary. In her attempt to reclaim women into history, she recently published *Tawaifnama* (2019), a book on the *tawaifs* (courtesans) of North India.

Selected Filmography

The Other Song (2009)
Naach (trans. The Dance) (2008)
Delhi-Mumbai-Delhi (2006)

Sita's Family (2001)
Barf (trans. Snow) (1997)
Khel (trans. The Play) 1994)
Nasoor (trans. Festering Wound) (1991)
Dharmayuddha (trans. Holy War) (1989)

What brought you to the world of documentaries?

I did my master's from the Mass Communication Center at the Jamia Millia Islamia University, New Delhi. When I joined Jamia, I was not previously exposed to documentaries. I didn't even know, frankly speaking, that I was going through a course on documentary filmmaking. At that time, I assumed Jamia as a film school. Film schools then meant feature films. In that sense, I was compelled into documentary by accident. I am talking about the 1980s. We were not exposed to the independent documentaries then. It is only at Jamia that I got exposed to documentaries. Some of the films that we saw there left a deep impression. Anand Patwardhan's *Prisoners of Conscience* had a deep impact on me. We could also meet Deepa Dhanraj and watch her films too. Meera Nair[1] also came there with her documentary *Indian Cabaret*. So, Jamia, in that sense, at that point in time, was a very vibrant place where many documentary filmmakers visited. It was a great chance to watch films and then to interact with them. Besides, we were very lucky that we had James Beveridge, who was a documentary filmmaker, as our teacher. Both James and his wife, Margaret Coventry, were instrumental in setting up the Mass Communication Research Center at Jamia. My love for documentary form is inspired by Beveridge.

Dharmayuddha *is your first independent film. It is a significant film along with* Nasoor *in the history of Independent political documentary films in that these films expressively represent the rise of Hindutva forces in India. These films were produced before the Babari Masjid demolition and before* Ram Ke Naam, *a documentary by Anand Patwardhan. Your film, in a sense, documents the impending danger of the rise of right-wing fundamentalism in India. Share the relevance, politics, and the reception of* Dharmayuddha.

When we shot *Dharmayuddha*, we followed some of the leaders of the Vishva Hindu Parishad (VHP)[2] in a small town of Uttar Pradesh during their campaign. There wasn't much importance given to this campaign in the mainstream media. Retrospectively, it is amazing that no one actually foresaw the kind of devastation that this politics would bring upon India. The demolition of the Babri Masjid followed soon after these films. We could somehow sense the menace. When we returned, we played those footage to the director of the Mass Communication Centre and also to other people. People responded saying, "Oh God! This is too shocking! How can anyone talk like this?" At that time, what VHP was saying was considered inconsequential, but they had a plan. In retrospect, I feel that it is a moment of history that we caught. In fact, it is almost archiving the moment. Babri Masjid was still there when *Dharmayuddha* was made. I remember some people then said these are very extremist and sensational views; therefore, they need not be taken very seriously.

As a middle-class woman filmmaker, how do you play with the form and language of the documentary? Do you think women documentary filmmakers engage a language of their own to fully address the issues they film?

In the late 1980s, it was very difficult. Once I finished my graduate studies, I began producing independent work. There weren't many women filmmakers in documentary or in fiction form then. So, it was a kind of adventure. I was exploring different aspects of communal violence in my early films called *Nasoor* (trans. *Festering Wound*) and *Dharmayuddha* (trans. *Holy War*). At this point in time, filmic spaces were not "meant" for women professionals. So, the journey was not easy. All of us, that is, the early women filmmakers, experienced our share of sexism from our own colleagues or even from the crew members. My early films were codirected with Rahul Roy, and it was just assumed that he was the boss, or the actual director. That is the way sexism operated. It was also difficult in terms of constantly having to assert one's place as a documentary filmmaker. Now, I hope women filmmakers don't have to encounter such forms of sexism. By the mid-1990s, so many women were even editors. Things have changed over the years. I think it has to do with the entry of many women into documentary and fiction films.

Khel is a sharp departure from the kind of films you made before. There is an identifiable shift from social self to personal self. How do you account for such a sharp turn from the social to the personal/intimate? The film is also significant in that it deploys innovative structure, constructed sequences, and voice-over. How did such a structure help you to communicate your perspective as a filmmaker better?

We had been very busy as filmmakers through the late 1980s and early 1990s. We did a lot of films including *Dharmayuddha* and *Nasoor*. We also did a series of lesser-known documentaries about the status of women in agriculture. The bulk of our work were looking at their sociopolitical situations. In the earlier part of our work, the urgency was the issue at hand. I don't think much thought went into the form during the making of our early films. Later, questions like *how* will you say what you say became a serious concern. As we grew as filmmakers, the questions of form and exploring form or of exploring filmic language became important. I think it was at this point of time that *Khel* came into being. It is one of the earliest attempts of Indian documentaries to be reflective. Such a formalistic innovation was not coming from any theoretical reading or understanding. Also, we were not exposed to world cinema or the diversity of documentary filmmaking. It was in the early 1990s. Whatever we were learning were in bits and pieces from some film festivals and from our personal explorations. *Khel* reflects the inner questioning that I as a filmmaker was going through at that point in time. It is more of a dialogue with myself and a means to engage social realities in complex terms. My early films had a straightforward answer to everything. It became very important to engage more deeply and not to be so anxious to have a simple straightforward answer. So you approach your subject with a great measure of respect and understand that everything need not fit into your worldview. And that is what *Khel* is doing. It is like a filmmaker who comes from a certain social reality and has a certain worldview engaging with a way of life, cultural factors, and even with spiritualism which are completely out of the filmmaker's way. I don't have an easy answer, and it is alright to say I don't.

Sita's Family *concerns with a crisis perhaps you went through. The form of the film was very innovative in that the filmmaker herself is filmed. What made you turn the camera to yourself? Moreover, the film is also a journey into the interiority of three generations in your family. Do you think it is an anthem to the struggles of middle-class women who are not sufficiently represented in the public sphere?*

Yeah. I am so glad you noticed it. In fact, *Sita's Family* is a continuation of what I was trying to do in *Khel*. The same concern is explored with more nuances in *The Other Song*. These three films treat the internal world. Although the journey started with *Khel*, it was extremely tentative. So, I tried to bring oneself to the narrative consciously. As filmmakers, we are always in the film. But when *Khel* was made, we felt embarrassed about putting ourselves or acknowledging that we are there. Somehow putting yourself seems like middle-class indulgence. When

Still 10 A still from the film *Sita's Family*. Image Courtesy: Saba Dewan.

I started working on *Sita's Family*, I was becoming confident as a filmmaker. I wanted to look at the history of middle-class women through the family and I chose my mother's side of the family. So, it is quite natural that I became the narrator. And questions like what brings me to that? Why am I interested in that? What are my issues which bring me to this subject? Why am I doing it all? What I actually wanted to say and how I wanted to say are enmeshed. They often dictate each other. *Sita's Family* is one of those films which conveyed what I wanted to say and how I wanted to say. I am a participant in the film. I think the most difficult part in the film was to have the camera on me. I am a shy person and it is about my private life.

Unlike the popular Bollywood films, Naach *focuses on the spectators who watch the dance and the events going around them. Interestingly, you leave the dancer and instead film the viewer/audience. In that sense the viewer is being gazed at and not the body of the dancer. Explain your creative decision.*

I always had a problem with the arguments around male gaze. I have a feeling that it reduces the agency of women. When we say that these bar dancers are mere characters of the male gaze, it reduces their agency. Such a perspective has been constructed by the male viewers. The fact is that women are also constantly looking at men (audience) and manipulating them to a great extent. The film was after all from the point of view of these dancers. I choose to have the camera from their point of view rather than the other way around. In the early days of shooting, I remember, the audience used to go away. Over a period of time, because *Naach* was shot for a long period of time, the regular audience became part of the performance.

Your third film in the trilogy is The Other Song. *You took more than eight years to complete the film. Was it part of building a respectful relationship between the filmmaker and the subjects in your films?*

The difference actually is in how you make the relationship with the people you work with and how you approach them. I have always approached the people I work with as equals and with respect. I am entirely leaving it to them as to how much of their life they wish to share with me. Especially for these three films, it was as if they had the power. In fact, watching the rough cut, I took their suggestions. Then, I shot it. And they have the right to tell me, "I don't want this. I might have said this to you then. But I don't want this now. Please remove it." I think people are not stupid. If you are honest and respectful, people can figure it out. *Tawaifs*[3] are the smartest women around. They draw their boundaries, and I always respect those boundaries. As far as *Naach* is concerned, I shot those spaces that they were comfortable in. I didn't shoot stripteasing scenes, although I could have shot them as well. The woman I was working with didn't want it. I don't want to violate that space. There are choices that as a filmmaker I have always made. I have respect for people I have worked with. Their dignity, more than anything else, should be respected. I believe that completing a film is not the most important thing. I shoot in particular circumstances but someone's life and sense of comfort override my film sequences. I would never impose that on them. I have a continuous relationship with each woman, and it is a relationship between women who are equal.

You have been making films for the last thirty years. Have you ever felt a creative exhaustion?

I was exhausted after making *The Other Song*. So, I started working on a book (*Tawaifnama*) which is a completely new medium for me. I have never written before. The book also took a lot of time. Now the book is done. It is time to get back to filmmaking. So, I am thinking of new ideas and I really want to get back to the medium.

Notes

1 Meera Nair is an Indian American filmmaker based in New York. She is known
   for her films like *Salaam Bombay!* (1988) and *Monsoon Wedding* (2001). Her
   documentary *Indian Cabaret* (1985) explores the life of cabaret dancers in Bombay.
2 Vishva Hindu Parishad (VHP) is an Indian right-wing Hindu organization
   committed to the cause of Hindu nationalism.
3 Tawaifs are courtesan women who excelled in music and dance particularly during
   the Mughal rule in India.

Paromita Vohra

Figure 11 Image Courtesy: Paromita Vohra.

Paromita Vohra is a Mumbai-based documentary filmmaker, curator, columnist, and screenwriter. Unlike social documentaries that dominated 1980s, her films are affective, reflective, and expressive visual narratives which creatively mix fragments of poetry, fiction, and drama to uncover the plural nature of all reality. Shaped by multiple aesthetic and feminist sensibilities, her films winningly engage with issues related to gender/sexualities (*Unlimited Girls*), cultural politics (*Q2P*), and popular culture (*Cosmopolis: Two Tales of a City*) in a fluid performative style. Particularly, her film, *Unlimited Girls*, a significant work in the genealogy of feminist films in India, is an intellectual wandering into the everydayness of feminine voices. In her quest to generate a visual language of desire, she not only inserts herself into her narratives but also follows unconventional methods, thereby constituting new political and aesthetic possibilities. Known for her sophisticated formalism, Vohra creates her own visual templates often traversing the realist moorings of documentary practice. She is the cofounder of *Agents of Ishq*, a web-based platform that seeks to challenge the puritanical approach to sex, body, and desire.

Selected Filmography

Partners in Crime (2011)
Morality TV and the Loving Jehad: A Thrilling Tale (2007)
Q2P (2006)
Cosmopolis: Two Tales of a City (2004)
Unlimited Girls (2002)
Annapurna: Goddess of Food (1995)

What makes your films significantly different from many other documentary filmmakers is the way you mix the popular with the artistic. What do you accomplish in mixing and transgressing genres and discursive boundaries?

I do believe that there is some abstract art which not everybody will easily understand and some popular work which functions at an absolutely basic level of enjoyment. And there are popular works that are poetic and complex in their own way. However, being elite does not automatically equip and improve your understanding of anything. I don't like to precategorize anything. I also don't believe that just because you have employed a particular style in your film you are by default political and an intellectual. For me, Bollywood[1] films can be extremely intellectual and poetic too. And Bollywood songs, so mocked because they are not realistic in aesthetic, are extremely sophisticated work. They also debate the politics of love, the context of love, and its poetic and philosophic dimensions. These are all quite intellectual pursuits. Audience are capable of engaging them as well, of understanding this popular form of abstraction that uses a more sensual, erotic medium. People use different languages to say the same thing. No form is inherently better or worse than the other. For me, low art and high art is a result of colonial mindset. It comes from the imagination that the native mind cannot understand superior things and that their forms are primitive and naive. What is so complex about realism? After all, it is the reliance on realistic aesthetics as a mark of rationality or "reason" that brings us into a world so literal minded, so ill-equipped to interpret form. I want to eventually communicate what I am thinking. I am not interested in pandering to people but I do wish to communicate. I think the aspect of pleasure in cinema is very natural. In fact, humor and music in film are a mark of respect for the audience, of drawing all their senses into a discussion. For me, pleasure is the greatest form of intelligence and it brings all of us to a common place to engage with each other. It is an inclusive frame, not a condescending one.

What made you a documentary filmmaker? Was that conscious choice or a systematic entry?

It was not a systematic entry. I grew up in a preliberalization period of the 1980s, and my decision to pursue arts was not easy. Today, arts—or perhaps we should call it arts and media—is a more systematized and much more corporatized field. Since both my grandparents were successful in film, Bollywood or fiction films would have been a potential place for me at that particular point in time, at least in terms of filmmaking imagination, although, then, it was a far more feudal and more inimical space for women than it is now. As a middle-class kid, I did not have much awareness about art films. I had seen only a few art films in Doordarshan (public service broadcaster founded by the Government of India). And, for some time, I was in Andhra Pradesh (a state in the southeastern part of India). Here I used to watch Telugu (the language spoken by the people of Andhra Pradesh) films regularly without understanding much Telugu. So, cinema meant mainstream commercial film. In one sense, I entered the field of documentary by a process of elimination. But another way of looking at it is that I followed a vague desire which had no obvious manifestation, which did not stand before some evident professional choices I could make. I studied literature and everyone felt I was a good writer and should become a journalist, a prospect I found uninteresting. After college, I had no real sense of what to do, but I did want to do something creative. So, I studied Mass Communication in Mumbai, which was a new course then.

The first Mumbai International Film Festival (MIFF) of Documentaries and Short Films[2] happened when I was in college. In that particular year, MIFF had several retrospective sections, both Indian and international. During this period, it was Anand Patwardhan who was the model documentary filmmaker and template for us. Like most young people then, I admired Anand's filmmaking, his passion, and sense of justice. He was an inspiration in that sense. But I am a sort of person who loved songs, pleasure, humor, poetry, and entertainment. In that festival, I saw many other forms of films as well. After watching all these films, I sensed a certain possibility in documentary form. Documentary form combines both the political and the creative. The independence of the form also appealed to me. In some sense, it was a very open-ended and unmoderated medium then. I even felt that the medium is almost like me: unfinished, immoderate, and doesn't have a plan for the future. After that choice, my journey became complex and layered by much experience. And my choices (political and artistic) emerged layer by layer through a diversity of encounters.

Many of your films like* Cosmopolis: Two Tales of a City *and* Q2P *are contextualized in Bombay and explore the city's character. In* Q2P, *for instance, you call Bombay as "a future city" as you capture the many riddles of it. How influential was the city of Bombay, its everydayness and fluidity in your films?

I came to Bombay in the 1990s. Bombay is a difficult city to live in. It was a post-liberalization period. New things like television began to happen that time. In fact, my first documentary was made for a television channel BiTV, which is now shut down. On the one hand, you can say that Bombay is a difficult city to live and not a place for documentary filmmakers. Documentary, for many, over here was almost like some kind of government thing. Having said that, it was much better for me to be an artist in Bombay than anywhere in India. For me, documentary at that time was a choice for living. So, I did whatever I could. I worked with Anand for three and a half years. I worked with Ruchir Joshi[3] and Reena Mohan.[4] At the same time, I also worked—for television, for music TV, for fiction series—and was writing not just to earn money but also because of my interest in different contemporary forms. Even while working, I tried to work with filmmakers who have different approaches to documentary films. This heterogeneity had undoubtedly changed my critical perspective. I also felt some disagreement with some hegemonic approach to what documentary is and what it should be. Had I been in some other place, for instance, Delhi, I would have felt seriously suffocated. In Bombay, you can belong to so many professional and, in fact, personal contexts, simultaneously.

I also found that there is a sort of elitism in progressive politics. In India, progressiveness is often defined in terms of the relationship with the state or national ideas. I came from a progressive family but not by those nationalist standards. My maternal grandfather was a Hindu Bengali Brahmin,[5] a very well-known composer in films, and my grandmother was Khoja, a Kutchi Muslim, and an actress and producer. The intermarriage was not upheld as an example of anything. It was just there. They were bohemian and very urban and did not perfectly fit into any categories. Later, they separated from each other, lost some of their success and much of their money. But they didn't hark back to their glorious past all that much. They were not representative of any emblematic trajectory. I also don't find myself relating to the politically correct categories available in progressive discourse. I didn't want to fix myself into this extremely boring box. As a woman and as an artist, I could not connect much to that "high-minded" lofty idea of documentary as a self-denying form.

Coming from an elite background and telling "ordinary" people about their life was not a comfortable idea for me. It also seemed like people were making the same kind of films, even after the audience had changed. It led to a situation like you make films to prove that you are progressive. People also watch it to prove that they are progressive. It was a ritualistic performance of progressiveness. I never want to be a filmmaker of that sort. I have political positions and I express them through my films, but films are not merely an illustration of politics. Rather, politics drives your exploration and your filmic desires to create a different conversation. I want people to love the film, to experience it with complete sensory openness and experience the world from another perspective. I wish to engage with the audience, not to pander to them, but to have a passionate and pleasurably intellectual conversation with them.

One of the things that happened to me was that in the quest for affordable housing, I ended up living in a working-class tenement for over a decade. My neighbors were working-class folks—bar dancers, auto rickshaw drivers and onion sellers. It was a very transformative experience for me. They were my neighbors with whom I had varied relationships. I think it is important that I had to leave the privilege of my class context, out of my own choices, not as some kind of political posturing. It changed the way I thought about things and how I formed relationships with people. It's a kind of redrawing of yourself, away from the familiar structures of your origins, with their logics, moralities, and connections. You have to learn to explain yourself as an individual. It is during this time of great professional and personal polyphonic exposure that I evolved my visual and narrative language which is eventually developed in my films.

Unlimited Girls *is an intensely personal film. It defies the logic of early feminist films which are preoccupied with the idea of a collective self. Explain your creative intention.*

I agree with your observation on *Unlimited Girls*. What I have tried to argue is *personal is not private* but the amalgamation, or the meeting place, of the public and the private. Can we really distinguish between the public and the private? There is a "publicness" that enters in our privacy that makes it very personal. In the so-called political documentaries, it is only about the public self. I think it is an important moment in feminist consciousness: to arrive at the identification of gendered experience and to express oneself as a collective. But as a filmmaker this cannot be a permanent approach. These politics evolve as more and more doors open in the mind, as women make a series of different choices, confronting all the contradictions that intersectionality speaks to. I am a feminist. I am living an everyday feminist life complete with questions, commitments, pleasures, sexual desire, and interactions with others, as well as the claiming of rights. I am not just a claimant to rights, but also part, along with the rest of the world, of creating a new understanding of what it means to live in the world. This experience is political. Politics is not only that which is moderated by the state and the citizen-subject. Many things create change in the world, some tangibly, some intangibly, and we play these things out in our lives in immensely varied ways. I want to build that everyday experience and aesthetics in the film I make.

Still 11 A still from the film *Unlimited Girls*. Image Courtesy: Paromita Vohra.

Your films are "a parody of the ordinary." For instance, **Cosmopolis** *and* **Q2P** *focus on food politics within Mumbai housing and the gendered nature of public toilets in Mumbai, respectively. Is this style some sort of dialogue/ critique of the existing practices of documentary filmmaking in India?*

I don't think of it as a critique. I think of it as a conversation with the more orthodox documentary. As I already said, I do not believe any form is invalid— they all have different validities. I am only uncomfortable with the orthodoxy of documentary form and its claims to being politically superior via sobriety, pan-national politics, and masculinist realism. I don't believe you can just drop any content into a preestablished form and express a different perspective. Form expresses politics. While *Cosmopolis* is of course a highly unusual film in which I play the goddess Annapurna in a conflict with the goddess Lakshmi, played by Renuka Shahane, even as the city battles over vegetarian and nonvegetarian communities, *Q2P* is more linear, more conventional even. In fact, it is rather like, after making very different films, I arrived at the traditional social documentary, one that talks about classical themes of inequality, and a city built on the basis of inequality, but then treated that form a bit differently, more associatively. Such forms often function through juxtaposition, but I suppose I have found a way to be associative, a concatenated form, which examines the interstices, which looks at what is not being said in order to open up the political mindset we inhabit, not in order to accuse and make easy heroes and villains of people. I want people to think about the world around them, and, by doing so, perhaps arrive at different choices and solutions even. I do not want to predetermine, but to catalyze, tease, pleasure, and invite the viewer into the luxury and deep truth of thinking. There are, of course, elements of parody in some films, elements of farce in others, which query all pieties.

At the same time, it is very important to give choice to the viewer of your documentary not to agree with you. There are many ways by which you can do that. In many films, the strategy is to erase the filmmaker's identity or else to render it literally through a first-person narrative. I suppose I do neither, working instead with being an unreliable narrator. When I am making a film in which I appear pointlessly here and there (for instance, as a goddess, as a woman searching for Sandra from Bandra, as Fearless, as a woman you see only via parts of her body and her smudgy reflections), it becomes hard for the viewer to completely rely on me. They may find the narrator amusing or charming or intriguing, but not authoritative. It enables or encourages the viewers to decide by themselves. I am performing some character in the film. As a result, viewers won't be able to trust me. If you are very sure that you cannot trust me, then whom do you trust? You have to trust yourself. For trusting yourself what will you use? You have to use your own senses. The film pays deep respect to the senses. This is how I engage with the audience. I try to produce a sensory intelligence in my films. That's why the film is constructed in such a way that the audience is asked to bring their sensory intelligence to the table, to trust their senses to make sense of a situation. The purpose of art is to strengthen our senses, or ability to "sense" the world, and hence make sense of it, to its unspoken currents, to the way power functions in invisible ways, and to the way love, possibility and belief also function as intangible determinants of a moment or a choice.

What a conventional documentary does is that it says I care about the world. It equates the desire of the filmmaker with the desire of the subject. Truth is, a filmmaker is making a film for his or her sake. Their identity is not the same as the identity of the person in the film. So, I feel it is better to create a form which respects the filmed person's dignity of deciding how they want to represent themselves to the extent possible. I, as a filmmaker, sometimes invite them into performing the version of them that I see, through my questions, through my gestures. Let that be transparent to the viewer. Let them see that this particular filmmaker rendered this particular version of the person. The person is many things outside the frame of the film. That's one of the reasons why I keep questions in my films. I am very interested in thinking. For me, thinking is a luxurious and almost a sexual activity. Everybody should have that enjoyment in my film; it need not be reserved only for the filmmaker. I am interested in contemporary politics not doctrinaire politics.

Do your films assume a particular class of audience? Who are your intended audience? Do you imagine a particular category of audience while making a film?

I want my films accessible to as many people as possible. I am very well aware that rural audiences may find it difficult to watch my films barring one or two. So I am not pretending that I am reaching that audience. I don't want to preach to the oppressed. I am trying to engage with my sort of sociocultural class and drive a discussion about our political choices. I don't really have a fixed viewer in mind. Whenever I do a film, I always think about the questions that it answers in people's mind. My films are responding to people's feelings. If people say that my film addresses only the middle class, I see it only as mother-in-law criticism. I am making it for the middle class to question themselves, their privilege. I am not a sentimental filmmaker. I do address the middle class. I have a deep feeling that the middle class needs to change the way they think. But I don't think that it's the formal experimentation that makes the films urban. It is merely their setting.

Your web-based innovative project called Agents of Ishq *is the first of its kind in India which explores desire and sexual culture.* Agents of Ishq *cannot be considered as a documentary in the strict sense of the term? How should we treat it? Also comment on the future of documentary filmmaking in the age of ever-increasing digitalization.*

I am in a particular phase in my life where questions concerning reality and truth have become complex. I won't say that documentaries have no future in India so let's try something else. *Unlimited Girls* is suffused with digitalness. Digital was not even properly developed then. Since I was excited by the digitalness, I wanted to incorporate digitality in my film. For me, digital has opened up a language and a landscape. Simply put, it is the presence of many simultaneously open windows. Digital language is the language of multiple identities, selves, and forms. Whatever I do on the internet is more or less like my films. There is a sort of actuality, literature, feeling, and politics there. It's all hybrid like my films. But it is done in a different way. I think no form is over ever. But what is over is the limited perspective or definition of documentary as one particular thing. You can imagine documentaries in many ways. People are shooting their reality 24-7. They no longer need you to represent them. Therefore, you have to represent yourself. Your point of view. This is what I am doing in *Agents of Ishq*, cocreating a documentary of Indian sexual lives through text, video, audio, and graphics. There are questions; there are narratives; there are songs. Multiple voices and perspectives enter and coexist. But the central philosophical, aesthetic and political frameworks are laid out by me.

Notes

1 Bollywood refers to the industry of Hindi cinema in India.
2 MIFF was initially called BIFF. BIFF stands for Bombay International Film Festival.

3   Ruchir Joshi is a filmmaker and a writer from India.
4   Reena Mohan is an independent documentary filmmaker and an editor from India.
5   A Brahmin/Brahman is a higher-caste person in the hierarchy of caste system in India.

Rahul Roy

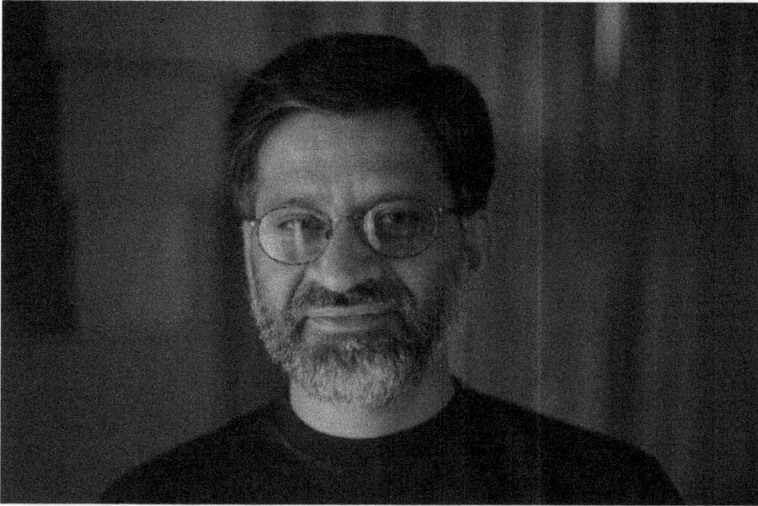

Figure 12 Image Courtesy: Rahul Roy.

Rahul Roy is a Delhi-based independent documentary filmmaker who has contributed extensively to the discourses on masculinity. After his graduate studies at the Mass Communication Research Center, Jamia Millia Islamia, Roy worked as a relief worker in New Delhi during the anti-Sikh riots in 1984.[1] Oscillating between subjective renderings of reality and social vision, his films are predominantly explorations of the inner selves of an individual. Although his interest concentrates on the subjective and the intimate, he has also produced some location specific and ethnographic films like *The City Beautiful* and *Majma*. His thematic preoccupations such as subjectification, neoliberal subjectivities, identity, gender, and intimate relations in private spaces finds expression in *Till We Meet Again*, *The Factory*, *When Four Friends Meet*, *Majma* among others.

Selected Filmography

The Factory (2015)
Till We Meet Again (2013)
The City Beautiful (2003)
Majma (2001)
When Four Friends Meet (2000)

Unlike typical Bollywood films which celebrate masculinity, your films such as **When Four Friends Meet** *and* **Majma** *show masculinity in crisis. For instance, in* **Majma** *we see male characters as victims and powerless. What is your artistic vision behind these films?*

I come from a place where masculinity is seen and conceived as a sense of entitlement to power. I am using the word "sense of entitlement" intentionally. We live in such a circumstance where you feel you are entitled to power, if you are a man. So, your whole life is in a way trying to deal with that power. There is no way you are going to experience the power in the same way as you think you are entitled to. But you are constantly putting yourself in situations of violence and conflict because of that sense of entitlement. So, in a sensual way, my films deal with that dilemma. *Majma* is about the push that comes from the ideology of masculinity for men to project themselves as privileged through their bodies and relationships. So, the central issue in *Majma* is about the performance of masculinity across several registers and the inability to perform to the standards of what masculinity sets out to you. Besides showing how inadequate you are insofar as sexuality is concerned, it also starts affecting other aspects of your life. You have to perform masculinity not just in the context of your sexuality but it's a performance that has to be done in all other relationships as well.

When Four Friends Meet *is perhaps the first Indian documentary film that dealt with masculinities. You made this film at a time when masculinity studies were emerging in Indian academia. What motivated you to make this film? How did you find those four friends? As a middle-class representative, how did you refrain from objectifying these working-class men?*

When I passed out from Jamia Millia Islamia in the late 1980s, many films were produced about women and their lives. I found myself uncomfortable dealing with women's issues, and, that's when, I figured out working on a documentary on masculinity. It was also a period of huge struggle for the documentary filmmakers in the country. There was a sudden drying up of resources, and there was little support. Second, there was also a major questioning of documentary form and practices during this period. If you look at the development of documentaries between 1992 and 1995, there were only a few documentary films. But from 1995 onward, there was a significant shift happening in the field. Everyone started making films in different ways. One of the fundamental issues was about political documentaries: How to make it? What is the purpose of political documentaries? among others. There was a criticism that in political documentaries the subjects were part of the projection of the filmmakers. That is, the subjects were completely instrumentalized and used as a tool. Since many of us in the filmmaking were from different political backgrounds, we had certain perspectives about the working-class struggle, about the importance of solidarity, and about the marginalized (on the basis of caste and color) people. In fact, some of the narrative threads of my films are developed by the people who are in the film. What kind of story do they want to tell about themselves to the world was also a major concern during that period. While watching my films, I want people to know that they are watching stories of normal human beings not of the heroes. All my films are made from their perspective. I see myself as a medium and as somebody who echoes their voices.

Till We Meet Again *is a sequel to* **When Four Friends Meet.** *We rarely see sequel films in documentary films. Why did you do that? The film also moves from a class-specific desiring male to a universal man who is victimized by his situation or a man who is affected by the struggles of his life. Elaborate on the shift from the class specific male to a sort of "universal" male.*

When Four Friends Meet ends with a promise that we will meet again. It was about a bunch of people who are yet to face the weakness or the fragility of life. But they did not feel that life was weak during the cinematic time. They were dreaming and were aspiring. The focus of the film was more on their fantasies and aspirations. On the other hand, the focus of *Till We Meet Again* was very different. The film is actually very depressing in the sense that it was all about the difficulties of life rather than the pleasures of it. It was more about confronting and experiencing the real.

Was your sense of documentary cultivated in the classroom? How do you look back at your early influences that shaped you as a documentary filmmaker?

I received BA (Honors) in History. After completing my undergraduate course in History, I was trying to figure out what to do next. I was in a way inclined to academics. However, I wanted a break before joining a graduate school. Mass Communication and Research Center at Jamia Millia Islamia had just started then. I thought of applying there. I did not have any definitive plan to become a filmmaker when I joined there. It was more an accident. In the 1980s,

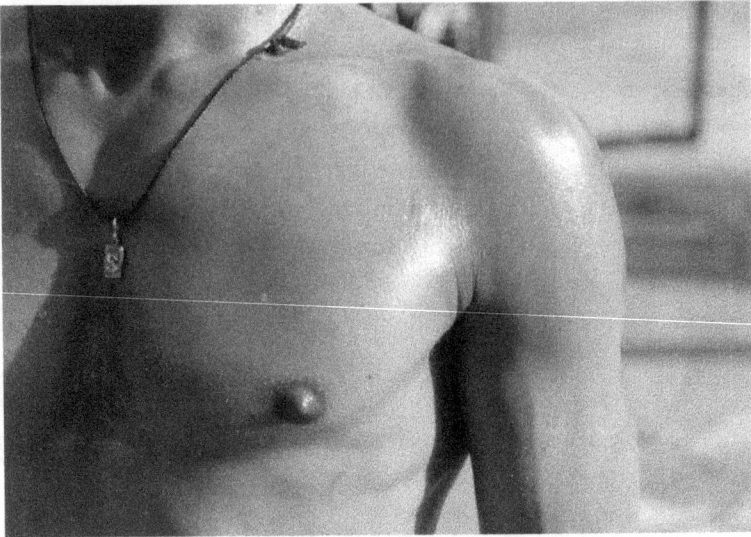

Still 12 A still from the film *Majma*. Image Courtesy: Rahul Roy.

documentary and independent cinema in India were fairly weak. The Films Division of India used to make certain structured films. Moreover, we were not exposed to a variety of documentaries across the world. We were more exposed to fiction films before we joined Jamia Millia Islamia. Film society movement was pretty strong then. Documentary films were sort of absent from the cinema education during that period. The Film Society Movement, on the other hand, did not focus on documentaries because documentaries were perceived as a tool for propaganda. In the 1970s and 1980s, I think documentaries were considered more as a propaganda tool. Documentary gained attention in the context of films made by Tapan Bose and Suhasini Mulay. Anand was also making films in that period. Except for them, there were not many documentaries. I was introduced to the documentary form at Jamia Millia Islamia. It is only after the completion of the course that I started looking avidly and specifically at documentary films. That time, filmmakers were looking at the medium more instinctively. It was also a period when a couple of very important films were released: Nilita Vachani's *Eyes of Stone* (1990)[2] and Ranjan Palit and Vasudha Joshi's *Voices from Baliapal*[3] (1988). These films were important because they were instinctive, observational and practiced an intimate look at people's life. *The Eye of the Storm* (1970) was another important film to me as it explored the possibility of the form. These films impacted me and gave a new sense of direction.

The City Beautiful *explores the crisis of two working-class families. Do you think it's the working-class population who are the worst affected by globalization? There is a moment of hope in your film in spite of the bizarre situations that your characters are in. Could you elaborate on this?*

When Four Friends Meet is set in Jehangirpuri.[4] The geography and history of the place is very much part of the film. But the space these four men create for themselves is liminal. It is actually about desires, aspirations and dreams. The film is looking at the intimate space and how working-class people operate in that space. I did *Majma* looking at how these feelings work in a public space. It is set in a market place where intimacies are very public and everything is absurd. In a sense, *Majama* was a response to the closed intimate space. Once I finished *Majama*, the next space was the closed family space and how the same idea operates inside families. So, the background of *The City Beautiful* was the large-scale changes that are happening because of globalization and Westernization. It is dealing with what these changes do to the families and how they react and deal with them. "Hope," which you could decipher in my films, is not an ideological position. But it is more about how people in their everyday life are able to survive and work through everything because they have dreams and they want to do better in their prospective days. Put differently, "hope" comes out of how people make small decisions and how they negotiate the everydayness in their lives. Irrespective of their crisis, they should move on.

Unlike your previous films, **The Factory** *addresses the struggle of a group of factory workers. Maruti is perceived and interpreted as the harbinger of modernity in India. In scrutinizing Maruti and their nexus with authorities, the film problematizes all the popular narratives about Maruti company. In that sense, it is not only a critique of the practices of the company but also of the state which is insensitive to the basic rights of its citizens/laborers. What draws you to this film?*

I am so glad that you asked this question. Because most people who want to hold enough in the 1970s and 1980s don't think critically about the significance of Maruti Suzuki company and what it symbolized for Indians especially for the middle class in the 1980s. When the Maruti car was introduced into the market, it emerged as an important feature story for the most popular writings about how India is progressing. If you start looking at the literature of the 1980s about what Maruti cars had done to India/Indians/the middle class, it is almost like a fantasy story. It was a symbol of a new and emerging India. In that sense, I guess, for many of us, Maruti is not just another factory. It was a very important figure of what was being projected as the New India. Maruti was presented as the most progressive company and was seen as the best that capitalism could do in India. Besides the car as a symbol of many other things such as modernity and mobility, the factory space was projected as a radical and revolutionary space. It was also seen as the most democratic space within the strict structures of capitalism. If you look at literature, they present how the management and the working-class dine in the same canteen and the kind of democratic relationships they had. So, the point is it is a significant institution. These imaginings were in the back of my mind when I was making the film. From 2010 onward, there was a lot of interaction between the Maruti workers and the outside world. Workers stood against the company. It was a new revelation. In a sense, it was against what we were thinking about the company. Strike at the factory and the response of the management brought us to the realization that it was just like any other multinational company. Sadly, I was making the film at a time when the movement had been defeated. I had no access to the factory.

As a filmmaker who has written on the course of documentary filmmaking in India, how do you see the present and future of documentary practices?

The documentary image is actually the most powerful and intimate image in the world. In that sense, one of the promises when video technology came in during the 1980s was that it will democratize the medium. Accordingly, the whole emphasis of the 1980s was on teaching how the medium should be used by the people for raising their own issues. Such issues are settled now. Now it is the concern of professional documentary filmmakers to produce images of relevance. People started deciding for themselves what is relevant for them, and they produce images around it. You don't need to be a filmmaker to produce images now. We have platforms like YouTube, which is actually built by people's effort. In that sense, the practice of professional documentary making has been challenged now as it was in the past, although in a completely different sense.

I think the form is a response to contemporary crises by professional documentary filmmakers. Documentary filmmakers should respond to it. The whole issue is how we separate the professional from the nonprofessional. There is a certain way in which an "artist" has to carve his or her own space versus "non-artists." I think the form is going to be a central concern and how filmmakers respond to it really matters now. One direction that we have seen clearly is the museum space where the moving image and the documentary images entered in a big way. What is interesting is also the whole idea of reality and evidence, which is a central concern in documentaries, and how they can be presented and challenged in different ways. That is why, I am arguing that magical realism (where different elements are negotiated) could probably be the big shift that could happen as far as the documentary is concerned. It is where the hyperreality of the form actually jumps at you much more than in the past. I think that is the future of documentary films.

Notes

1 Sikh riots of 1984 refers to a series of violent attack and killings of Sikhs in India in response to the murder of Indira Gandhi, India's then prime minister, who was assassinated by her Sikh bodyguards.
2 *Eyes of Stone* (1990) is an Indian documentary by Nilita Vachani. It deals with the life of a young rural woman named Shanta in Rajasthan, who believes that her life is possessed by spirits.
3 *Voices from Baliapal* (1988) is an Indian documentary by Ranjan Palit and Vasudha Joshi.
4 Jehangirpuri is a place in New Delhi.

Surabhi Sharma

Figure 13 Image Courtesy: Surabhi Sharma.

Surabhi Sharma is an educator, curator, and independent documentary filmmaker based in Abu Dhabi and Mumbai. Although she started her career as a theater artist, she has been working on several feature-length documentary films and video installations since 2000. An alumna of the Pune-based Film and Television Institute of India, she is also a curator of independent films and the Films Division films for Films Division Zone. Informed by feminism, her interest includes migration, music, and labor. Blending the techniques of cinema vérité and the ethnography of everyday, her films examine environmental crisis/ extinction of species (*Aamakaar, The Turtle People*), the precarious situation of the unorganized migrant laborers (*Bidesia in Bambai*) and surrogate motherhood (*Can We See the Baby Bump Please?*). As an attempt to make visible the unseen and the marginalized, her films are conscious efforts in mapping the margins. She also teaches Film and New Media Program at the New York University, Abu Dhabi. Her films have been screened at many international film festivals including Dubai International Film Festival, Yamagata International Documentary Film Festival, and MAMI Mumbai Film festival, among many others. Her best-known installations are *Airplane Descending over Jari Mari*

(2008), *Tracing Bylanes* (2011), and a five-channel video installation, *Riyaaz* (2016).

Selected Filmography

Returning to the First Beat (2017)
Bidesia in Bambai (2013)
Can We See the Baby Bump Please? (2012)
Pregnancy, Prescriptions and Protocol (2008)
Jahaji Music: India in the Caribbean (2007)
Aamakaar, The Turtle People (2002)
Jari Mari: Of Cloth and Other Stories (2001)

Do you think your training in anthropology informs and determines the theme and structure of your documentaries? Or is it that you wish your works to be ethnographic? And how do you address the question of "real" in documentary filmmaking?

My training in Anthropology more than Psychology informs the way I conceptualize my films. Yes, ethnography is a great influence on how I structure my films. I don't believe in the "real." I am critical of the argument that documentary deals with reality. It is very less real in documentary films just like any other medium. I believe we are putting forward an argument, a thesis, a worldview in our films. The camera (and sound) is the tool to express what one has observed or want to say. The camera is only bringing you closer to the way I see the world not to some objective reality. So, the question of objectivity is quite questionable in the documentary. On the other hand, I am also acknowledging the archival value of the footage we shoot. That doesn't mean that we have an absolute claim to reality.

As a woman filmmaker, do you think the language of the film has to be different from other male documentary filmmakers?

This is not a formula where you choose form over content or the other way around. My understanding is that form emerges from your content and content is not a fixed variable. Form emerges from the way you seek out stories, the questions you ask, and how you ask them. If I am making a film a few days after riots, then the urgency of the moment will make me ask questions in a particular way. I will carry the charge of wanting to piece together the narrative of violence to see who is responsible. My form would emerge from the urgency of holding people accountable. If I was to revisit that space and those memories five years later, ten years later, twenty years later, they would be a very different set of questions I would ask. I would attempt to make meaning of the scars that a community carries so many years later. I would tread lightly on people's memory and their sense of outrage or injustice. My form would emerge from being reflective. I am a woman. I am a feminist. Most of my films are not looking at the feminist subject, but the manner in which I structure my films comes from a certain understanding of filmmaking that is certainly influenced by being a feminist. Perhaps that's why I abhor filmmaking that has presupposed conclusions and are aggressive in their approach to present that conclusion. They are fitting their material to put forward their case. I am open to finding many truths.

It is always a "tough" choice to be an independent documentary filmmaker and this needs a certain amount of perseverance. How did your love for documentaries begin?

My influences in college made me a filmmaker. We had professors who introduced us to world cinema and also pushed us to think of ways in which we wanted to engage with the world. We were trained even at the undergraduate level to do research seriously. So, reading, seeking references for whatever project/assignment we were working for, going out and meeting people were an essential part of what we were expected to do. This training and an excitement about cinema led me to think of entering this world. We were exposed to both fiction and documentary cinema and did not see them as necessarily distinct and separate worlds. A lot of exciting work done in India were mostly documentaries at the time and that was a huge influence. I was a student of anthropology, sociology, and psychology. So much of the work we were doing in class was connected with our immediate world. We remain very connected and are constantly referencing each other's work. Apart from the fact that I grew up watching films with my parents and read a lot, I am not sure what exactly my early influences were. My parents constantly pushed me out of my comfort zone. That is, if I was used to watching Hindi and English mainstream films, I was also taken to watch strange art house films. If I was reading the regular books that kids read, I was also made to read stuff that was way beyond my understanding. If we traveled to typical tourist destinations, we also went way off the usual path to places that had never been seen by the tourists. I guess this influenced me to become overly curious about things that lay outside my bubble.

In **Jahaji Music: India in the Caribbean,** *you have equated political and racial tensions with Jahaji music. How did you come up with such a curious combination?*

Music tells us about both contemporary tensions and the history of the islands. Music is very central to the public life in Trinidad and Jamaica. Questions of race, identity, and sexuality are the themes that are dominant in the music. I was interested in the social history of this vibrant music.

The imaginary world of Bhojpuri migrants and their vibrant musical culture is the focus of **Bidesia in Bambai.** *Could you elaborate on your choosing of such a point of view? Why is migrant psyche and their cultures important? And how complex is migration and migrants' situation in India?*

After *Jahaji Music*, I was interested in understanding how music reflects social histories. *Jahaji Music* was filmed in Trinidad, and a large part of the population are descendants of indentured workers mostly from the states of Uttar Pradesh and Bihar. The colonial government got them to work on sugar plantations in the Caribbean. So, contemporary music carries that history and the sound of that journey. I was curious about what I could understand listening to the music of Bhojpuri workers[1] in my city, Mumbai. My guiding questions were: What history of migration was visible? What stories of love and longing would emerge? What understanding of the precarious lives of migrant workers in Mumbai? These issues and questions led me to make *Bidesia in Bambai*. As a filmmaker, I never offer a conclusion. That is, I have no grand conclusion on the migrant psyche and on the issue of migration in India. I explore ideas and questions. My films are a sum total of that search. No one can romanticize migration. My attempt was a journey into the psyche of these migrants, how they negotiate with their sense of displacement, and how their music carries the very culture they are from. It was also an attempt to explore how music gives them a sense of purpose.

Still 13 A still from the film *Bidesia in Bambai.* Image Courtesy: Surabhi Sharma.

What is your objective in making documentary films on laborers, slums, and surrogate women who are pushed to the seamy side of everyday life?

I don't know what my objective is but I believe my role as a filmmaker is to make meaning of stories that are whispered from the edges. The stories might not be clear and more often undramatic. This is what I seek. I don't see myself as an investigative filmmaker. I am not attempting to make visible the lies that our government and media spins. My effort is to engage with the mundane and the everyday that might not seem outrageous but is embedded in an unequal society.

Is independent documentary immune from the influences of the commercial industry especially with the coming of many online screening platforms such as Netflix?

It depends on the filmmaker. And this is a recent phenomenon. Earlier, the whole community was immunized because no one in India saw the commercial possibility of documentary films. But the world market for documentary film is huge and powerful. They see the potential to market Indian documentary films. That brings with it the burden of making things intelligible and simple to an international audience. A certain density of ideas gets simplified. That precarious balance is tough. And since the international documentary market is interested in Indian films, local commercial industries sit up and take notice too. Then they look for heartbreaking and thrilling documentaries that tell simple stories which appeal to everyone. That is an interesting development but one that I am wary of.

Before becoming a filmmaker, you were a theater artist. Could you share your experience of your transition from a theater artist to a documentary filmmaker?

I worked as an actor with Satyadev Dubey[2] and Sunil Shanbag[3] in Mumbai from the late 1980s until mid-1990s. Both directors are very important to the alternative theater movement in Mumbai. The manner in which these directors worked with texts and brought them to stage was a huge learning experience for me. This learning was happening parallel to my college life and my life as a young trainee in the film world. This part of my life has been the foundation to my approach in cinema as well.

Slums have always been a favorite theme of Bollywood filmmakers. It is also used by some Hollywood films to represent and stereotype India. Your portrayal of a slum in Jari Mari: Of Cloth and Other Stories *differ from those stereotypical representations. Share the politics and aesthetics of such an outlook.*

Bollywood films see slums as the site for crime and poverty. They are not interested in the day-to-day experience of living in an insecure settlement. My film was centered on what it means to be a worker whose home is illegal, whose work is not secure, and whose citizenship is invisible to policy-makers. What does that even mean in a city hankering to be the next Singapore or Shanghai. My approach and my questions were different from what a Bollywood film or a Hollywood film is interested in. That is perhaps what accounts for the totally different experience of both the films.

You graduated from the Film and Television Institute of India (FTII). Do you think such a structured training in film school helped you to become an independent documentary filmmaker?

My training in FTII has been the biggest influence in my filmmaking. This connects to my answer about form and content. My training in cinema at FTII makes me see that my form emerges from my content. It is an organic process in that your material gives one insight into how to shape and structure it into a film. I don't begin with the form and then find material to fit into it. That may be a perfectly valid approach for some but that is not how I work. Seeking the form within the material is what my training at FTII gave me. I have the confidence to play within my material.

What persuaded you to engage with an environmental issue of North Kerala in Aamakaar, The Turtle People?

C. Saratchandran,[4] an important film activist in Kerala, told my producer Sunil Shanbag about the village and their struggles. Sunil urged me to visit the village because I was living in Bangalore at the time. I was unsure since North Kerala was an unfamiliar place for me. Generally, I do not go in search of "interesting" subjects. Sunil was really moved by what Sarat had told him and so I went along. I spent two days at the village with Sarat. I returned totally overwhelmed by the group and the village. That's how I began to work in this film. Sunil Shanbag was totally involved and supported me every step of the way.

Notes

1 Bhojpuri workers refers to migrant workers who speak Bhojpuri language and typically belong to the states of Bihar and Uttar Pradesh.
2 Satyadev Dubey is an Indian film and theater director, screenwriter, and playwright. His notable screenplays include *Bhumika* (trans. *The Role*) (1977) and *Aakrosh* (trans. *Anger*) (1980).
3 Sunil Shanbag is a theater director, filmmaker, and screenwriter.
4 C. Saratchandran was a documentary filmmaker and a civil rights activist from Kerala, a South Indian state.

Nishtha Jain

Figure 14 Image Courtesy: Nishtha Jain.

Born in New Delhi, Nishtha Jain is a multi-award-winning filmmaker, producer, and writer based in Mumbai. Jain created an independent documentary outfit named Raintree Films, together with Smriti Nevatia. In her efforts to engage the everyday world, feminism, and progressive politics of the day, her films, as they problematize the established hierarchies, also embody the feminist clarion "personal is political." More importantly, Jain's films are a sustained analysis of gender and its imperatives in everyday lives. For instance, *Lakshmi and Me* is a critical take on the master-servant relationship and the pervasive caste thinking that prevails in a typical middle-class Indian family. Besides gender, her films also discuss issues like domestic labor (*Lakshmi and Me*), women's movement (*Gulabi Gang*), and politics of image-making (*City of Photos*). She is one among the early filmmakers who politically and aesthetically addressed transgender issues. Unlike "objective" and realist documentary narratives, her films are intimate and reflective, and thus offer incisive insights on quotidian realities of life. Coproduced by like-minded individuals and institutions, her films are widely distributed across the world. In 2020, she received the prestigious Chicken & Egg Award[1] for her outstanding work in documentary.

Selected Films

The Golden Thread (2021)
Submerged (2016)
Gulabi Gang (trans. *Pink Gang*) (2012)
Family Album (2010)
At My Doorstep (2009)
Lakshmi and Me (2007)
6 Yards to Democracy (2006)
Call It Slut (2005)
City of Photos (2004)

As a woman filmmaker, do you think the language of the film is different from male documentary filmmakers?

When women question the male gaze and replace it with theirs, the language naturally changes. Godard once said something to the effect: with passage of time, films become like documentaries about the actors, director, and the times. Our films hold a mirror to us. For example, *Lakshmi and Me* is a testament of my politics and the state of my art/craft from a decade ago.

Women's experiences are different from men's experiences. And this gendered experience gets reflected in our films provided the filmmaking is a conscious process. This may not happen in commercial projects. Ekta Kapoor's[2] serials, for example, draw on patriarchal notions only to feed them further.

Trace your filmmaking career as an independent documentary filmmaker? How difficult and exciting was that journey for you?

We were a family of film buffs fortunate to have four theaters in the five-kilometer radius of our house. A few kilometers of walk to the theater was no deterrent to buy tickets in black to watch the first-day show. There was no separation yet between parallel and mainstream cinema then. So, a theater could play a mainstream film like *Raampur Ka Lakshman* (1972)[3] and the next change could be *Bhuvan Shome*[4] (1969) or *Mrigyaa*[5] (1976). Even Doordarshan[6] in those days broadcast a wide range of films in their Sunday slot. From Raj Kapoor's *Bobby*[7] to Mani Kaul's *Duvidha*[8] and *Uski* Roti,[9] we grew on a healthy mix of entertainment and art house films. The black-and-white images from Utpal Dutt's[10] performance in *Bhuvan Shome* left an indelible mark as did the social realism of *Mrigyaa*. However, it was the temporality in Mani Kaul's films which intrigued me and stayed with me, even though I was only eleven years old when I first watched it. Doordarshan would also broadcast films of the European masters and FTII Diploma films in late-night slots during the International Film Festival in Delhi. I would stay up late to watch these films. Many of them were masterpieces. FTII diploma films intrigued me. They were raw and unconventional. Often, I would miss school to watch Hollywood Romance in the matinee show. My mother was a ready accomplice. We saw *Roman Holiday*, *My Fair Lady*, and *Sound of Music*. By the time I was in my late teens, I too was a film buff but never thought that I would be making films one day. I joined Jamia Millia Mass Communication Center for my postgraduate studies. We were taught a little of everything in radio, television, and film. After my graduation in the late 1980s, I began work as an editor and correspondent for video newsmagazines (*Newstrack* and *Eyewitness*). In those days, Doordarshan was the only source of news, and they carried the "official" version of the news. The video news magazines became a popular source of alternative news until 1994 when cable television started in India. Politically, it was a very important period. Sample this: the demolition of the Babri Masjid, anti-Mandal agitation, militancy in Kashmir, Sri Lankan civil war, and the assassination of Rajeev Gandhi.[11] As an editor, I was privy to hundreds of hours of footage from these troubled areas. The world as we knew was changing in front of our eyes and we knew that these events would change Indian polity forever, and they did. We are seeing its fullest impact today. But while the content of these stories was gripping, they would be edited in a typical BBC television documentary format. I felt these formatted shows suffocated the power of the footage. I wished to work as an independent filmmaker and longed to enter the world of cinema. I joined FTII in 1995 to specialize in film direction. Since 1998, I've been making independent films, mainly documentaries.

Gulabi Gang is an exceptional documentary in terms of both craft and content and in the way it showcases women's collective movement against corruption, caste oppression and gender violence in a remote region in Uttar Pradesh. How

***did the nonmembers of the gang in the village respond to it? Sampat Pal Devi is
the backbone of the Gulabi Gang. Will the gang survive after her? How did you
arrive at the subject which should have demanded intense research?***

In 2008, I was attending a film festival in the United States. A fellow filmmaker
told me about the grass-roots women's movement in Central India called the
Gulabi Gang. Some of the news channels in the United States and Europe had
run news stories about them but not many people had heard about them in
India. Upon my return, I began researching them. I found their story powerful
for several reasons. This wasn't a revolution brought by urban radicals but
growing from inside in the most backward and patriarchal areas of India. This
region has seen many brave female warriors. In fact, it has thrown up many
women leaders—both famous and infamous—Jhansi ki Rani (an Indian queen
of the Maratha princely state of Jhansi in Uttar Pradesh), Phoolan Devi,[12] and
Mayawati.[13]

Sampat Pal Devi's brand of feminism was entirely her own creation. It took
into account the rural realities, the constraints that women face because of
their economic dependence. In some sense, they do not have support systems
like the women in urban areas. On our very first meeting, Sampat Pal Devi
and I realized that we had differences on many issues, like whether a woman
should return to an abusive husband or not. Sampat Pal Devi's efforts were to
reconcile the couples and not let the marriages break up. Of course, I had a
different opinion about these "compromises." But soon I realized that to judge
a rural reality with my urban parameters would be unfair. The lack of access
to justice via the legal system because of corruption or cost made mutual
settlements practical. We learned a lot after spending time in the area. We also
witnessed first-hand the difficulties of the people who live there. Like the Wild
West in the United States, Bundelkhand is a region in which guns speak before
people can open their mouths. We were fortunate not to have an untoward
incident, thanks to the authority that Sampat Pal Devi commands. However, we
encountered violence on a daily basis. Stories of women's deaths were common
and often passed off as suicides. When we began filming, Gulabi Gang claimed
a membership of 70,000. It had increased to 400,000 by the time the film was
released. Gulabi Gang had several regional leaders but none as charismatic as
Sampat Pal Devi. But her overarching political ambitions and lack of vision
proved to be detrimental and ultimately led to a split within the group in 2014.
She's still active, although the movement has lost its initial momentum and
popularity.

Still 14 A still from the film *Gulabi Gang.* Image Courtesy: Nishtha Jain.

Lakshmi and Me *is about domestic workers in India from the point of view of Lakshmi, your household maid. How feudal are Indian households? The film radically problematizes class-caste structure at both social and family levels. Share the political vision of the film.*

The film examines the issues surrounding the subject of domestic work in a patriarchal and feudal society like India. I'm looking at how unconsciously the people, even those who question the feudal and patriarchal system, are drawn into the exploitative system as a matter of either convenience or habit. So, instead of making an objective film about domestic workers, I decided to turn the camera on myself because I was exactly that sort of leftist, feminist, single woman who employed another woman to come in for an hour for cleaning and washing. In retrospect, I really didn't need any help but it was the convenience and affordability that stopped me from questioning this need. The monthly wages of domestic workers at the time I made the film were equal to the cost of fancy dinner in a restaurant. In contrast to my generation, the women of my mother's generation were used to doing housework. In fact, they took pride in doing it. But it was different for my generation. Some of my school/college friends did not know how to make tea because they always had house help. In my home, we could not afford house help and my mother expected me to help her out, but she never had the same expectations from my brothers. This definitely was a point of contention. Until she asked my brothers to work, I would not help her and, eventually, she would land up doing all the work herself. The idea that feminism also meant being relieved of housework had taken root in my mind. So, as soon as I started working and could afford to employ help, I did. I was one of those benevolent and friendly employers who was not indifferent. On the contrary, I was engaged with problems with my domestic worker(s).

A friend visiting from abroad unwittingly became a catalyst for my film. Upon introduction, he extended his hands toward Lakshmi. She was embarrassed. Perhaps, no middle-class or *savarna* (communities that belong to the four *varnas* or classes as per Hindu texts) people had ever shaken hands with her. It was her response to such a simple gesture which started a process of self-reflection. And that is the gist of *Lakshmi and Me*. It looks at how class, caste, and patriarchy come together to determine actions and choices. The film recognizes our privilege and questions our entitlement as middle-class and savarna people. Lakshmi and I had a friendly, even warm relationship, but there was no denying the social and economic divide. We inhabited very separate worlds. In India, domestic work is called "help" and the workers "servants." They are around us all the time and yet, in a sense, invisible. The film holds a mirror to us and shows up an uncomfortable reality. At the time the film was made, wages were paltry and there were no unions to determine fair pay or laws to enforce minimum wages. Most employers, knowingly or inadvertently, tended to treat their domestic workers as if they are inferior or less-entitled beings. Things have improved since then for domestic workers but the attitudes of the employers are more or less still the same.

In one of your interviews you said making Lakshmi *and* Me *was like "walking a tightrope throughout the process of filming, editing, and questioning yourself, Should I film this? or Could this be invasive"? How do you put together a plan to make a documentary like this?*

It would have been an easier task to make an objective film with interviews of domestic workers talking about how they are maltreated juxtaposed with employers talking about how unprofessional the workers are. Instead, I decided to turn the camera to myself, to make a self-reflexive film that lays bare our indifference and occasional brutality to those who serve us. At the outset, I did not realize how morally exhausting the making of this film will be. But it was not all wasted. There was a handsome pay-off. That is, any employer who watched the film could not escape the moral and ethical questions that the film raises.

There is a Lakshmi in nearly every middle-class home in India. The film also addresses the other power relationship between the filmmaker and the subject.

City of Photos *uses a number of frozen moments as the medium for a dynamic exploration into the politics of image-making and the ethos of photo studios in India. What prompted this fascinating journey into the city of photos through a narrow line where the political meets the personal?*

In the late 1990s, when the Indian middle class had almost stopped using photo studios for portrait photos except for an occasional passport or matrimonial photo, I was surprised to find that photo studio business was flourishing in small towns, village markets, fairs, and the poor localities of big cities. Muslims formed a big part of the clientele because photography is a taboo in Islam. This was also a period of transition from analog to digital photography. Some of the old practices like hand-painted fantasy backdrops were getting replaced with digital backgrounds. The fantasy backgrounds not only reflected aspirations for a better home, or a desire for a holiday in Swiss Alps but also gave a chance to the people, who have been left out, to show that they are up with the times. So, backgrounds highlighting contemporary reality or events found their way into people's portraits. The film is about politics of self-representation. I consider the photo studio portraits to be early-day selfies. Clients worked closely with the photographer to create an image of themselves which they would be proud to show off to the world. They dressed up and used make-up, and the photographer would light up and direct them. Photo studios served as little fantasy breaks in an otherwise mundane life. Today, all the services that photo studios provided are available in a simple application. But a photo taken on a phone does not have the timeless quality that a good studio photographer could provide. The film enters into the world of small photo studios that you are most likely to miss. It stops and looks at hundreds of dust-ridden photos on the walls which reveal a world that exists only in photos. Like a photo that captures the moment that's gone, the film captures a world that was passing away.

At My Doorstep *explores the predicament of being displaced from one's homeland to survive and the implications of social and economic inequality. As such, migration has become a global phenomenon and an inevitable twentieth-/twenty-first-century episode. What is your take?*

Most of the migrations are inequity driven. In India, people are forced to leave their villages to come to the cities in search of livelihood and better education.

These migrations could have been avoided had the successive governments paid better attention to our rural areas. And then agriculture is getting riskier and young people don't want to do laborious work like farming. Millions migrate to the cities every year. The cities are overpopulated, and there's not enough jobs for everyone. People have no choice but to take up available work which is not well paid, and they live in hovels. The film looks at the lives of watchmen, garbage collectors, laundry men, delivery boys—all those who serve people like us, the residents of a typical middle-class housing society. Most of these workers are not unionized so there's a lot of undercutting in wages and other forms of exploitation. The sum total of all this is a certain form of emasculation, which in turn manifests itself as alcoholism, identity politics, sexual violence, depression, and so on.

Call it Slut *is a take on patriarchy and conservative values from a transgender perspective. It is framed as a conversation between you and Lakshmi. Why is it structured as a dialogue? Don't you think feminine sensibility is also under attack when we deal with transgender issues?*

No, I don't think feminine sensibility is under attack. On the contrary, *Call It Slut* celebrates femininity. The starting point of the film is my envy that Lakshmi, a transgender woman, is able to flaunt femininity in a way that I as a woman can't owing to our inhibitions about our bodies. I'm not as free with my body as Lakshmi is with hers. And that's because she has a male body even though she has a female mind. She dresses as a woman but carries herself with the ease of a man. And that's the privilege which is subtly shown in the film. Her comfort and my discomfort are counterpoints but a beginning of discussion.

Notes

1   Chicken & Egg Award recognizes those films/filmmakers that are committed to social change, art, and craft in filmmaking.
2   Ekta Kapoor is an Indian film/television producer and director.
3   *Raampur Ka Lakshman* (1972) is a Hindi film directed by Manmohan Desai.
4   *Bhuvan Shome* (1969) is a Hindi language film directed by Mrinal Sen.
5   *Mrigyaa* (trans. *The Royal Hunt*) (1976) is a period film directed by Mrinal Sen.
6   Doordarshan is the official government-owned and -controlled public service broadcaster in India.

7 *Bobby* (1973) is an Indian film directed by Raj Kapoor. It was a trend-setting movie casting Rishi Kapoor and Dimple Kapadia in the lead roles.

8 *Duvidha* (trans. *In Two Minds*) (1973) is an Indian film directed by Mani Kaul.

9 *Uski Roti* (trans. *Other's Bread*) (1969) is an Indian film directed by Mani Kaul. It is considered as a seminal work in the Indian parallel cinema/New Indian Cinema.

10 Anti-Mandal agitation refers to a series of protests in the 1990s against the implementation of the Mandal Commission report that recommended caste-based reservations in the government jobs.

11 Rajeev Gandhi, son of Indira Gandhi, served as the Indian prime minister in 1984. He was assassinated in 1991 while campaigning in an election rally.

12 Phoolan Devi was a bandit who later became a member of Indian Parliament. She was assassinated in 2001.

13 Mayawati is a former chief minister of Uttar Pradesh, a Central Indian state.

Sridhar Rangayan

Figure 15 Image Courtesy: Sridhar Rangayan.

An alumnus of IIT Bombay, Sridhar Rangayan is an independent filmmaker based in Bombay. Although he started his career as a television screenwriter and director, Rangayan later became an independent filmmaker to direct films of his choice. As a gay activist, he is one of the forerunners in the LGBTQ+ movement in India. He started making LGBTQ+ films even during criminalization of same-sex practices in India. In 2001, he founded Solaris Pictures, an independent production company along with his partner Saagar Gupta. Rangayan's films (including his fiction films such as *The Pink Mirror*, *Yours Emotionally*, and *Evening Shadows*, and documentaries such as *Purple Skies* and *Breaking Free*) have consistently addressed LGBTQ+ issues and, thus, remain landmark works in India's emerging queer cinema movement. His documentary *Purple Skies*, coalescing multiple stories of pain, pleasure and hope of LBT lives, addresses every day and unattended struggles of LBT community in India. His *Breaking Free*, in a related way, chronicles human rights violations faced by the LGBT communities in India because of the Section 377 of the Indian Penal Code which criminalizes same-sex activities. Using personal testimonies, *Breaking Free* exposes and criticizes the homophobic social mores of Indian Society. Additionally, he is the founder director of KASHISH Mumbai International Queer Film Festival, South Asia's largest LGBTQ+ film festival.

Selected Filmography

Breaking Free (2015)
Purple Skies (2014)
Bridges of Hope (2008)

You had a successful career as a television screenwriter and director before becoming an independent filmmaker. Why did you become an independent filmmaker of LGBTQ+ issues?

When I was doing television for almost four years, I felt that there was no space for any stories that were non-heteronormative and that was frustrating for a gay man who was bursting with stories about the community that needed to be told urgently. This was between 1999 and 2000 when Saagar Gupta (writer, art director, producer) and I proposed to one of the television channels a simple gay love story in their slot for love stories. We said it was high time we told stories about same-sex love too. But the channel vetoed it saying such stories were not meant for family audiences. That's when Saagar and I decided that enough was enough and quit television to form our own production company Solaris Pictures in 2001. Our first production was *Gulabi Aaina* (*The Pink Mirror*), which went on to become a huge festival success, screening at more than eighty international film festivals and winning two awards. That was the beginning of our focus on making LGBTQ films.

You are a gay filmmaker and have been working for LGBTQ+ rights in India for the last twenty years. How challenging it is to be an LGBTQ+ filmmaker in India?

Since we started making LGBTQ-focused films from 2001, there has been no looking back. It is indeed a huge challenge to continue making LGBTQ films, but what drives is our passion and our commitment to highlight stories about our community. When we started making movies, there were hardly any films that were made on the subject. But, now over the past few years, there have been numerous short films, documentary films, and independent features in the subject and the nascent Indian LGBTQ cinema movement has truly kicked off.

As a filmmaker, you have made documentary as well as fiction films. How do you see documentaries as a cinematic medium? Is it because of the limitations of the medium that you started making fiction films?

It is the other way around. We made several fictional films before turning to documentary films. It was in 2008, seven years after we started Solaris Pictures and had made three fiction films that toured film festivals across the world, that we focused on making our first documentary film. It was definitely by chance it happened. I was covering a press conference in Mumbai in 2008 to protest against the arrest of *Hijras*[1] in Bangalore. It suddenly hit me that the real world was a bigger concern than telling fictional stories about the community. Following the press conference was a protest by a group of Hijras and *Kothis*[2] who shouted down Section 377[3] slogans. This turned me to introspect what Section 377 meant for the community and how it impacted real lives so drastically. From then on, because of the lack of budget, whenever I would travel to any work to any city, I started shooting LGBTQ+ events and LGBTQ+ activism. From over six to seven years of such documentation came two feature-length documentaries, *Purple Skies* (2014) and *Breaking Free* (2015).

Purple Skies *is a journey into the lives of women, transmen, and gender queer persons who negotiate their nonnormative gender and sexuality. The film gives a glimpse of the layers of violence that LBT communities in India suffer. How did you come to this film?*

After the Nirbhaya incident, Public Service Broadcasting Trust (PSBT) India, an organization in New Delhi doing amazing work producing documentary films, put out a call for films dealing with violence against women. Saagar and I thought it was important to discuss violence against lesbian and bisexual women in the larger context of violence against women. So, we applied for a grant to PSBT with our film *Purple Skies—Voices of Indian Lesbians, Bisexuals & Transmen*, and we were happy that our proposal was accepted to make a feature-length documentary. So, keeping the backdrop of Section 377, for which we had already been documenting many stories, we went ahead and shot several candid portrayals of lesbian and bisexual women and transmen across Mumbai, New Delhi, and other cities. It was very heartening that so many LBT persons managed to share their stories in screen with us candidly, without fear of stigma and discrimination it may bring to them. While the film covered stories of anguish and pain of lesbian women and violence and alienation they faced, it also brought out happy and empowering stories of younger LBT persons who have managed to overcome all odds and are living a life happily with their partners. We were very happy when the film, apart from screening at several film festivals, also was telecasted in Doordarshan, India's National

Network. *Purple Skies* is perhaps the first ever film on lesbian and bisexual women to be telecast, thereby reaching the story of LBT lives to millions across India. We did ensure availability of a counsellor to help the protagonists to deal with any adverse reactions post the telecast, but thankfully there were none. We were all flooded with calls and messages from people across the spectrum and the helpline number we had listed in the film received numerous calls for help and support. The film, screening on YouTube currently, continues to inspire younger LBT persons, and also offers a window to mainstream society about LBT lives.

Breaking Free *is a personal journey that exposes the human rights violation faced by the LGBT community in India. The film was made in a period when LGBTQ+ desires were criminalized in India. While your* **Purple Skies** *is very optimistic, the mood of* Breaking Free *is different. Why did you use a particular form in the film where the filmmaker himself becomes the part of the film? What prompted you to make such an intense film on LGBTQ+ rights in India?*

As I mentioned, we started documenting LGBTQ events, activities, and activists over seven years, and from it is born *Breaking Free*. The main focus of this film is Section 377 and how it victimized the community and pushed the community underground for centuries since colonial times. It traces the history of legal challenge to Section 377 in the courts by speaking to lawyers and advocates from its first petition by ABVA[4] till the reversal of judgment by the Supreme Court in 2013. It also traces the history of the civil movement by the LGBTQ community to move out of the shadows and become empowered, by speaking to activists, community leaders and also LGBQ community members across numerous cities in India. What was heartening was that we managed to get real-life testimonies of people who were chargesheeted with Section 377 and suffered greatly. The stories of Kokila, Madhumita, Pandian, and Arif Zafar and Sudeesh Singh are real eye-openers, as well as countless stories of misuse of Section 377 by police and blackmailers. It took a lot of effort to track down these persons and encourage them to share their stories candidly. And we are highly obliged to everyone who participated in the film *Breaking Free* and lent their voice to this narrative. In fact, at every screening of the film, at festivals, at community centers, the main reaction by people is that we didn't know much about the actual violence and discrimination caused by Section 377. The younger-generation LGBTQ members have no clue of the long struggle that has brought about the current freedom they enjoy. It definitely gave them a sense of whose shoulders they stand on. Yes, the film ends with the negative judgment in 2013. But I feel it leaves the viewer with the hope that the changes brought in by the community is irreversible. And that got proved by the 2018 verdict by the Supreme Court reading down Section 377 and finally decriminalizing same-sex relationships.

I was also a protagonist driving the story. It was a device that came much later because I felt I cannot remain invisible if I was telling the story of Section 377 and how it impacted the LGBTQ community. Second, as a gay man who has been impacted by Section 377 and has been an intrinsic part of the movement since I came out in 1991. My life has been intertwined with the LGBTQ movement for rights in India. In fact, "I," as the narrator, lends credence to the stories I tell in this film. The film won the National Award for Best Editing (nonfiction) for editors Pravin Angre and me (Sridhar Rangayan) at the Sixty-Third National Awards presented in 2016, and the citation read, "an orchestrated cuts and curves to depict the hardship of the oppressed" (which involved editing more than 400 hours of footage into an 82-minute film). This was the crowning glory for the film apart from a couple of awards and a good festival run. The film is currently screening on Netflix and also shows up in the Trending in India section, which is rather surprising. But it is also extremely gratifying for an independent film which was crowdfunded and self-funded.

Still 15 A still from the film *Breaking Free*. Image Courtesy: Sridhar Rangayan.

You are the founder director of KASHISH Mumbai International Queer Film Festival. In a country like India why do you think there should be a festival like KASHISH? What is the mission behind this film festival?

KASHISH Mumbai International Queer Film Festival was founded in 2010, right after reading down of Section 377 by the Delhi High Court, which we felt gave us the freedom to host an LGBTQ film festival in the public domain. There have been LGBTQ film festivals in the past which were organized in colleges or cultural institutions, but KASHISH became the first ever LGBTQ film festival to be held in a mainstream theater with the complete clearance from the Ministry of Information and Broadcasting, Government of India.[5] The idea for the festival was twofold: first, to create a safe-space within a mainstream space for the LGBTQ community to celebrate their lives on the big screen, and, second, to formulate a better understanding of LGBTQ lives for non-LGBTQ audiences. Both these ideas have been fructified by the success of the festival in terms of number of films being programmed and the number of audience members attending the festival increasing manifold over the years. Thirty percent of KASHISH audiences are non-LGBTQ members, thereby signaling a growing interest among mainstream audiences to participate in LGBTQ events. KASHISH has definitely been instrumental in mainstreaming queer visibility and enabling rational attitudes among general public about LGBTQ lives. KASHISH remains apolitical, though the films we show are political in nature. Also the very fact that we are organizing an LGBQ event in a mainstream space is a political expression. The only politics of KASHISH has been to be inclusive of the diverse segments within the LGBTQIA+ community and offering a platform to nurture filmmakers in this genre.

Your documentary **Purple Skies** *is the first LBT documentary screened in Doordarshan, the public service broadcaster founded by the Government of India. Your film* **Breaking Free** *was given a National Award. In a country where LGBTQ+ desires are criminalized, how do you negotiate your gay identity with the apparatus of the state?*

It has definitely been a challenge making the films that we make. Lack of financial resources being one among the many barriers. In the initial years, when we did our first two films (*The Pink Mirror* and *Yours Emotionally!*), we were even scared to carry out the filming and editing processes, and everything had to be done underground. Also finding actors to play gay or transgender parts was a huge challenge, and the Indian film industry back then wasn't evolved to support production, exhibition, and distribution of our films. So, at Solaris Pictures, as we continued to make LGBTQ-themed films over the past two decades, we continued to create new paths of our own—to fund our films, to produce our films, and to distribute our films. We sincerely hope we have created these new paths that are able to benefit the nascent Indian LGBTQ filmmaking community.

One of the hurdles has also been censorship by the Indian Board for Film Certification—where they deem anything to do with homosexuality or trans-sexuality to be adult and certify it with an "A" certificate,[6] though the film portrays both these with sensitivity and empathy. We have had quite a few run-ins with the censor board: from our first film *The Pink Mirror* still denied a certification (literally banning the film) to our later projects getting an "A" certificate, thereby reducing its potential distribution and outreach. Only our two films *Purple Skies* and *Evening Shadows* received a "U" and a "UA" certificate, respectively, that too after much intervention. The antiquated rule book of the censor board needs to be revamped urgently to include contemporary sensibilities.

We carry on with our work with passion and dedication, and do not bother with the state agencies unless they cross paths with us, which we negotiate through conversations, instead of confrontation. That has been our way of working, as we continue to weave our rainbow dreams into narratives, to reach out to audiences across India and the world.

Notes

1 *Hijras* is a term used in India to refer to transgender persons.
2 Kothis is an Indian slang for an effeminate gay man.
3 Section 377 is a section in the Indian Penal Code established during the British rule in India which criminalizes homosexuality and other nonnormative sexual practices in India. In its landmark judgment dated September 6, 2018, the Supreme Court of India decriminalized homosexuality and other nonnormative sexual practices in India.
4 Founded in 1988, AIDS Bhedbhav Virodhi Andolan (ABVA) was the first HIV/AIDS activist movement in India that advocated civil rights for LGBTQ people in India.

5 Ministry of Information and Broadcasting is a ministry under the Government of India that regulates and manages information, broadcasting, press, and cinema in India.

6 "A" certificate is a film certification given by the Central Board of Film Certification (CBFC) of India that restricts the exhibition of a film to those who are below the age of eighteen. The CBFC also issues certificates such as "U" (unrestricted public exhibition) and "U/A" (unrestricted public exhibition subject to parental guidance for children below the age of twelve).

3

Documenting Inequality

Casting the Caste

Caste is a form of social stratification that results in ostracization of a group of underprivileged people. As a disconcerting sociopolitical reality, caste functions as a discriminatory force in India. Predicated on the cultural ideologies of purity and ritual status, caste as a mode of social exclusion is practiced in India irrespective of stringent laws against them. Although caste has been central to the power relations in India, it has hardly received any critical attention in the mainstream commercial films or in the Films Division documentaries. For instance, although *They Call Me Chamar* (1980) addressed the contentious question of caste, it was filmed from the point of view of a dominant caste person. Independent documentary films, which were seen as an alternative to the commercial and state-sponsored movies, are equally guilty of evading the question of caste till the 1990s. However, inspired by the writings of B. R. Ambedkar[1] and his vision of casteless societies, a group of independent documentary filmmakers since 1990s began addressing caste-based discrimination, descent-based social hierarchy, and ostracization in documentary format. *Lesser Humans* by Stalin K., *Pee* (trans. *Shit*) by Amudhan R. P. and *Kakkoos* (trans. *Latrine*) by Divya Bharathi, for instance, delineate caste-based labor and untouchability in contemporary India. These films, including the testimonies of affected people, not only question the middle-class complacency of denying the reality of caste oppression but also critique the despicable institution of the caste system itself. Furthermore, while these films vindicate the emergence of a radical new Dalit politics in India, they also expose the role of the state in promulgating caste ideologies. Put together, these filmmakers as independent voices foreground unseen faces and unheard voices of India, and thus galvanize critical attention into the lives of Dalits and the marginalized.

Note

1   B. R. Ambedkar is a social reformer and the chief architect of the Indian Constitution
who inspired anti-caste movements in India. He fought against the social
discriminations of the "untouchables" (people who belong to the lower castes) who
are now politically addressed as Dalits.

Amudhan R. P.

Figure 16 Image Courtesy: Amudhan R. P.

Based in Madurai (a major city in the Indian state of Tamil Nadu), Amudhan R. P. is an independent documentary filmmaker, media activist, and the founder of a media collective called *Marupakkam*. As a documentary filmmaker, he sheds light on socially relevant issues such as caste, untouchability, and refugee crisis. For instance, his film *Pee* (trans. *Shit*) was a cultural shock to the complacent middle-class Indians who refuse to see the brutal side of caste-based discriminations and forced labor. In 1998, he organized the Madurai International Documentary and Short Film Festival and has been part of the festival since then. Known for blunt aesthetics and rhetorical politics, his self-funded films are an expression of societal issues that require immediate political, social, and direct action. Besides, he commissions films and organizes media-related workshops to empower marginalized groups.

Selected Filmography

My Caste (2019)
Dollar City (2015)

Hey Mr. Gandhi, Leave the Indians Alone! (2012)

Mercury in the Mist (2011)

Radiation Stories Part 03: Koodankulam (2009)

Radiation Stories Part 02: Kalpakkam (2008)

Radiation Stories Part 01: Manavalakurichi (2008)

Seruppu (trans. Footwear) (2006)

Mayana Kurippugal (trans. Notes from the Crematorium) (2005)

Pee (trans. Shit) (2003)

Theeviravaghigal (trans. Terrorists) (1997)

Your film Mercury in the Mist *concentrates on mercury contamination in a Kodaikanal[1]-based thermometer factory owned by a multinational corporation. In the film, the camera against a pensive music follows the workers and maps their bodies in order to expose the intensity of exploitation and violence. Although there is no direct critique of the practices of the factory, you expose the wounded, affected bodies through their testimonies. How do you characterize your practice of filmmaking where the camera functions as a means of justice?*

First, it might be because of my conviction and sense of justice. As a filmmaker, my sentiments have always been with the "other" who is marginalized, victimized, and hurt by injustice. That sensibility runs through my films however subtle or explicit. Second, maybe my politics prompts me to do so. In any art form, even if it is a fairy tale, there is a discernible ideology and counter-ideology at play. Some are subtle, some are direct, some are black and white, and some talk about gray areas. Although treatments vary, there lies a sense of justice in every art form. The idea of art is very much ingrained in the sense of justice. In that sense, every art is political. I doubt whether those art forms that don't talk about some form of justice can be called art. The treatment may vary. For me, any significant art that stood the time has always talked about justice. I engage with such art forms.

Migration, refugee crisis, repatriation *are hardly discussed in documentary films. Your film* Theeviravaghigal (trans. Terrorists) *is an early attempt that deliberated the predicament of repatriates. With an activist zeal, the film shows how nationalism becomes a tool in the hands of the state to categorize its citizens in terms of their origin in the Sri Lankan context. Why do you think that the state's treatment is inappropriate and often violent?*

Theeviravaghigal is a sociocultural documentary. The film deals with the predicament of a group of peasants who are the repatriates from Southern Sri Lanka. They were brought back to India under the Sirima–Shastri Pact[2] and were made to settle in the hills of Kodaikanal, a famous hill station near Madurai. Most of these repatriates wish a dignified life. However, their situation became worse since they are Dalits. They are in a "state of exception" and are doubly marginalized. When repatriates ask for their rights, the government doesn't like it. Moreover, governments and politicians here are essentially anti-Dalits. They get angry if repatriates demand their rights and justice. It is in such contexts that they face such brutal responses from the police and the government. When the judicial commission was appointed to inquire about their situation and demands, one of the members of the commission called repatriates as people with "terrorist" mindset. As such, the idea of racial hate is at the heart of the problem. It is in this context that the idea of belonging becomes relevant.

Although caste has been a grotesque reality in India, it is rarely addressed in the mainstream commercial cinema. Your film **Shit** *was a cultural shock in that it bluntly exposed caste and problematized the very idea of hygiene. Why is caste so exploitative in the sense that it breeds injustice and discrimination?*

India's biggest problem is the caste system. It is impossible to think of social justice without the annihilation of the caste system in India. Caste operates subtly in India. It is very much ingrained in the psyche. So the question of justice is a distant reality here. Although we feel that there is no caste in manual scavenging, caste is at its very root of it. If you search for the background of people who are doing manual scavenging, we can see that they are all from "lower caste" backgrounds. There is an assumption that some are destined to do it. It is definitely a thought that was built along casteist lines. In that sense, the popular idea of hygiene is very casteist and elitist. As long as we are stuck in our caste holes, India can never create a just society. Our caste affinity influences all our activities which by default creates imbalances in the social system.

Your films boldly problematize caste and depicts how it is used as an oppressive method to marginalize Dalits in Tamil Nadu. Why do think Dalit issues are central to our times?

Dalits are the worst victims of the caste system. Dalits are at the bottom and are not even treated like human beings. They are denied basic facilities, rights, and opportunities. They face brutal violence whenever they breach caste hierarchy. As such, the caste system is legal in social terms. Like African Americans who face racist violence and discrimination, Dalits in India face casteist violence and discrimination. These issues are hardly discussed in the media. We need to address this issue since we are in some way or the other affected by the caste system.

Vande Mataram, the national song of India, is sung as a tribute to the nation. But your difficult-to-digest Vande Mataram: A Shit Version *lampoons the patriotic song and sheds light on the seamy side of India like poverty, caste, and gender discriminations. What compelled you to make such a difficult-to-digest music video?*

It's really tough to be a critical filmmaker anywhere in the world, not just in India. Especially when you criticize the state. State is the biggest legalized threat to our freedom. It is a huge, modern, supposedly inevitable, and dangerous trap. Some clever, savvy, and intelligent woman or man can take over the country and she or he can dictate us in the name of law. One has to constantly engage with the idea of the state else we would become a party to the state-sponsored violence in the name of nationalism or patriotism. I do not mind getting killed or arrested by the state for being anti-national. But I will seriously feel sad if I knowingly or unknowingly support any form of violence by the state. Besides, the state is only an arrangement to manage our territories and people. It need not be given too much love and adoration. People have left their states and become citizens in other states. How do we explain that? Are they disloyal? Are they anti-national? No. We are modern citizens of this globalized world. We should be able to go anywhere and find our peace without affecting local people and the environment. My problem arises when I criticize people who are my friends. In my latest film, I criticize the position and strategy of trade unions in Tiruppur (a district in Tamil Nadu). Many of my Left-leaning friends and groups are not convinced by that criticism. I lost a few friends because of the film. However, as a filmmaker, I should make films from my point of view. My films have to reflect my sensibility.

Advancements in technology have completely revolutionized documentary practices in India. As an independent documentary filmmaker, elaborate the changes that have happened in documentary filmmaking practices in terms of process, audience, reception, and technology.

In Tamil Nadu, things have changed a lot. We have many more filmmakers than the past. People here make all kinds of documentaries. We also have many film screenings and film festivals. Political documentaries are being well appreciated in Tamil Nadu. People's movements have started making their own documentaries instead of waiting for some television or urban filmmaker to intervene. Documentary films are considered as people's medium now. The advent of cheaper and accessible digital formats has revolutionized the medium itself. It has removed the aura of filmmaking. For example, a film titled *Kakkoos* on manual scavenging by Divya Bharathi had drawn everyone's attention. DSLR technology, digital projectors, digital formats, and audio equipment have enabled filmmaking, film screening and dissemination much easier and accessible. People are watching independent documentary films in India more than ever before. Although the number is minimum compared to the viewership of commercial films, people are still watching and appreciating documentary films. It is really a change.

Hey Mr. Gandhi, Leave the Indians Alone! *is about three villages in Madurai where 1500 acres of fertile land is segregated for founding a Special Economic Zone (SEZ) project. Although Gandhi is revered, Gandhism[3] is at a critical turning point in India. His critiques of development and vision for the village economy are often neglected by those who claim to be his followers. Put boldly, the celebration of Gandhi and neglect of his teachings is a contemporary Indian paradox. How do you characterize such selective reification and the paradoxical claim on the legacy of Gandhi?*

We have pragmatically used Gandhi and his teachings. Gandhi wanted us to protect the village economy. But we have destroyed the village economy. We expose our rural life to modern industry which is more organized, brutal, sophisticated, and clever. *Hey Mr. Gandhi, Leave the Indians Alone!* talks about villages which are going to be exposed to a SEZ project. In the name of the development, we are ready to sacrifice our villages to modernity. Both the left and the right parties here want to replace the village economy with industries. That's why I asked Gandhi to leave us alone, as we have moved on. We are all on our masochist trip. Gandhi's presence will prick our conscience. It is like asking my grandfather to look away as I am going to sacrifice my grandchild for a greater cause. It is definitively a paradoxical situation we are in now.

Dollar City *presents industrial firms in Tiruppur*[4] *and illustrates the idea of manufacturing consent among the workers. In many ways, the film is reminiscent of Charlie Chaplin's* **Modern Times**. *Although it is contextualized in a South Indian city, it is in many ways reflective of every other place in India. Since the idea of development and growth are so normalized in India, those who speak against it are perceived as anti-state, development and progress. Why do you think a film like* **Dollar City** *is more relevant in a period when everybody is talking about growth, progress, and development?*

I think it is very relevant. The attempt was to expose how false this dream of development is. In this context, the idea of manufacturing consent is very relevant. They are being alienated from themselves. Their aspirations and desires are set by somebody else. The film is about a town called Tiruppur, which consists of thousands of small, medium, and big garment-manufacturing units. Entrepreneurs are the kings. They decide everything. Their aspirations are preferred over workers and environment. You can *feel* the consensus. This is constructed by the powerful. The poor people and the workers are the real sufferers. Even the established trade unions are silent spectators. Government agencies behave like facilitators. They just love that industry. They are ready to sacrifice their rights for "growth." It is so paradoxical. The fact that there is consensus doesn't make a situation or a thing right. As a filmmaker, I try to expose the paradoxes behind this consensus.

Still 16 A still from the film *Dollar City.* Image Courtesy: Amudhan R. P.

You are behind Madurai International Documentary and Short Film Festival. The festival has been creating an alternative space for the independent filmmakers. Why do you think such independent festivals and screening platforms are relevant?

I make my films for those who are not "converted." They are my ideal "target" audience. By "not converted" I mean those who are ready for a dialogue. Those who have patience to listen to me. I want to show my films to that person or group of people who are ready for a dialogue or an argument or even a fight. With that intention we have started a festival in Madurai called the Madurai International Documentary and Short Film Festival. It has completed twenty-two editions so far. It has been envisioned as a noncompetitive film festival since its inception. Since the primary intention of ours is to create a space for dialogue and discussion through films, we never felt the requirement for a competition. Winning a prize or an award should not affect the quality of the discussion. The festival should focus on quality films, sensible viewing, and participatory audience. The idea behind such a festival is to initiate discussion around the exhibited films and create a community to plan some positive action such as learning, traveling, reading, screening films, making films, and joining some social or political or cultural group for direct action. When it started in 1998, there weren't many film festivals for documentary films. It is an independently organized festival. We don't take corporate or state funding. It is an alternative platform for many filmmakers whose films are otherwise rarely seen or exhibited. Many people come here and watch films. As a filmmaker, I make use of such alternative screening spaces to exhibit my films as well.

Notes

1 Kodaikanal is a hill town in Tamil Nadu, a South Indian state.
2 Sirima–Shastri Pact is an agreement signed between prime ministers of India and Sri Lanka (Lal Bahadur Shastri and Sirimavo Bandaranaike) in 1964. This pact granted Sri Lankan citizenships to many people of Indian origin in Sri Lanka.
3 "Gandhism" is a term used to refer to the teachings, practices, and philosophy of Mahatma Gandhi.
4 Tiruppur is a city in Tamil Nadu, a South Indian state.

Divya Bharathi

Figure 17 Image Courtesy: Divya Bharathi.

Divya Bharathi is a documentary filmmaker from Tamil Nadu, a South Indian state. Known for thought-provoking films, her documentaries are intense social critiques which probe issues such as manual scavenging, caste-based discrimination, and government failures. Influenced by the Argentine film director Fernando Solanas,[1] her films are political statements that awaken social conscience. Financed through crowdfunding and often released on YouTube, her documentaries at once trouble and provoke the audience. Her first controversial documentary, *Kakkoos* (trans. *Latrine*), using nauseating visuals, probes into the life of manual scavengers and deliberates on how caste determines the social predicament of these workers. No different was her second film titled *Orutharum Varela* (trans. *Nobody Came*), which ruthlessly chronicled the failure of government resulting in the death of hundreds of fishermen in Tamil Nadu and Kerala during Cyclone Ockhi.

Selected Filmography

Orutharum Varela (trans. Nobody Came) (2018)
Kakkoos (trans. Latrine) (2017)

How did you come to documentary filmmaking? As a "not much sought after" medium, what compelled you to become a documentary filmmaker? Was this a conscious choice?

I come from Aruppukottai, a village in the southern part of India. Documentary films are not so popular here. But as a part of the cultural movement, many documentary films were screened in my village. So, I was lucky to watch documentary films from a very young age. On every first Sunday, debates and discussions were organized in my village. I used to be part of them. But my father was unhappy with my revolting self. Maybe because I am a girl. I used to argue with him. I was not ready to obey him completely. He was the first person in my life to seriously disagree with me. He wanted me to behave as if I am an ordinary girl. When the fight became intense, he stopped financially supporting me so that I could not go to film screenings. But I disobeyed his orders and went to the movie hall which was a little far away from the village. I was a disobedient child. You can also sense disobedience in my films too.

After my schooling, I pursued visual communication. My intention was primarily to produce a film with a difference. Growing up in Tamil Nadu, it's quite natural that you have a desire to make films. Films are so influential in Tamil Nadu. But my desire was something else. To produce films for people. I don't know how that went into my mind. But my only desire was to produce a film that speaks for people. People on the margins were my prime focus. My father was a cotton mill laborer. I was born and brought up in indignant circumstances. In certain ways, the exuberance of commercial cinema won't suit me. Thus, documentaries were a natural choice. I seriously wanted a medium that speaks for myself. Documentary gives me a space to vindicate my anguishes after seeing and experiencing injustices.

Kakkoos is an unique documentary in terms of its theme, production, exhibition, and the controversy connected to it. What motivated you to make Kakkoos?

Although I joined the Visual Communication course, I was thrown out of college. However, my passion for filmmaking led me to learn editing independently. My economically poor condition restricted me from continuing Visual Communication course and I ended up in a law college which charged a very nominal school fee. Moreover, I thought knowledge of law would greatly help my activism. The main issues addressed by the law students in those five years varied from Dalit issues through assaults on women to genocide in Sri Lanka.[2]

My life-changing event occurred in October 2015. Two sanitary laborers died after they fell into a septic tank while working. I never considered the woes of sanitary workers as my own before that. To be honest, I hadn't given the slightest thought before this incident, if they hadn't approached me to draft a complaint. In reality, I never considered it to be an issue concerning me. And I was clueless about the laws and amendments in their favor. It took me some time and a few wise words from my seniors to realize that there are indeed strong laws that restrict manual scavenging. I helped them file an FIR (First Information Report; a document prepared by police), and soon we embarked on a journey to get them justice.

One of the victims was named Muniandi. His wife Mahalakshmi couldn't accept that her husband had died. She kept talking to the body at the morgue as if he was still alive. I couldn't just take it. Her two kids were running around her and the media was photographing her. I kept looking at her. I thought about the meaning and purpose of life. While taking the body to the yard, it had a stench. It had been in the morgue for three days. All of us moved except Mahalakshmi. She was seeing her husband after three days and for the last time. She pushed everyone aside, hugged the body of Muniandi, and cried inconsolably. I realized that all the human rights issues that I have been addressing till then were of no help to this woman. I thought if I couldn't address her pain, what is the point in being an activist. That desire finally led me to the making of *Kakkoos*.

Still 17 A still from the film *Kakkoos*. Image Courtesy: Divya Bharathi.

Mainstream discourses, in a limited way, discuss the struggles of manual scavengers. Even the government formulates laws and regulations against manual scavenging. But it still continues. Is it because of caste determinism?

Although I was into political activism, manual scavenging never drew my attention. These sanitary workers and manual scavengers are in front of us. Whether it is morning or evening or night, they are on the streets. But we don't see them. We refuse to see them. It is a conscious refusal. That's why I say it is casteist. We need someone to clean our shit. Since we are all casteist, we think that manual scavengers are destined to do it. We are the benefactors. Such a system benefits the government as well. So they ignore such human rights violations. Although every one appears progressive, they directly or indirectly make sure that manual scavengers and sanitary workers are doing their duty. Ultimately, it is a system that favors us. Manual scavengers are the sufferers. Look how intense and inhuman the caste system is! A dead body is given respect only if one belongs to a dominant caste. Nobody gets arrested here for caste violence. Because it is not an issue neither for the authorities nor for the legal system. In Tamil Nadu every month someone dies because they are caught up in a manhole or a septic tank. It is treated only as unfortunate accidents. Nobody is ready to look into the safety conditions of the sanitary workers. We are all responsible for these murders.

You use songs in your documentary films. Documentary films usually don't use songs in their filmic text. Could you elaborate your creative choice?

Songs are so central to my films. Songs are usually used for entertainment. But, I thought, let me use it for a political purpose. The whole predicament of people, their anguishes and revolting voices are captured in the song. I don't think songs are inimical to the form of documentary. So I was very conscious about lyrics, music, and voice. *Kakkoos* ends with a song. What you see in the song is their (i.e., manual scavengers') statement, their resilience, and their demand for justice.

Given the controversial nature of your films, how did you generate funds for your films? When you analyze the economics of independent documentary filmmakers in India, many follow crowdfunding to get finances and resources to support their vision. Did you use a crowdfunding model to finance the documentary?

When I set out on this journey, it was just me. Very soon, I realized that I couldn't do it alone. A few of my friends joined the project. I raised funds for the film by myself. Although I had confidence in my project, nobody was ready to produce it. I pawned my gold ornaments and raised some money. But that was not enough. I used to update the daily progress on social media then. Seeing my situation, some of my Facebook friends donated a small amount. By the time the movie was complete, it cost me approximately Rs. 3.5 lakhs (approximately US$5000). Vijay Sethupathi, a popular actor from Tamil cinema, saw the trailer and contacted me and offered me Rs. 35,000 (approximately US$460). Since many have contributed their money for this film, I did not wish to release it under a single name. This is how I could complete my film.

Given your non-Dalit identity, how do you think you represent issues related to caste and the situation of sewage workers? Aren't you appropriating their voice? Put differently, how do you see your identity vis-à-vis the themes that you address in your films?

I am always conscious of this issue. I am not a Dalit. That doesn't mean that I cannot make a film on caste-related issues. I decided that sanitary workers should speak for themselves. In fact, they speak in the film. Their voices are heard. Their protesting voices, anguishes, and revolts are heard in the film. I come from a leftist background. I am also aware that the Left in India failed to address caste issues. It is not just workers' problems or class issues alone. Finally, if you can point out one instance where I am doing injustice to the lives of manual scavengers, I will apologize and withdraw my film.

What is your take on the relevance and future of documentary films?

Nowadays, many youngsters are into moviemaking. However, nobody encourages or guides them into documentary filmmaking. Documentaries tell the histories of nations. They demand hard work and research. It can create huge social change. Although everything appears very normal, there are many fissures in society. Whenever and wherever there is injustice, I believe there is a space for documentary films. I believe there will be filmmakers who can seriously address inequalities and injustices that usually don't appear in the mainstream. Many documentary films in India are existential and are a product of a particular situation. Since documentary films are comparatively less costly than popular films, it is people's medium. So, I believe there will be some good films in future too.

You either use your characters as talking heads or try to contextualize their experience in a larger framework. Technically speaking, your way of telling resembles cinéma vérité. Do you have any favorite way of filming/telling stories? And how did you raise funds for your films?

I accidently came to filmmaking. My film *Kakkoos* was a result of an emotional experience. Although I wanted to make documentaries, I was not aware of it as a medium. Since I know a little more of editing, I thought of producing films. Documentaries have been often tagged as boring. I wanted to pause such a stereotype. Hence, I took special care while editing *Kakkoos*. My main objective was to engage the audience for two hours. My husband and I sold gold and raised money. It was very minimal. But we wanted to make the film. So, we tried to meet as many people as possible. It's only when we had some money, we could request our cameraman to join us. We traveled to more than twenty-five towns. We had no preconceived notions. No script. Nothing. We spoke to people and the film is made out of their dialogues and what we saw there. My initial plan was just to focus on ten families who have lost their dear ones in manual scavenging. Later, I thought I should not just address the incidents alone but should show the injustices and exploitation involved in the act including the caste system. It was very tough to shoot in the public toilets. I thought if we cannot even stand in these toilets or see these visuals, imagine how it must be working in them! When you are into filmmaking and see such a situation, you cannot sit there and cry. It is not a perfect cinema. But I think it has something that makes people watch it.

You are threatened, ghearoed, and abused for exposing unrelenting caste discrimination and violence. In particular, how challenging was the making and screening of Kakkoos?

Yes. There were several threats. Even now it is no different. While I was shooting *Kakkoos*, sanitary inspectors and supervisors stopped me. Once they broke my camera. As the film is about government's apathy and the politics of manual scavenging, authorities denied screenings and, at times, interrupted screenings at many places. Government and the affluent don't want to stop manual scavenging. They are the benefactors. They need someone to clean their shit. In fact, it is the entire system that sponsors and favors such killings. So it's no wonder that I am arrested in the name of the film and labeled as a Naxalite[3] and anti-national.[4]

Notes

1 Fernando Solanas was an Argentinian filmmaker who is known for his political films like *The Hour of the Furnaces* (1968) and *Tangos: The Exile of Gardel* (1985).
2 Genocide in Sri Lanka refers to the brutal killings of Tamil population in Sri Lanka during the Sri Lankan Civil War.
3 Naxalite is one who believes in the ideology of Maoist communism and is usually a member of revolutionary leftist political groups.
4 "Anti-national" is a controversial term used in India to refer to those who oppose majoritarian nationalism/extremist nationalist policies.

4

"Remain True to the Earth"

Mapping the Post-Natural India

The early nature-documentary films such as *Nature's Nectar* (1961), *Malnad—A Gift of Nature* (1963), and *Nature's Symphony* (1977), among others, produced by the Films Division of India were didactic, apolitical, and merely fostered an awareness about agro-biodiversity of India. On the other hand, independent nature-documentary films produced particularly after the 1990s sternly dealt with nature in that they took into account the profound impact of human activity on nature, geological actors and the state's contentious relationship with land and capitalism. These documentaries can be broadly classified into three categories: first, the films that critique the Nehruvian idea of big dams[1] as "the temples of modern India"; second, the anti-globalization documentary films that depict the devastating impact of global/transnational corporations on the local environment; third, films that celebrate "unspoiled" nature. If the first two categories produced argumentative films that laid bare the fissures in development paradigm,[2] and, by extension, the idea of progress itself, the last category celebrated uncorrupted and "naturalness" of nature. Departing from the intentions, aesthetics, and politics of the educational/wildlife films produced by the Films Division of India, Sanjay Kak, Shriprakash, Meghnath, Biju Toppo, K. P. Sasi, among others, through deploying the Anthropocene as an analytic lens, examine the complex interactions of ecologies and societies. With an activist zeal, many of these filmmakers critique the prevailing notions of development programs of the state which jeopardize not only nature but also its original inhabitants such as tribals/Adivasis. In particular, their films delineate the plight of tribals (*The Land of the Diggers*), ruthless mining and nuclear radiation (*Buddha Weeps in Jadugoda*), human rights of the indigenous people/displacement (*Development Flows from the Barrel of the Gun*), and the nexus between the state and corporates (*Iron Is Hot*). Their documentaries boldly reflect on the untenable developmental policies of the state and its free hand in helping the corporates to exploit nature. Again, unlike the purists, who treated nature as an exclusive space, these filmmakers imagined a rightful and ethical place for humans within nature. In so doing, these filmmakers while visually expressing sustainable development as a way forward also advocate reasonable change in the way we treat nature.

Notes

1 Nehru, while laying the foundation stone for India's first major river valley project, the Hirakud Dam in Orissa in 1948, asked the people to face the grim prospect of displacement thus: "If you are to suffer, you should suffer in the interest of the country." (See Roy, Arundhati (1999), "The Greater Common Good," *Frontline*, 16 (11), 22 May. Available online: https://frontline.thehindu.com/other/article302573 33.ece (accessed on September 07, 2019)).
2 Anand Patwardhan's *The Narmada Diary* (1995) is a typical example.

Sanjay Kak

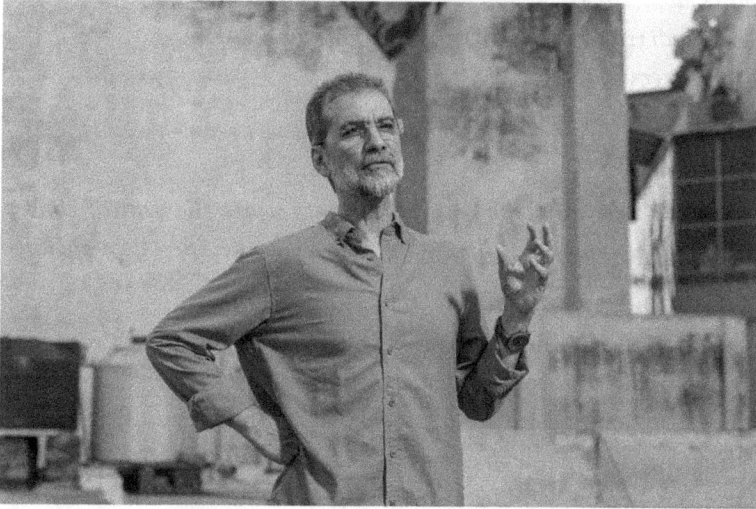

Figure 18 Image Credit: Shovan Gandhi.

Best known for his films *Red Ant Dream, Jashn-e-Azadi* (trans. *How We Celebrate Freedom*), *Words on Water*, and *In the Forest Hangs a Bridge*, Sanjay Kak is a self-taught filmmaker who started his career with a brief stint in television. As a political and environmental filmmaker, his documentaries address wide-ranging issues such as ecology, resistance politics, the Maoist insurgency,[1] and the struggle in Kashmir. His films are an attempt to historicize and situate the sites of dissent as a means to contest the hegemonic narratives of nation, people, and nature. Although several attempts were made to censor his films by ultra-right groups, his films continue to probe the ongoing ecological, political, and cultural issues impinging India. Central to his oeuvre is depiction of nature and the multiple realities of tribal cultures in India. *In the Forest Hangs a Bridge* and *Words on Water*, while foregrounding the ecological politics, also lay bare the complexity of nature/culture interface, thus expanding the meaning of the term "political" beyond the limited contours of the term. He is also an occasional writer and has edited two volumes on Kashmir: *Until My Freedom Has Come: The New Intifada in Kashmir* (2011) and *Witness Kashmir 1986-2016: Nine Photographers* (2017).

Selected Filmography

Red Ant Dream (2013)
Jashn-e-Azaadi (trans. *How We Celebrate Freedom*) (2007)
Words on Water (2002)
In the Forest Hangs a Bridge (1999)

***Ecology, wilderness, and the fragility of nature are the central concerns in
some of your documentary films. What takes you to nature as a documentary
filmmaker?***

Even the most extreme crisis that we are going through in our lifetime is probably
incomparable with the ecological catastrophe that the world is facing today. The
scale of destruction that we are up against is enormous, and that makes every
other struggle of ours futile in comparison with what nature is undergoing.

Nature has been a significant and long-standing concern in my films. In
1986, I had done a series of films on the Ganga River, a sort of travelogue
from its origins in the mountains, all the way to where it empties into the
sea at Ganga Sagar.[2] Our preoccupation was not with the sacred nature of
the river but more an attempt to look at the river as a means to understand
the civilization it has supported. Of course, even then we could see what was
happening to it, dammed up in the mountains, or down in the plains, in places
like Kanpur, where it was already drying up. And what we were seeing of the
river even then could not be seen after five years. So an engagement with
the environment was always there. When I went to do a film in Arunachal
Pradesh,[3] in what became *In the Forest Hangs a Bridge*, maybe my own politics
had evolved; I too had changed.

Of course, my first reaction was one of shock: for we were facing a thriving
tribal culture, a living one, not a tribal culture defeated or destroyed as you
might encounter in other parts of India. At the same time, you could also see
how fragile it was.

I remember when we finally got to the editing room after the shoot, Reena
Mohan, my editor, asked me what the plan was, what the film should be. I recall
telling her that in the making of a 1,000-foot bridge of cane and bamboo we had
witnessed something extraordinary, and I wanted us to be able to convey a sense
of that. Even if it turns out to be something of an idealization, I'd be fine with
that. I had a feeling that we must communicate what it is that we are losing.

Eventually when the film was done and we started screening the film, several people did find it "too romantic." But I was up for that. It was important for me to convey the full splendor of what traditional society had to offer us. And only in a relatively protected place like Arunachal Pradesh could you see that, and talk about it. It is probably easier to dismiss the viability of Adivasi life in Bastar[4]—or in Kerala—because what you encounter is a culture in retreat, in defeat. We did some screenings in Arunachal Pradesh, even in the village where we had shot it, and, even then, people there knew that this was a tradition that was passing, that it was already lost. Meghnath, who is a fellow documentary filmmaker, and a popular teacher in Ranchi, in Jharkhand, once told me that he regularly screens this film to his students, many of whom are Adivasi. For him it was a way of showing what there is to value and preserve in Adivasi culture.

So yes, nature is very much there in all my films, it's just a question of how much it is front-ended and how much of it is background. You could see this in the film I made in Kashmir, *Jashn-e-Azadi*, or in *Red Ant Dream*, which are not primarily "about nature."

What can we talk about where nature and ecology don't come in? Whatever happens in Kashmir is also about rivers, about water, about hydropower, is it not? The preoccupation with nature may be subtle or explicit. That depends on where the focus of the lens rests.

How do you interpret the idea of looking back at your own films? Have you ever felt the urgency of redirecting your own politics when you watch it after a few decades? Revisit your film **In the Forest Hangs a Bridge** *after twenty years of its making?*

The good thing is that when I see that film, I rarely feel embarrassed. I can see that there is something in it even now, which is a relief. I think this act of looking back is an important one. When I look at my older films, and not just *In the Forest Hangs a Bridge*, I still find that something rings true, that the arguments I made in the film still remain valid for me, that I will stand by If I look at the two films I made about Indian migrants, in England, and in South Africa, what we said in those films about the cultural and political space for immigrants in 1992 is still valid in some ways. Two decades on we might have found more sophisticated ways of articulating things, but even those earlier ways of telling still remain valid.

I think this is the power of the documentary form in some ways, this is what makes the medium so valid in our times. This is why I believe that documentary film work is important work. Because it is our privilege as documentary filmmakers to distil our time. Why is that images that can be on television every day, or every hour, are not thought of as threatening, but when Anand Patwardhan puts them into a film it is threatening to the state? When you get it right, those are the truths which are not going to disappear overnight, which have a long shelf life. I think whether a film is well made or badly, the least we require of a documentary is that it contains truths that last! And you can sense every time you watch a good documentary.

I was speaking to Meghnathji about Anand Patwardhan's latest film, *Reason.* "What did you think about the film?" I asked him. His reply was quite amazing for me. He said I am very glad that I lived through an era when documentary films have been there to make a record of our times. From Anand's *Prisoners of Consciousness* to his *Reason,* and with literally hundreds of films and dozens of filmmakers, there is a short record of what we have lived and experienced. Somehow Meghnathji's response both reassured me and made me very happy. Whatever we think of the documentary film in India, with all its limitations, we cannot dismiss the fact that a kind of history has been recorded by these films. In the same way, what you are doing by putting these interviews together is also important, since this kind of reflected history is also very important. Because everyone may not be able to see all those films. But such conversations would certainly bring out different dimensions of the history of our times.

Documentary filmmakers around the world since the 1960s were conscious of environmental catastrophe. And many of the environmental movements in India in the 1980s were "purist" in nature. But the approach of the independent documentary filmmakers was different from that of the purists'. Although there was an element of romanticization of nature in your films, it was done only to account for the life of indigenous population. To what extent is "pure nature" present in your films?

In India, at least in the beginning, people who spoke for the environment were, perhaps, the purists—the good people who were raising the alarm about "save the Tiger," "save the Forest." But the complexity of human-nature interactions, the place for understanding power, and politics, was not always apparent in that approach. It is true that many of us as filmmakers were instinctively reacting to that, saying, "Look! It's important to save nature, but India is a poor country and there should be some place for people as well." I can understand that it was important for the purists to be narrow, and rigid, but on the other hand it was equally important for us to suggest that there was another side of the story. In that sense, I don't think I could ever make a proper "wildlife" film! I must also say here that when I went to Arunachal Pradesh, I certainly saw this thriving tribal culture but it is also true that I was shocked to see that there was absolutely no wildlife around the villages in the Siang Valley. And this is equally true of Bastar. Because people have literally hunted and eaten everything that might be construed as wildlife! Earlier when people only had bows and arrows, there was a sort of auto-balance. But once the air guns and rifles arrived, whether it was birds or squirrels, they were all decimated.

I'm very careful in my films to not say that whatever tribal culture deems is right, to promote a blind nativism. In Bastar, for example, when the Maoists first went into those areas in the 1980s, there was a tradition among the Adivasis of the area that at a certain point of time in the year everybody would go hunting. All the men that are. They would pick up their bows and arrows and disappear for almost a month. No other work would happen. And the Maoists said this is crazy, this is unsustainable, and cannot go on. And although many of the other reformist agendas of the Maoist ran aground in Bastar, here their intervention worked. And as a result, the Adivasis of Bastar eventually withdrew from that practice.

Of course, while it is true that some traditional Adivasis practices are unsustainable, they simply cannot be compared to what we are doing to nature now. Can we compare their act to what the mining project is doing to nature? That is where I pull back from the position of the purists. The responsibility must be put at the door of the form of capitalist development that we seem committed to. How much control do ordinary people have in this? There is a small group of elites who collude across the world to reap up all the benefits, and the price is paid by the people. So, I do think that too much space is taken up by the damage caused by ordinary people. What is the point of trying to control pollution caused by these people without any regard for the large-scale polluting agencies which are several thousand times larger than what the ordinary people are doing? I am not arguing that people are not callous. But sometimes drawing attention to the callousness of the people is exaggerated; in order to cover up something even worse than that.

Narmada Bachao Andolan (NBA) is one of the important green movements in India that worked against building dams on Narmada River. It was one such rare environmental movement where native tribes, farmers, environmentalists and human rights activists all came together against the development that puts the life of the indigenous population at risk. Many documentary films including your **Words on Water** *emerged out of the movement. How do you revisit those films especially in the context of Gujarat government's recent decision to raise the water level at the Sardar Sarovar Dam?*

I think that the real achievement of the NBA is not just that they succeeded as a movement against dams but it brought together for the first time a gathering body of understanding. It made possible a critique of modernity from a third-world perspective. It is not a coincidence that the World Bank eventually commissioned their first ever study on large dams based on the development and displacement of the Narmada Valley. They conceded that dams should not be developed. It is not a coincidence that the NBA became known internationally. I think it is this curious combination of the wisdom of the Adivasi people, the understanding of the farmers of the Nimad region,[5] the engineers from the IITs who joined the movement and supported it from within, even those from the media who wrote about it, all of this made this movement very relevant. Today people talk about open architecture and open platforms. I cannot think of a more remarkable example of that than the NBA. It managed to attract a lot of thoughtful people and really welcomed them in an open sort of way. What initially emerged as a critique of rehabilitation, the impossibility of rehabilitation, segued to issues related to large dams. Say No to Dams. The questions raised there were profound.

I went to the Narmada Valley when I was forty, and yet my politics was profoundly shaped by that experience. And it was not just a single person who affected me, but the whole flux of it that had an important influence on me, and made it highly rewarding personally. I think that even today in any part of India if you meet anybody interested in the social sector, chances are that they have gone to the Narmada Valley. Incidentally there are six or seven films about the Narmada movement. I was once at an environmental festival in Turin, in Italy, and they had a whole section of films there on the Narmada. If you watch all the films together, you get this strong sense of the changing character of the movement. *Words on Water* was almost the last in the list they screened, and there was certainly a sense of despair in that film. Recently someone was working on a book and asked me for a copy of the film to understand the place of the NBA in contemporary social movements. I got a message from her later that she found the film very moving. It's a reassuring feeling that when someone sees the film even a decade after it was done and still finds it relevant. If it can move people even now, I would believe that there is something in it.

In **Words on Water** *(2002) you speak about the possibility of a nonviolent Gandhian protest. But when you reach* **Red Ant Dream** *(2013), it's more radical. Do you have faith in radical revolutions?*

In the closing scenes of *Words on Water*, which I finished in 2002, there is a note of pessimism, in the context of the so-called "War on Terror." Following the devastating Supreme Court[6] order of 2000, and in the course of the two years which it took me to finish the film, the nonviolent Gandhian methods seemed to have been completely ground down. It was quite clear what the message of the Court to such movements was: Forget it, they seemed to say. So yes, I can now certainly see the limits of that earlier approach in our present times. But *Red Ant Dream* came about not because the Maoists offered a certain, glorious alternative, but because they represented a strand of what we call "revolutionary possibility," and this includes a dignified right to self-defense. That's my same attitude to the Kashmir insurgency[7] too. After all you have to grant people the right to self-determination. Even your adversaries should have that right. And if they take up arms to defend their rights, how could I judge them to be wrong?

Still 18 A still from the film *Red Ant Dream*. Image Courtesy: Sanjay Kak.

Your recent documentaries are pretty long. Could you state the significance of length in your documentaries? Is it a conscious choice of form?

Yes, the last three films have been long, feature length. And you're absolutely right in that the length is not there because we didn't know how to trim it down, or because there are masses of "information" to get across, or because there is a story, a narrative, that needs to be worked out. It has to do with the poetics of the film: What is the state of mind in which you want the viewer to receive the image, sound, and text; and how much time does it take to unfold that space in which a complex, ambiguous politics can be laid out? A politics which does not force a conclusion upon you but invites you to engage with it, slowly, sometimes in circular patterns, but in ways that will stay in your mind, hopefully.

Your film Jashn-e-Azadi *was a poetic take on the ongoing conflicts in Kashmir. Extending Theodore Adorno's famous statement, "there can be no poetry after Auschwitz," do you think poetic engagement with the Valley is lost now in the context of the recent developments in Kashmir including the abrogation of the Article 370 of the Indian Constitution?*

I'd argue this from the other end: it's precisely in such situations that poetry can—and must—emerge. Remember that in happy times we only thought of Kashmir as the backdrop of our adolescent fantasies, like Shammi Kapoor in *Kashmir Ki Kali*[8] (1964), yelling "Yahoo" on the meadows. Now, Kashmir has become the site of our present fears, and even our nightmares. Who says that is not ripe territory for poetic reflection? It's not just the narcissus that stimulates; so do the ashes.

Notes

1 Maoist insurgency refers to the ongoing conflicts between Indian government and various Maoist armed groups like the Naxalites in India.
2 Ganga Sagar is the confluence of river Ganges and Bay of Bengal.
3 Arunachal Pradesh is a Northeastern Indian state that shares international borders with countries like China.
4 Bastar is a district in Chhattisgarh, a Central Indian state.
5 Nimad region is the region around Narmada in Madhya Pradesh, a Central Indian state.
6 Supreme Court is the apex court of India.
7 Kashmir insurgency refers to a series of conflicts since the 1990s between Kashmiri separatists for an independent Kashmir and the Government of India.
8 *Kashmir Ki Kali* (1964) is an Indian romance film directed by Shakti Samanta.

Meghnath

Figure 19 Image Courtesy: Kolkata People's Film Festival.

Meghnath is an activist and documentary filmmaker from Jharkhand (a state in Eastern India). Although he began his career as a health worker in West Bengal, he later participated in various sociopolitical movements in Palamu district of Bihar (now part of Jharkhand state) and codirected films with Biju Toppo, the first Adivasi documentary filmmaker from Jharkhand. Inspired by the films of Fernando Solanas and Anand Patwardhan, he became a documentary filmmaker to represent the voice of those sections of people, especially indigenous population who remain unheard. His films focus on various issues confronting the natives of Jharkhand, particularly the destructive effects of development on nature and indigenous population. For instance, if his first film *Development Flows from the Barrel of the Gun* exposed five cases of developmental violence across India, his award-winning film, *Iron Is Hot*, is a bold exposition of the lopsided industrialization at the cost of human lives and environment. His only biographic documentary, *Naachi Se Baanchi*, traces the life story of Dr. Ram Dayal Munda,[1] a leading intellectual voice behind Jharkhand movement. Put together, his films are testimonies of the violence and exploitation that the Adivasis and tribal population suffer in India. He is also one of the founders of *Akhra*, an agency working in the field of culture and communication in Jharkhand.

Selected filmography[2]

Naachi Se Baanchi (trans. Dance to Survive) (2017), codirected with Biju Toppo
Accumulated Injustice (2015), codirected with Biju Toppo
Loha Garam Hai (trans. Iron Is Hot) (2010), codirected with Biju Toppo
100 Din Milega Kaam (trans. 100 Days of Work for You) (2009), codirected with
    Biju Toppo
Vikas Bandook Ki Nal Se (trans. Development Flows from the Barrel of the Gun)
    (2003)

There is a close association between activism and independent documentary filmmaking in India. In many instances, we rarely see any difference. You have been a staunch activist before you came to documentary filmmaking? How do you see the correlation between activism and documentary filmmaking in India?

Although there is a confluence of activism and filmmaking, I think documentary films are not completely about activism alone. In a larger sense of the term, "art" is also an activism, however minimal it is. There are artistic and activist sides in my films. I was part of a vibrant sociopolitical movement of West Bengal of the 1960s and 1970s. I started my career as a social worker. Although I was working in Bengal till 1979, I came to Palamu (a district in northwestern Jharkhand) and worked as a social and political activist till the end of 1980s. As I was working there, I felt that people's issues were not adequately represented in the mainstream media. Although there were a few exceptions, the majority of popular media has a colonial mentality. No different was Hindi media which also harbored such colonial bias. The voices of the marginalized especially Dalits and Adivasis were not part of their discourse. When I and my social work friends were alarmed by such glaring absences, we thought of taking their issues to the world outside. My earlier experience in still photography helped me to address the sociopolitical and subaltern themes. In my opinion, film as a medium is an extension of my social activism. I am convinced that film is my medium to represent and record people's voices. Inspired by the films and writings of Latin American filmmaker Fernando Solanas and the films of Anand Patwardhan, Sanjay Kak, K. P. Sasi, and others, I was convinced by then that documentary films suit me. I also felt that political documentaries have the space and possibility of becoming people's voices. On the contrary, commercial cinema never appealed to me. Although filmmaking and social activism are two different things, political documentary filmmaking has an interventionist aspect to it. My films are political and it makes visible the unseen images and the unheard voices of the poor and the marginalized. In that sense, there is an ostensible activism at work in my films.

With the introduction of new economic policies after the 1990s, India was undergoing a paradigm shift in terms of its economic policies and development. **Development Flows from the Barrel of the Gun** *is a critique of the enforced developmental policies of the state. The film begins with a montage of the car expo and fashion shows. Those images of the new India are contrasted with five other cases of displacement of the local/tribal population across India. How does mindless development affect nature and tribal population?*

Although imposed development was in vogue since the Nehruvian regime (for instance, aggressive building of dams), development policies after the 1990s were too critical in that the nexus between the state and the corporates became visible and explicit. Adivasis and the tribal population were the worst sufferers of this development. Their lands are looted, women are raped and their relationship with nature is interrupted. Our documentary deals with five cases of exploitation from all over India and is not limited to the geographical remit of Jharkhand alone. They include Utkal Alumina in Kashipur,[3] Orissa; the Koel-Karo Dam[4] in Jharkhand; the World Bank-funded forestry project in the district of Dewas,[5] Madhya Pradesh; the steel plant in Nagarnar,[6] Chhattisgarh; and the new port in Umbergaon,[7] Gujarat. All these are examples of the nexus between the state and the corporate.

Our documentary conveys how a new sense of development that engrossed India after the 1990s was inimical to nature and indigenous population. Most importantly, those developmental projects are implemented in environmentally volatile, fragile areas and on lands that are in "scheduled" areas (areas earmarked by the central government to safeguard the interests of tribes in the area) with large tribal populations. Ironically, the government which is mandated to protect these areas are the very perpetrators of such exploitation. Much of the film is narrated by the victims and the local social activists. In fact, the film is anchored on the testimonies of the victims. Fashion expos and automobiles booms are primarily for the rich and the middle class. Tribal people are excluded from such spaces. It is at the expense of their lives and land that current functionaries of development thrive. The film, in a sense, is a tribute to vanishing lands and indigenous population of India.

Iron Is Hot *shows images of sponge iron plants and big machines and how the industries affect the environment. Toxic waste is dumped on the farm lands and rivers. In fact, there is a song in the film where people sing, "land is our mother and forest is our friend." We also hear the slogans like "we will fight, we will win and we want food, not iron." What is the creative intention of Iron Is Hot? How do we balance development and environment? Are such resistances strong enough these days to challenge industries?*

Iron Is Hot is based on the fastest growing polluting industry called sponge iron. Although it is a profitable industry for the state and the corporate, it affects nature and tribal population. They are the worst sufferers of this industry. The internal regions of the state are plundered by the companies. These industries cause air and water pollution which affect the health of poor Adivasis and ecology. Eighty percent of the sponge iron factories are coal-based and they emit heavy smoke and dust and are also notorious for polluting the environment. Such pollution directly affects the fertility of the soil, environment, animals, cattle, and people. Although there is a pollution control board, it has become a pay and pollute board. Companies bribe the authorities and they do their business. The intention of the film is not just to show the predicament of the people but also to record their resistance. There is administrative connivance here. Those pristine lands are no more there and the tribal populations which depend on it are displaced. This is a form of developmental terrorism. As expected, Adivasis who live in those areas are affected by the pollution. You can see a large number of cancer patients and people affected by other serious illnesses as well. The situation hasn't improved. Government has become too autocratic and there is no scope for resistance these days. They employ terror tactics, and those who oppose the government are either killed or called Naxalites (a member of an armed revolutionary group).

Naachi Se Baanchi is a biopic which traces the life story of a visionary and a symbol of indigenous cultural reawakening, Dr. Ram Dayal Munda. Why did you think it is important to make a film about Dr. Ram Dayal Munda?

It is true that Dr. Ram Dayal Munda is a symbol of indigenous cultural reawakening. He is an Adivasi by birth and was educated in the United States where he also served as a teacher. What distinguishes him from others is that he returned to his native place. He founded and was a part of the Tribal and Regional Language Department of Ranchi University.[8] He later became the

Still 19 A shooting still of the film *Naachi Se Baanchi*. Image Courtesy: Megnath.

vice chancellor of the same university. He is the intellectual force behind the Jharkhand movement. Throughout his life, he lived for indigenous people and culture. Most importantly, in spite of his Western education and exposure to other cultures, Dr. Ram Dayal Munda lived and stood for our culture. In a sense, he is a symbol of Adivasi power. *Naachi Se Baanchi* is our first biography film. He is a source of inspiration for all Adivasi population.

You have been working with Biju Toppo who is the first documentary filmmaker from a tribal background. If we examine the history of documentary films in India, we rarely see such a long association. What keeps you working together for a long time? How do you characterize such association?

I met Biju Toppo in 1992 in Ranchi. I have been working together with him since then. I see him as my brother. He is such an outstanding and the first documentary filmmaker from an Adivasi community. We have been together for the last twenty to twenty-five years. In recent times, there are few other filmmakers from the Adivasi community, and they are making excellent films. The only problem is: we need to make these films reach large sections of audience. We don't have enough film festivals which can screen such films. There should be a federation among filmmakers irrespective of our differences so that documentaries like ours will reach large sections of population. Our association has been productive. Although we are producing films together, it doesn't mean that we produce films all time together. We have our independent productions too. It is very important for me that Biju's vision is available in my film as he is a representative of the Adivasi community which in turn offers a strong political voice in my films. Hopefully, we will make a few more films in future too.

Your films **Accumulated Injustice, Iron Is Hot** *and* **Development Flows from the Barrel of the Gun** *focus on tribal people,* **Adivasis** *and issues like mining, farming, and exploitation. Why do you think it is important to make films on Adivasis, tribals, and the vulnerable? And how far do your films do justice to their cause? Again, you are an outsider in the sense that you belong to a different background.*

Your question is partly right and partly wrong. You are right in the sense that I am an outsider and I come from a different background. I am a Bengali born in Bombay. It is wrong because I am careful with this aspect and dimension of my filmmaking. As such, I have been trying to do the work of recording an event. I have documented resilience and resistance of the indigenous population. I have been with this community for the last forty years. I was with this community even before I started my filmmaking in the 1990s. The problem is only when you do a top-angle point of view of their life. Even Satyajit Ray (one of the greatest filmmakers of all time in India) in *Aranyer Din Ratri* (trans. *Days and Nights in the Forest*)[9] offers a top-angle point of view of them. My approach is an eye-level approach. My films are the result of my camaraderie with the tribals. If you make films with this attitude, I think you can make films for them. Otherwise, there will be resistance. If you can work among them as part of them, I think there is a space for you. Moreover, I am working with Biju Toppo, who belongs to a tribal community.

Akhra *is one of the few independent media collectives in India which distinguishes itself through its involvement in people's movements. Share the context of the origin and growth of the collective in the 1990s. Do you think you could materialize your vision through* **Akhra?** *Do you think a collective like* **Akhra** *is still relevant in a period when we have easy access to other well-established platforms around the world?*

It was formed during the Jharkhand movement in 1992–3.[10] The intention behind *Akhra* was to organize artists, journalists, filmmakers, and friends to creatively participate in the people's movement that was happening then.

Amid many resurgence movements in Jharkhand, we felt that the artists, activists, filmmakers should come together and report the issues to the world. It was necessary at that moment to report news and do media work since the acts of resistance hardly appeared in the mainstream media. We used whatever medium possible including filmmaking, print media, journalism, photography, and so on. We used to go out and participate in people's movements and experience the force of people's resistance. On returning from the fieldwork, we wrote articles for newspapers or prepared photo stories or made films on the movement. We approached our friends and critics to review our work. *Akhra* was formed at a critical juncture in that a collective movement was formed to counter the colonial mentality of the mainstream media and journalists. As such, all our (with Biju Toppo) films are associated with some movements/struggles. Be it *Where Ants Are Fighting Elephants* or *Yet Another Accident*. In fact, many of our films are a consequence of our participation in demonstrations. Being a small group, I doubt whether *Akhra* can be called an organization. But for making films we need to find funding. Initially, our friends (usually social or political activists) helped us in the way of buying us video tapes. Since we cannot raise money as in the past, we, nowadays, admit some commissioned work. While doing a commissioned project we make sure that we don't receive any money from big corporations or individuals who are against people's causes and movement. Looking back, *Akhra* is really a great feeling. Since filmmaking is a collective activity, *Akhra* helped us to come together and make films informed by our philosophy. We were making films on alternative issues that usually don't appear in the mainstream media. I think here lies the relevance!

Notes

1 Dr. Ram Dayal Munda was an Indian scholar and activist from Ranchi who fought for tribal rights.
2 Meghnath codirects with Biju Toppo.
3 Kashipur is a city in the Indian state of Uttarakhand.
4 Koel-Karo Dam is a dam project in the Indian state of Jharkhand.
5 Dewas is a district in Madhya Pradesh, a Central Indian state.
6 Nagarnar is a village in Chhattisgarh, a Central Indian state.
7 Umbergaon is a town in Gujarat, a Northwestern Indian state.

8 Ranchi University is a public university located in the city of Ranchi.
9 *Aranyer Din Ratri* (trans. *Days and Nights in the Forest*) (1970) is a Bengali drama
   film directed by Satyajit Ray.
10 Jharkhand movement refers to a political movement in India for a separate state of
   Jharkhand.

Shriprakash

Figure 20 Image Courtesy: Shriprakash.

A filmmaker from Jharkhand, Shriprakash has been producing documentary films since the 1980s. Produced with an activist zeal and grounded in social reality, his documentaries problematize dominant discourses about nature and tribal population (Adivasi) and address unbalanced power dynamics. Broadly, his films are critical of the new economic policies of the government and show how unbridled commercialization and privatization of natural resources in the name of development takes toll on nature and the Adivasi community. With a vision to reclaim the lost voices of tribal communities in India and to preserve nature from the vagaries of modernity, Shriprakash uses documentary as a means for social change. For instance, *Buddha Weeps in Jadugoda* exposes the devastating impact of uranium mining on the tribes (such as genetic mutation and slow death) living near Jadugoda mining area. To further deepen his engagement with the tribals, he works as the chief coordinator of *Kritika*, an organization which works in the areas of culture and communication in Jharkhand.

Selected Filmography

Eer—Stories in Stone (2011)
Buru Gaara (trans. The Wild Rivulet) (2009)
Buru Sengal (trans. The Fire Within) (2002)
Buddha Weeps in Jadugoda (1999)

Do Not I Have the Right to Live? (1998)
Addo Miyad Ulgulan (trans. Another Revolt) (1995)
Kiski Raksha (trans. In Whose Defence) (1994)

Majority of your films concern the lives of the tribals and the issues related to their livelihood such as mining, farming and radiation. Why do you think it's important to make such films? How do you assimilate an insider's perspective of a community with regards to identity and sociopolitical exploitation? Also, briefly describe the challenges faced by you as a filmmaker.

I am always confronted by this question. Am I eligible to make a film on Adivasis and their issues? I was born in a tribal-dominated Jharkhand. Although I don't belong to the Adivasis community, I have been living very close to them. I have witnessed the crisis they were going through as a community. I think I can connect to them better than people living in the urban spaces. Adivasis are a group of people ignored by the government and its policies. They are a perpetually marginalized section of society. They had access to education only recently. The missionaries came here and educated them. But they had their own intentions. When I started filmmaking, there were no Adivasi filmmakers. Sustenance was more important to them than making films. When I tried to understand them more deeply, I felt that they are the only hope in this world. They live happily with nature. They know how to live with nature with minimum utilization of its resources. That gave me a lot of confidence to work among them. I really felt that these people are important for the world. I decided to work with them. I was threatened by the powerful since I started working among them. I felt it was important to tell what I witnessed here.

Independent documentary filmmaking in India flourished during the 1990s. It was also a period when there were several people's movements that thrived in India. There was hope among the people. But I had to undergo a lot of trouble to make a film because of the lack of experience and professional knowledge about the technical aspects of filmmaking. There were no editing facilities here in Jharkhand, and I had to frequently go to Delhi or Mumbai for editing my films. Finding an adequate budget was another real struggle. If this is what I experienced, imagine the situation of a filmmaker from an indigenous community. But things are changing. The younger generation from the Adivasi community are making their own films that counter the mainstream politics and points of view. My films, on the other hand, have their own relevance as a record of a particular time in history.

Another Revolt *registers the struggle against the Koel-Karo hydel project*[1] *in Jharkhand, which threatened the lives of thousands of tribals living in the area. In a sense, hydel projects in India are an extension of the developmental policies of the government and a very Nehruvian ideal. Why do you take such a critical stand on the development schemes of the government?*

I am critical of the development plans of the government, especially the idea of building dams at the cost of nature and indigenous population. The idea of building dams was done without taking into account the concerns of the ordinary people. *Another Revolt* depicted how people defeated the policy of the government which affected them. The intention was to show how people could emerge victorious against the government and its wrong measures collectively. But the situation is quite different now. Do people have a space to protest against what is happening against them? In that sense, I am not critical of Nehru for everything that he has done. There is a conscious attempt to discredit the contributions of Nehru in our times. I am not aligning with them. But I am critical of his developmental plans and programs. I agree that Nehru was more a romantic and that the affluent class really enjoyed the benefits of development. I am critical of Nehru's idea of building dams without taking into account the concerns of the displaced people. Same thing happened in Jharkhand. We are surrounded by people from other states. They are the ruling class. They exploit our resources. In a sense, they have made use of the naivety of the Indigenous population. But can we compare it to what is happening after globalization in India? My later films discuss such issues. I think what the corporate and multinational companies are doing in Jharkhand is beyond any comparison to what hydel projects have done in the past. Nature and the lives of the people are in danger more now than ever.

Buddha Weeps in Jadugoda *documents the effects of radiation on nature and the* **Adivasi** *population who are residing in the region. No other independent documentary filmmaker in India has consistently worked on nuclear radiation and its impact on the lives of people like you. You have used many testimonies of the affected in the film. How did you come to this film?*

I have made five films on radiation till now. They probed the impact of uranium mining on health and environment. We can see that, in the last decade of the twentieth century, there was a growing anger against government projects especially against uranium mining in India. It all started in 1996 when around thirty Santhal houses were demolished by the Uranium Corporations of India in Jadugoda (in Jharkhand) for the construction of the fourth-stage tailings dam. When I went there, I had no idea what to do. Except the fact that I have studied basic sciences, my knowledge about mining and radiation were limited. Everybody trusted the company. People believed that the company is good for them and for the nation. Nobody was ready to question the intention of the company. Even the impact of radiation was not so evident. People were basically divided on this. I spent three years there. At that time, I could watch a few films with similar concern. One was a film called *Half Life: A Parable for the Nuclear Age* by Dennis O'Rourke. These films have influenced me to think about the impact of radiation on people. In my research, I could find people who are affected by some kind of illness. It took almost three years to have enough material to convince people about the effects of radiation. I also realized that if I go with scientific data alone, I won't be able to counter the corporations and convince people. They are scientifically more advanced than me. They have legal and technical arguments to defend their activities. So I was thinking about a better approach to counter their arguments. I thought I would make a film on people's experiences and how the uranium company is affecting nature and indigenous population living there. To accomplish this, I made up my mind to understand more about tribal population, their ways of life and their relationship with nature. So I lived with them. I confronted many questions and documented them as well. During this time (1998), India also explored nuclear bombs. People were celebrating India's success. And it is during this period that I was making an anti-nuclear film. So you could imagine the kind of pressure I had to face then. I was trying to tell the story of a helpless community unaware of what is happening around them. They were asking some genuine questions. Soon I realized that those who ask these questions are very small in number and they are fighting against an unimaginable nexus of individuals, scientists and vested interest groups. They need much larger support. I became part of the movement. People are suffering. They had cancer and many other diseases. Marriage has ceased in this particular area. In 2006, I again visited the same place where I found that uranium mining has affected many indigenous communities. I could witness a lot of instances which substantiated how this mining impacts people and nature. I could understand that it was the same situation everywhere in the world where there is uranium mining. So I wanted to make another film. If I had the social capital, I could have made the film in two years of time. But it took almost ten years to complete the film. I could complete the film only in 2017–18.

Still 20 A still from the film *Kiski Raksha.* Image Courtesy: Shriprakash.

It is here the question of social capital becomes relevant and your connections with people outside really matters.

It is generally observed that film is both a political and an artistic medium. In many of your public talks, you claim that you are an activist filmmaker. But you have also used the possibilities of different cinematic techniques in your films. In **Buddha Weeps in Jadugoda,** *you use tribal music and their narratives. The beginning of the film is very suggestive in showing the march of the people in a wide-angle shot against the backdrop of nature. How important is aesthetics in your films?*

I have returned my National Award against the policies of the BJP government and against what they were doing against the people in India. I rarely get funding from any agencies because my films are oppositional and activist in nature. Throughout these years, I have been confronted by these questions: that is, whether aesthetics is important in the kind of films I make. Initially it is the aesthetic dimension of the film that distanced the medium of filmmaking from me. You can't expect something great in aesthetics from a person who comes from a rural background and has no formal training in filmmaking. The aesthetics in India have got a lot to do with technology and access to technology. This sometimes discourages people. For a person who comes from a different social order, it is very difficult to do justice to the aesthetics. But, for me, aesthetics alone won't make a film. If you work with aesthetics alone, how could you do justice to the content of your film? I know, as a filmmaker, my weaknesses and strengths. My relationship with the people in film is the strength of my films. I am able to understand what is happening inside them. In many instances, I had disagreements with filmmakers who are successful in the field. My perception of making films is completely different from them. I cannot compromise my filmmaking ethics for the sake of awards or aesthetics. I have a strong feeling that films need to be judged not by aesthetics but by the way it represents its subjects and issues concerned. There should be a balance between the content and the aesthetics.

In spite of the efforts of activists and filmmakers like you, the exploitation of nature and the indigenous population still continues. Do you still believe in people's activism/protest movements and documentary filmmaking as means to initiate (radical) change?

Since globalization, it is a reality that big companies are more powerful than nations. They can easily overpower poor people. It is happening all around the world. All the economic policies of the government are controlled by the corporate companies. Fortunately, I could record what people have experienced, their struggles, and their resurgence, which gives a feeling that you have done something in your life. I was not just filming but was a part of the movement itself. People are still fighting; and I will be with them in whatever possible way I can. I was more of an activist than a filmmaker. Maybe it would take some time to change things. But the fight should go on.

We don't have any powerful tribal leaders in the Indian Parliament who would seriously influence decision-making or the policies of the government. I see young doctors/engineers from the tribal community voicing and conscious of such lack of representation. I seriously believe that there will be a change. Things cannot go on like this. What is awaiting all of us is a big catastrophe. The younger generation is more aware of this. Within five to ten years there will be strong voices from the Adivasi community who would determine the policies of the government. They will raise questions against the Indian elites and the crimes they have committed against the Adivasis. They are going to raise questions which no Indians can easily ignore. On the other hand, there is a serious worry that those who have benefited from education and other things unconsciously develop a tendency to move away from the rest of the Adivasi community. They try to join the mainstream. I don't know how they negotiate tradition versus modernity debate. Irrespective of such genuine doubts and concerns, I still believe that there will be a change. The future of documentary films depends on how we respond to such challenges. Documentary filmmakers have responded quite well to this challenging call. They will respond in the future too. The fact that filmmaking has now become an accessible thing, I hope, will bring some radical change in the field. The emergence of Adivasi and indigenous filmmakers are the greatest hopes for the years to come.

Note

1 *Half Life: A Parable for the Nuclear Age* (1985) is a documentary film by Dennis O'Rourke. The film examines the consequences of nuclear testing at the Marshall Islands.

Biju Toppo

Figure 21 Image Courtesy: Biju Toppo.

Jharkhand-based Biju Toppo is perhaps the first Adivasi documentary filmmaker in India. Dubbed as an "anthropological filmmaker," Toppo's documentaries mostly codirected with Meghnath, sheds light on multiple unaddressed concerns of indigenous population such as displacement, human rights, destructive development, Naxalism, resilience of Adivasi communities, among others. Toppo's solo award-winning production, *The Hunt*, documents the tribulations of tribals in the Naxalite-hit areas of Jharkhand and Chhattisgarh. Broadly, his oeuvre registers the impact of unfettered industrial growth on the environment and the well-being of indigenous population. He is also a founding member of *Akhra*, an organization that works among indigenous people in Jharkhand. As a representative Adivasi voice, his films not only promote social change through detailing complex indigenous issues but also reclaim ethnic culture and indigenous history.

Selected Filmography

Jharia (2019)
The Hunt (2015)
Sona Gahi Pinjra (trans. The Golden Cage) (2011)
Kora Rajee (trans. The Land of the Diggers) (2005)

In Collaboration with Meghnath

Naachi Se Baanchi (trans. Dance to Survive) (2017)
Accumulated Injustice (2015)
Loha Garam Hai (trans. Iron Is Hot) 2010
Vikas Bandook Ki Nal Se (trans. Development Flows from the Barrel of the Gun)
   (2003)

You are perhaps the first Indian independent documentary filmmaker from an indigenous/tribal background. How did you come to documentary filmmaking and how difficult was this journey for you?

While I was pursuing a bachelor's degree in commerce during 1991–2, we had a student organization. Many students from my hometown Palamu[1] were part of it. In fact, it was called Palamu Students Association. I was the vice president of the organization. We were chalking a plan to help students who come from faraway places. We used to identify their problems and did whatever we could do. This was also the period of *Jharkhand Andholan*[2] (the Jharkhand movement), which sought separation from the state of Bihar, a North Indian state. Later, we were faced with a much bigger dilemma. It was August. I went to my hometown. My friends discussed the displacement issue there. They asked me if I could create awareness among students about displacement. When I returned to Ranchi,[3] we held a meeting. A few activists were also present. In 1993, in the name of development around 245 villages were displaced. The objective of the displacement project was to provide a field-firing range for the army. And the name of the project was "Netarhat Field-Firing Range." We became part of the movement. We were in a dilemma as to how to take development-induced displacement issues forward. We soon realized that there were very few from our community in the media. There was barely anyone in the print/electronic media. So I thought I could work in this field. I knew the power and impact of the media and hence I chose this line of work (documentary filmmaking).

Development-induced displacement is a significant theme in documentary films in India. In a way, individual sufferings are ignored for the nation's glory. How critical is the issue of displacement in Jharkhand? And how did displacement become a major preoccupation in your documentary?

During the 1990s, many corporate houses were established in our place (i.e., Jharkhand). There were mining companies and huge factories like sponge iron factories among them. There was intense pollution because of these factories. People were initially forced to move out of their place. Some of them became victims of the pollution. This was not unique to our place. It was happening throughout India. We dealt with this issue in our film *Development Flows from the Barrel of the Gun*. The situation was critical. When displacement was happening because of new industries, everyone said we should protest. During that time, Shriprakash, a fellow documentary filmmaker, came here after completing his studies in filmmaking from Delhi. He was filming the development programs and its resultant displacement. While assisting him, I understood the power of visual media and thought of making use of it for the betterment of society. So, after my studies, I started pursuing my career in filmmaking. As an individual who represents an area which is critically affected by the issue of displacement, it became one of my serious preoccupations as a filmmaker.

Your films like Accumulated Injustice, Iron Is Hot, The Land of the Diggers, and Development Flows from the Barrel of the Gun *focus on the lives of tribal people and issues like mining, exploitation, among others. Why do you think it's important to make such films?*

The concept of representation is a bit problematic. I don't believe that I can represent and speak for Adivasi communities in general. However, the fact that I belong to a similar background creates an impact. But it would be wrong to say that filmmakers who don't belong to this place or community cannot address tribal issues. In fact, there are many cases of significant efforts from the filmmakers who do not belong to a particular place or community and still address the issues of tribal population. It would be absolutely wrong to believe that I am the voice of the population. I am just documenting the issues. Documentary as a medium has a power to express itself. As an individual who comes from such a background, I can relate to their problems. Because these problems are my problems as well. It affects my family and relatives. We have our ways of looking at land, forest, water, and nature. We are all against these development policies and its resultant displacement. With regards to the question of identity, I think it is more intense and powerful when you speak for yourself. I have been doing films with that intention. When I am shooting,

I, as an Adivasi, cannot shoot with my camera as a voyeur. There is something which connects me as a filmmaker to the filmed. It is not a theoretical or forced connection. In that sense, I think Adivasi filmmakers can speak much more about themselves as subalterns.

Modern state as an extension of colonialism has failed to address the larger concerns of the tribal population. Notion of development was forced on them. It was more beneficial to the mainstream than the indigenous people? They were often the victims of the charade of development. Don't you think there is a problem in the way the state has addressed issues and concerns of the tribal population?

I think it's a genuine issue. State hasn't really understood our concerns because it treats Adivasis as a homogenous community. It is wrong to look at us from a mainstream perspective. The whole discourse of the mainstream and marginalized is a consequence of biased point of view of the elites. Then this binary breaks. This is the problem of the notion of state. It needs this binary of mainstream versus marginalized to function. We are a heterogeneous group with our own philosophy and ways of seeing the world. In the film *Kora Rajee*, I have discussed this issue. What I have been trying to address in my films are the problems of the people of my tribe. The film deals with life of the workers of the tea estate from Jharkhand, Orissa, and Chhattisgarh. Their current situation is portrayed in the film. I have used songs in the film. It is through songs that these workers express their struggles. These songs are still being sung there. In *The Golden Cage*, I have argued that our natives who go to work in towns and cities are actually trapped there. Although the government promises social upliftment of tribals, these provisions and promises never see the light. We are appropriated to their (mainstream) culture. We are forced to quit our culture and lifestyle. Such a notion of upliftment is even theoretically wrong.

Development Flows from the Barrel of the Gun *is a critique of the state-corporate nexus that undermine Adivasi resistance against thoughtless development policies. Are Adivasis the prime victims of the much celebrated Nehruvian model of development? In fact, we don't see much solidarity from other sections of society/media against the mindless development policies of the government. Do you think documentary film plays a major role in foregrounding such issues?*

State as well as the social reformers contend that Adivasis should be mainstreamed. Modern state takes an effort in this direction on its own terms.

But they forget the fact that we have our customary laws. Why don't they talk about inculcating our laws and custom to their laws? It is this attitude that irks me. Because of the current model of development in Jharkhand around fifteen lakh people are being displaced and relocated. It happens due to building dams. Worse still, those displaced are not reimbursed. State completely ignores the sacrifices of our ancestors. Development should not be one-dimensional. It should benefit all. But the development in India is one-dimensional and hierarchical. Development should be applicable for all. No city dwellers are asked to move out of their homes and leave behind their land. It is only Adivasis who have to give up their land and culture. The government is bent upon taking over the land in the name of development. And the most tragic thing is that in spite of all these sacrifices we are not benefited in any way. Governments in the name of development have made amendments in laws which were made by the British to protect tribal land. These amendments have made it easier for the authorities to take over tribal areas. If we organize any peaceful protest/movement against such activities of the state, we will be charged as Naxalites. We are tortured and ostracized. This is happening all over Bastar and Dantewada districts of Chhattisgarh. Almost 640 villages have been displaced for mining of minerals and metals. When these people return to their land to farm or anything, they are shot down as Naxalites. It is only a very few of us who are trying to bring out the real situation in these states. Mainstream media is with the state and they are the carriers of state ideology. As a documentary filmmaker, I have tried to foreground these issues.

The Hunt *is an independent documentary which registers how* Adivasis *are charged as Naxalites. Do you think Naxalism is used by the state to crush down dissent and resistance of the tribals?*

To an extent it is right. It is quite natural that when people are denied justice, they will react. They may conduct some agitations to regain their rights. It is their basic right to live in their place. But the authorities think that by stamping us as Naxalites, they can overcome all protests. They believe that they can subdue us by terming us as "Naxals." Many among us are hunted down and killed. It is their intention to create fear among us. But it is absolutely wrong to crush dissenting voices by killing us. Such actions don't even have common sense. How can they term 40,000 people who participate in a rally as "Naxals"? Naxalism is a way for the authorities and the state to curb and subdue us.

Still 21 A still from the film *The Hunt.* Image Courtesy: Biju Toppo.

Naxalism in India emerged as a corrective force against the landlords and their exploitations. If you look at the emergence, growth, and history of Naxalism in India, one could argue that Naxalism was predominantly influential in tribal areas. Do you think the state/government is responsible? Don't you think the Naxalites also exploit tribals for their political interests?

It is a complex issue. But the ultimate victims are Adivasis or the tribal population. It is the negligence, corruption, and exploitation of the authorities and those in power that led to the emergence and growth of Naxalism in India. Government is directly responsible. The government system is failing and that is why these ideologies (i.e., Naxalism) spring up and nurture themselves. Government says that Naxalites are taking money forcefully from the tribals. Inversely, for any government related work, are we not forced to pay bribes? How far is our state and its apparatus inclusive of tribal people and their sentiments? Aren't they marginalized? If the state is not addressing their concerns, what right does it have to accuse tribals? If at all tribals support Naxalites, I would consider the state as responsible for such a predicament. It is because of the exclusion and discrimination practiced by the state that Adivasis are forced to listen to the Naxalites and their ideologies. How do we deal with Adivasis' life and their customs? Why can't they include our laws and customs when it comes to the question of development? Notion of development in India has always been exclusivist and biased. We had a prime minister who asked us to suffer for the development of the nation. We have built huge dams in the country. The benefactors are those who live in the cities. It is the Adivasis who are the real sufferers. Millions are relocated because of building many dams. Worse still, 90 percent of them are not reimbursed. You are displacing us from the land of our ancestors. What about the sacrifices of our ancestors? This is a serious problem. No government understands this.

Notes

1   Palamu is a district in northwestern Jharkhand.
2   Jharkhand Andholan refers to a sociopolitical movement which demanded separate statehood for the state of Jharkhand.
3   Ranchi is the capital city of Jharkhand.

5

Thinking through Regions

Nation and Its Discontents

"Thinking through Regions" foregrounds the paradoxical and complex exchanges between different regions and nation. In demanding the audience to treat the region as a distinctive space within the nation, Iffat Fatima, Haobam Paban Kumar, Bilal A. Jan, Stanzin Dorjai, and Mukul Haloi, among others, in this cluster emphasize the affective and the situated nature of geography and culture. Vibrantly fresh, politically nuanced, ethnically diverse, and aesthetically innovative, these documentary filmmakers defy easy categorization. In bringing together filmmakers from specific and unrepresented regions across India (such as Kashmir, Ladakh, Manipur, and Kachchh), this cluster, while attempting to pause the homogenizing and ultra-nationalistic discourses of the postcolonial nation-state as echoed in the commercial films and the Films Division films, exposes the exclusive imaginings of the nation as one that is unaffected by regional dynamics. Put differently, these filmmakers question the dominant treatment of the region merely as a bureaucratic unit and as an apolitical space, and, in so doing, bring to relief the heterogeneity rooted in regional/ethnic identities and culture. For instance, enforced disappearances and the consequent empirical realities of Kashmiri Muslim women recur in Iffat Fatima's documentaries to underscore the human side of the ongoing conflicts in Kashmir. Again, Mukul Haloi, a filmmaker from Assam, in his *Tales from Our Childhood* persuasively presents Assam insurgency in the 1990s through utilizing real and imagined individual/collective memories of the time. In addressing divergent regional issues like linguistic plurality, ethnic diversity, and cultural resistance, these filmmakers demonstrate the dynamic relationship between regional voices/subjectivities and the nation-state. Using the regional specificity and everydayness to address many engaging questions such as the exchanges between the nation and regions and the enactment of ethnic subjectivity beyond certain fixed national imaginaries, these filmmakers further radically challenge the homogenous identity promoted by the state. In essence, these filmmakers, in treating regions in ethnic, social, and cultural terms discover India in its plurality, diversity, and sophistication, and thus avoid the dangers of a single story about the nation.

Iffat Fatima

Figure 22 Image Courtesy: Kolkata People's Film Festival.

Kashmir is often stereotyped in dominant narratives as a seat of terrorism—a position that not only fails to capture the granular realities of the place but also, in the process, displaces Kashmiris of their aspirations and political self-determinism. Although independent documentary filmmakers (such as Bilal A. Jan, among others) based in Kashmir dismantle such tropes, and thus offer a complicated history and politics of Kashmir, Iffat Fatima, perhaps as the only independent woman documentary filmmaker in Kashmir, is distinct in that her films focus on the largely overlooked role of women. Born in a Muslim family in Kashmir, Fatima grew up highly influenced by conflicts in Kashmir in the 1990s. While her earliest film *Boojh Sakey to Boojh* (trans. *Figure Out if You Can*) is a contemporary retelling of thirteenth-century Sufi poet, Amir Khusru, her film *In the Realm of the Visual* concerns with Dashrath Patel (an artist from India). *The Kesar Saga* documented the storytelling traditions in Ladakh[1] through the Tibetan epic *Kesar* Saga.[2] However, her political disposition was evident in *Lanka—The Other Side of War and Peace*, which traced the tragic consequences of the Lankan civil war. Since 2006 Fatima has been associated with the Association of Parents of Disappeared Persons (hereafter APDP) on the issue of enforced disappearances. *Where Have You Hidden My New Moon*

Crescent, for instance, featuring Mughal Masi narrates her longing for her lost child Nazir Ahmed Teli, who was allegedly abducted by the Indian forces in the 1990s. Her films *Khoon Diy Baarav* (trans. *Blood Leaves Its Trail*) and *The Dear Disappeared* are also concerned with enforced disappearances and the logic of the production of insecurities among Kashmiris. Having said that, Kashmiri women in her films are not permanent victims but agents who reconfigure their immediate realities and everyday conditions. In doing so, her films reinstate the agency and categorical voices of the Kashmiri women and deftly illustrate how they exercise their subjectivity in spite of living in a militarized zone. Situating herself in such a precarious space, Fatima in the present interview discusses her filmic self, her engagement with resistance movements in Kashmir, and women's protest movements in Kashmir.

Selected Filmography

The Dear Disappeared (2018)
Khoon Diy Baarav (trans. Blood Leaves Its Trail) (2015)
Where Have You Hidden My New Moon Crescent (2009)
Lanka—The Other Side of War and Peace (2005)
The Kesar Saga (2000)
Boojh Sakey to Boojh (trans. *Figure Out if You Can*) (1996)

It is fantastic to think about a woman filmmaker from a conflict zone like Kashmir. Perhaps you are the only woman Muslim documentary filmmaker in Kashmir who makes political documentaries. What are the risks/challenges you face as a woman filmmaker in a place that has been a cauldron of conflicting perspectives and emotions? And as a woman filmmaker from Kashmir, how different is your filmic language from the (native) Kashmiri male documentary filmmakers?

I started making documentary films in the 1990s. To be able to work as an independent documentary filmmaker is a struggle but more so a privilege. To me what is most valuable about making documentary films is that it has given me access to lives and situations which is immensely educative. It's a vantage point which makes one think and rethink to make sense of what is happening around on one's own terms. To make autonomous choices and create a piece of work in a way you think appropriate is an entitlement and a responsibility simultaneously. Challenges and risks are part of a process and have to be negotiated as they come along. All modes of communication are gendered; film language is no exception.

How gender gets deployed in films depends upon the sensibility, politics, and imagination of the filmmakers—both male and female. There are feminist films made by men as there are misogynist films made by women.

Your film **Where Have You Hidden My New Moon Crescent** *is a journey into a repertoire of (un)seen violence narrated through intensely personal/political testimonies of Mughal Masi, who dies after waiting for twenty years for her son to return. How challenging was it to retrieve, relive, and transfer those experiences of violence to the medium?*

The challenge I think for filmmakers and artists is to be able to transfer an experience. You can record narratives, but on screen they can be flat. How do you transfer and translate that experience? The decisions and choices one make are part of a process which is simultaneously intuitive, conscious and deliberate. Mughal Masi was a poet, surrounded by tragedy and sorrow. I met her during the sit-in protest organized by the Association of Parents of Disappeared Persons (APDP), a collective of the families of the victims of enforced disappearances in Kashmir. APDP is an ongoing movement against the heinous crime of enforced disappearances in Kashmir, which started in the early 1990s. The APDP organizes a sit-in protest every month in a public park in Srinagar. Mughal Masi was always present at these protests—sometimes hopeful, sometimes angry, and sometimes desperate and always in deep distress—her poetic sensibility, the ability to articulate her grief without rancor was a very special quality which drew me to her. About a month before she died, I spent a day with her with my camera. I recorded a long conversation where she talked about herself and about the events that shaped her life—both personal and political. *Where Have You Hidden My New Moon Crescent* emerged organically from Mughal Masi's insightful recounting of the social and political events of her times and her deep longing for information about her only child Nazir Ahmed Teli, who was disappeared by the Indian security apparatus in Srinagar in the 1990s. The film is a tribute to her unrequited quest for justice. She was in deep anguish but remained hopeful and resistant till the very end.

What distinguishes documentary filmmakers like you from the rest is the immediacy and materiality of your experience in a conflict zone. How challenging is the act of making a documentary film in a conflict zone like Kashmir?

I usually respond to the demands of the situation and the available resources. In Sri Lanka, for the film *Lanka—The Other Side of War and Peace* I did the camera myself. It was a very informal crew of three women. One of them was a translator. For almost a year, we regularly traveled up and down the A9 highway which connects North and South Sri Lanka and was a war zone for decades. I have hundreds of hours of footage collected from those travels.

The Kashmir films have been made over a period of almost ten years. During these years, I used multiple modes of acquiring material and resources for the films. I was intensely engaged with the struggle of the families of the disappeared and tortured in Kashmir. Enforced disappearances is a heinous crime recognized as such by international laws and conventions. It was less about the film and more about my engagement and involvement with the issues confronting the people I was working with and spending time with. In fact, advocacy work on disappearances is a lifetime commitment, and I continue to be engaged and involved in the struggle of the families of the disappeared and their campaign for justice.

In course of my engagement with the families I would sometimes do the camera myself, in a very informal manner. However, there have been several other camera persons who have worked on the film and some filming took place in formal settings with a proper crew, but I generally maintain and prefer a small crew; otherwise, it tends to get invasive and unwieldy. My objective is to reach out with the camera, and I try to minimize the intrusion of the camera.

he kept repeating "where is Fayaz Sahibs mother" I came out on the verandah

Still 22 A still from the film *The Dear Disappeared*. Image Courtesy: Iffat Fatima.

Khoon Diy Baarav *concerns enforced disappearances and the politics of memory in Kashmir. Could you unpack the meaning of the title? How critical is the situation of enforced disappearances in Kashmir particularly after the abrogation of Article 370?*

Khoon Diy Baarav is a term very often used by the affected people to express resistance as well as their demand for justice. It's on the tip of their tongue, so to say. It's a complex saying; translating it effectively is almost impossible. Broadly, it implies that blood that is spilled will not go waste, it will extract justice. In other words, innocent blood that is shed through oppression and violence sediments in memory and will remerge in the form of resistance. From memory comes an empowered form of resistance. "Resistance" is the key word in Kashmir where people are grappling with the impossibility of justice from the Indian state which hasn't been coming for the last sixty years, and there is little expectation of it in the near future.

Over the last seventy years, Kashmir is reeling under a military occupation, more so after the armed uprising in the 1990s. A very large number of people have been killed, disappeared, tortured, and maimed. And the memory of atrocities remains etched in individual bodies and keeps spilling on to the collective. As long as the demands of justice remain unrequited, the situation in Kashmir will continue to be critical. The state is bent upon erasure. Not only erasure, it wants to impose its own narrative. "It makes our truth into lies and their own lies into truth," remarks Parveena Ahangar, who has been leading the battle against enforced disappearances in Kashmir.

Kashmir is a political problem, and there cannot be a military resolution to a political problem. The Indian state wants to erase the Kashmiri aspirations for political self-determination by imposing a narrative of Pakistani terrorism. Incidentally, the problem is completely lost and erased in these narratives. However, it's not going to be easy; there are people who have for years formed a movement and they have made huge sacrifices. There is an aspiration and passion for *azaadi* (trans. freedom) in Kashmir. It's not something that will die down. If it had to, with the kind of military power that has been used there by now, it would have been dead and gone. But it reemerges, resurfaces, and transforms.

Lanka—The Other Side of War and Peace *is a different film in your body of work in terms of geography and perspective. As a film that explores the cultural functions of memory, forgetfulness, and violence, how do you situate your experience of making the film? And what does it mean to revisit the film in the context of the recent events in Sri Lanka?*

On February 22, 2002, after decades of brutal fighting, the Government of Sri Lanka led by Ranil Wickremesinghe, and the Liberation Tigers of Tamil Eelam,[3] led by Vellupillai Prabhakaran, signed a ceasefire agreement. Soon after, in April 2002, the A9 highway, which links the war-torn North with South Sri Lanka, was opened to civilian traffic after twelve years. It was a historic moment, ushering in a long-awaited period of hope for a negotiated settlement to the ethnic conflict, which for decades seriously embittered the relations between different communities—the Sinhalese, the Tamil, and the Muslims—living in Sri Lanka. For those displaced and separated by years of war, the A9 highway became the "Road to Peace" and a catalyst for the documentary film on which I worked from 2002 to 2005. The period between 2002 and 2005 was a rare time in Sri Lanka. The signs of peace had appeared after a lapse of many decades. Checkpoints were being dismantled, travel restrictions relaxed, death squads, and disappearances were few and far between and the displaced persons were returning to their homes. Based in Colombo, I traveled several times between Colombo and Matara in the south and Colombo and Jaffna in the north

The film set out to explore the possibility and the meaning of peace within the context of Sri Lanka's brutal history of violence. As it shifts between north and south, the film spans the history of decades of violence in Sri Lanka juxtaposing the multiple realities of war and peace that simultaneously exist here. Sri Lanka's history of violence is pervasive and protracted. The armed *Janatha Vimukti Peramuna* (trans. People's Liberation Front) (JVP) insurrection of the 1970s and the 1980s brutally suppressed by the government, communal riots aided and abetted by the government, and protracted civil war between the Government of Sri Lanka and the LTTE are bloody episodes, wherein hundreds and thousands have been killed, tortured, disappeared, and displaced.

In 2002, as the ceasefire agreement brokered by the Norwegians came into effect in Sri Lanka, it soon became evident that an official discourse that privileged economic rehabilitation and reconstruction over issues of democracy and human rights was being propagated to facilitate negotiations between the two warring parties. The official discourse left little scope to investigate into the causes and impact of years of multilayered violence and to find ways of healing the deep wounds in the social fabric. The plight of the thousands who disappeared, tortured, maimed, and displaced remained unacknowledged and forgotten. The main objective of the film was to provide space for people to remember and to reflect upon their past history of violence and brutality and thereby contribute toward the creation of an atmosphere for dialogue and reconciliation. The film was made through a consultative and collaborative process with lawyers, academics and activists in Sri Lanka.

In April 2003, the peace talks between the Government of Sri Lanka and the LTTE broke down, and the peace process was stalled. In July 2006, after a four-year fragile ceasefire the war resumed. It formally ended on May 18, 2009, with the killing of the LTTE leader Velupillai Prabhakaran. The Sri Lankan Army gained control over the entire territory held by the LTTE in the north and the east. Tens of thousands of civilians are believed to have been killed in the final months of battle. The government has denied allegations by the UN and human rights groups of committing war crimes and abuses during the final offensive against the Tamil Tigers and ignored international demands for an independent investigation.

Most recently, I traveled to Sri Lanka in 2015. Much has changed since then. In 2004, Tsunami devastated large parts of the southern coastline. LTTE was vanquished and postwar reconstruction reshaped much in the North. In 2015, Chavakacheri and Jaffna looked very different from 2002. But nowhere are the changes more dramatic than on the 100-kilometer stretch of the A9 that runs through Vanni. The site of many bloody battles for over twenty-five years has been rebuilt at a massive cost.

Traveling on the road from Colombo to Jaffna after all these years was surreal. As new episodes of violence begin, a large part of the past gets erased from public domain and public discourse in Sri Lanka. As Milan Kundera says, "The struggle of man against power is the struggle of memory against oblivion." The film *Lanka—The Other Side of War and Peace* remains a valuable account of personal narratives, images, spaces, and places linked to Sri Lanka's long history of violent conflict which is being officially and deliberately obliterated from public discourse.

Notes

1   Ladakh is an Indian union territory in the Himalayas.
2   *Kesar Saga* is an eleventh-century Tibetan epic.
3   The Liberation Tigers of Tamil Eelam (LTTE) is a Tamil militant organization based in the northeastern part of Sri Lanka.

R. V. Ramani

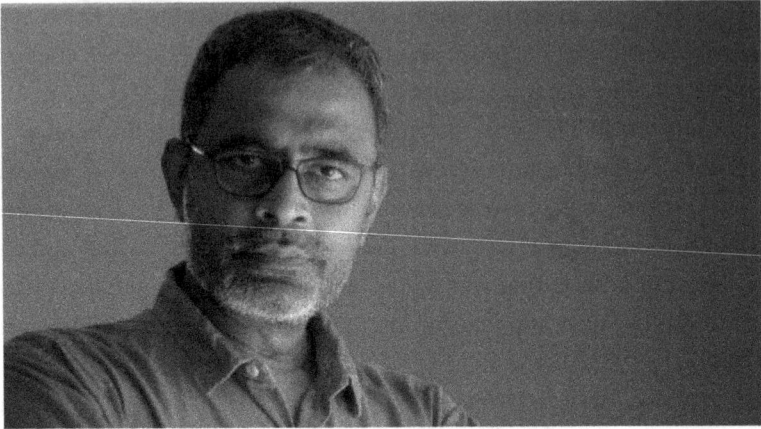

Figure 23 Image Courtesy: R.V. Ramani.

R. V. Ramani since the 1990s has produced more than twenty independent documentary films which are largely impressionistic and self-reflective, and hence defies easy classification. Moving beyond the documentary avunculate of fact/fiction, his films in crossing boundaries and generic conventions are lyrical, evocative, and poetic expressions. A graduate from the Film and Television Institute of India (FTII), Pune with specialization in Motion Picture Photography, his films, predicated on abstraction and innovative structures, offer heterogeneous points of view in a self-consciously stylized hybrid form. For him, filmmaking is an intuitive and instinctive work that questions meaning making within the structure of the film. Consciously working against dominant ideologies and consumptive modes such as television and treating filmmaking as an organic process, his oeuvre searches for innovative forms suitable for his narratives. Put differently, his films are visual and semiotic try-outs that engage the local and quotidian realities of life. For instance, if films like *My Camera and Tsunami* is a more aestheticized examination of documentary as a medium and notions of reality, *Nee Engey* (trans. *Where Are You?*) is an impressionistic ethnography on shadow puppeteers. His films and retrospectives are screened in many International Film festivals and other platforms like Mumbai Film Festival, Yamagata International Documentary Film Festival (Japan), Pusan International Film Festival (Korea), Munich International Film Festival, among many others.

Selected Filmography

Oh That's Bhanu (2019)
Santhal Family to Mill Re-call (2017)
A Documentary Proposal (2016)
Hindustan Hamara (trans. This Country Is Ours) (2014)
My Camera and Tsunami (2011)
Nee Engey (trans. *Where Are You?*) (2003)
Season (1997)
Language of War (1996)
Face Like a Man (1993)
Saa (1991)

What does independent documentary mean to you? And how did the Emergency shape the history of independent documentary filmmaking in India?

Discovering a form in the process of making a film, addressing concerns within oneself and ensuring that the film is completed as per your instincts is an independent documentary for me. It is a form of free expression. Earlier, Indian documentaries were largely a propaganda tool of the state with its own logic of production and distribution. The arrival of 16 mm and even 8 mm film formats created a major opening for many filmmakers to access the tools of filmmaking. One can safely say that the Emergency created and paved the way to the emergence of various unique forms of expression which were truly independent bypassing even the state control. There were, for instance, artists' who found innovative methods to express resistance to the Emergency or assert their thoughts in a highly controlled climate in publications such as newspapers, theater, poetry, literature, folk forms, contemporary art, and film.

How did you get interested in making documentaries? And how early did you become interested in film?

Probably it has to do with me as a photojournalist and my general impression about myself as someone good in candid photography. This is even before I thought of studying filmmaking in FTII. My preference was toward the unset rather than setup situations. I like rawness as opposed to polish, gloss, and control. This probably continued even after I joined FTII to study cinematography. Though I felt I am comfortable with all the aspects of cinematography and confident in any genre, the element of rawness, the unanticipated, the surprise, and an "image" created on the spot excited me. Gradually, I came up with a term to characterize such an approach. I called it "candid cinematography," which is completely different from candid photography in application.

I think it is by accident that I became a filmmaker. I never even remotely thought of becoming a filmmaker, when I was studying at FTII. I just wanted to be a cinematographer and excel in it. When I was at FTII from 1982 to 1985, the idea of documentary filmmaking was not even introduced to us in a formal way like the way it happens now. These days, I conduct documentary filmmaking workshops in FTII and many other places.

Share your early influences, particularly films and artists that shaped you as a documentary filmmaker.

Though I liked watching many commercial and action films during my school and college days, I was particularly influenced by Ritwik Ghatak's *Ajantrik*[1] and B. V. Karanth's *Chomana Dudi*.[2] These films were shown in an NFDC (National Film Development Corporation of India)–owned cinema theater in Churchgate (an area in South Mumbai) as morning shows. Such theaters do not exist now. Before I joined the Film Institute, I worked on a feature film titled *Pehla Adhyay*,[3] directed by Vishnu Mathur. The film was unique, avant-garde, and experimental, which revealed new possibilities in fiction form. After my graduation from FTII, I collaborated with Vishnu on a few documentaries including a short fiction as a cinematographer. A diploma film at the Film Institute titled *Kinhi Chuttiyon Mein* by Sameera Jain too revealed immense possibilities of fiction as an alternative form of expression. Importantly, my own classmate, Soudhamini, who was studying direction joined FTII with an intention of making a film on the musician M. D. Ramanathan.[4] I too was very fond of M. D. Ramanathan. But he passed away while we were at FTII. Making a film about M. D. Ramanathan became an obsession. It did finally happen in 1991. One more strong influence at FTII was Mani Kaul. He would visit FTII as a guest faculty. His films *Dhrupad*[5] and *Mati Manas*[6] were in fact premiered at FTII when we were studying there. Both of these films border on fiction and nonfiction. In fact, Mani Kaul deeply influenced many of us and shaped our journey in independent filmmaking. The first film that I worked as a cinematographer, after graduating from FTII, was a film on a mathematician called S. Ramanujan.[7] It was titled *Enigma of Srinivasa Ramanujan* and was directed by Nandan Kudhyadi. This film was wonderfully scripted as a play between documentary and fiction. In general, I do not differentiate genres of filmmaking. It's all the same for me: a deep engagement with the language of cinema with certain chosen parameters. I chose to work with documentary parameters. But I do call the experience of my films as fiction.

Your film **Hindustan Hamara** *is a visual conversation between you and Anand Patwardhan. Share Anand's influence on you as a filmmaker and on the documentary movement in India.*

When I was in my college, I came to know about Anand Patwardhan through some of my friends. But I didn't get to see any of his works. After joining FTII, I remember trying to convince the faculty to invite Anand Patwardhan for a session in our class. Anand Patwardhan later was a frequent visitor to FTII and even completed his film *Bombay: Our City* using the editing facilities in FTII. This film was screened in FTII, just as I was graduating from FTII. Also, one of my immediate seniors at FTII, Uma Sehgal, made a documentary titled *Shelter*. There was also Ranjan Palit, who had shot *Bombay: Our City* for Anand Patwardhan. He too made a documentary as his final diploma film in FTII on the Bhiwandi handloom workers. I felt good about all that.

I am generally drawn to certain noncommercial and independent film narratives. Anand Patwardhan's film *Bombay: Our City* threw up a huge challenge for me. Though I was supportive of his topical concerns and intent, I experienced a dilemma with his form and treatment. Over time, I started treating the form and treatment as the content. My first film *Saa*, made in 1991, was an exposition of that approach. I became obsessed with the way we portray characters, situations, the quality of intimacy, ideas of empathy, self-reflectivity, notions of equality in the film medium. Later, I wanted to create a documentary form free from any definitions and needs, stripping it from monolithic narratives and through a strong assertion of subjectivity. The film that I made with Anand Patwardhan (based on some of his screening events) is a culmination of my invisible dialogue with Anand Patwardhan all through my career since 1985. I completed the film in 2014.

Your film **My Camera and Tsunami** *is known for its innovative form and structure. It is self-reflexive and is about the process of making documentaries. It also radically questions conventional practices in documentary filmmaking.*

Themes can be anything. Treatment is what brings the essence of the theme. The form for every film has to be reinvented. The patterns need to be questioned. The meaning making needs to be questioned too. I try to do it in my films and it is inbuilt in the structure of every film I make.

My Camera and Tsunami *is a memory of a camera which perished in tsunami along with a final recorded footage in it. What prompted you to make an impressionistic film on tsunami and exclude the horrors of it?*

I was in a dilemma as to how to make a film based on my intense experience of tsunami. I witnessed something spectacular and beyond my imagination. I had lost my camera and friends. The footage I shot of the tsunami got destroyed. The magnificence and the mystery of this experience, the notions and perspectives of truth, along with absence of image churned metaphorical film for me. *My Camera and Tsunami* also became homage to my camera, which probably saved my life, a partner in image making, negotiating life and death. I wanted to create my experience of tsunami, revealing my personal life, moments of ecstasy in image making, without showing any footage of tsunami.

As an independent documentary filmmaker, how challenging is it to find and build a production budget?

I never even find my working budget. I just go ahead and make films with whatever one can find. There are two things: a working budget and the value of the product in a certain geographical territory. Working budget is not the budget of the film. It is more a personal diary note. Unfortunately, this is treated as a budget. And then if there is a partner as a financier for this working budget, they

Still 23 A still from the film *Oh That's Bhanu*. Image Courtesy: R.V. Ramani.

seal the working budget as the value of the film. Filmmakers are often cheated on this and lose the value of their work to somebody else. How do you value any work of art? It is not based on incidentals. The real challenge is retaining the ownership of the film or sharing copyrights.

Saa *is an exploratory journey into the distinctive rhythms of urban and rural India. Why do you think rhythms are central in the urban and rural lives of India?*

Rhythms are central to everything. It is a sense of life and a pulse. In this film, I gauge the pulse and the interconnectedness of my diametrically opposite, locations: the rural and the urban. Actually, it is a journey to find my own rhythm and my functionality as well. I was sure that I wanted to experiment with form, as we did in the film school. I did not change my style to adapt to industry and commercial requirements. After living in Mumbai for almost twenty-five years, I moved to Chennai.[8] My own working equations were breaking apart. I needed to resurrect my rhythm of working. I searched through the rural and urban rhythms, the pulse of local trains, the migrant labors, and assertion of belonging to seek and revive my own rhythm.

Most of your films like **Face Like a Man, Brahma Vishnu Shiva, Lines of Mahatma** *register multiple realities and worlds of art and artists. Even your recent film,* **Oh That's Bhanu (2019)** *is about a dancer and a theater actor, Bhanumathi Rao, in her mid-nineties. How challenging and intriguing is making films about the realities of artists? And how suitable is the medium (documentary) for such a journey?*

In my films, I look at aspects of expression, shades, and nuances of expression: blocked, distorted, leaked, flowering expressions. It doesn't matter who my protagonists are. I anyways treat all my protagonists as artists who are seeking an expression through a form. In *Face Like a Man*, reputed artists consciously express themselves in an artists' camp. I became the back-door entrant in this camp, discovering a form for myself, along with them. *Brahma Vishnu Shiva* started as an experiment to observe impermanence but ended as a philosophical narrative. *Lines of Mahatma* was again a kind of struggle to connect to an image, to an enigma. For the artist, K. M. Adimoolam, featured in the film, it was a struggle to reconnect to the "image" of Gandhi. For me, it was a challenge to connect with two of my favorite artists, Gandhi and Adimoolam, and to discover a form. The only need is to express and to find an expression.

In one of your interviews you said, "I don't even think of large audiences now; I don't even need them actually. I like small audiences. I like showing my films to a few people and having nice feedback and talk. I don't even like to show my films on television."[9] *Why do you think television is not suitable for your films? Do you think documentary filmmakers can stay away from the digital/online screening platforms?*

Television channels in their current desperate state are not suitable for my films. At the most, they do charity for documentary filmmakers in India. Their politics and their viewers are different. Television industry in India is functioning on its own survival politics. The only way to liaison with them is to work under their codes. That is a different kind of filmmaking. I strongly believe my film will work wonderfully in television or cinema theaters, if a slot for such films is nurtured by the television. But there are no takers. This space is not available to us and I have not made any dent on that. They are not ready to accept independent and tangential works. It threatens and confuses them. I enjoy small audiences and intense discussion. Big players are on a spree to acquire rights and ownerships, dictating what is good for them. Small funders take over all rights from the filmmakers. And, finally, one needs to find a balance of independence and self-respect.

Out of the many hours of footage, how do you arrive at the final length of your films? As a documentary filmmaker myself, I am curious to know the process.

Well, either one goes by the dictates of television standards or by the logic of your narrative. I choose the latter. There is also the idea of how much an audience can watch.

Many of your films such as Santhal Family to Mill Re-Call *employ multilayered narratives. Why do you think it is important to have multiple perspectives?*

The only truth is the perspective. Multiple perspectives is the area I am interested in. It offers possibilities as opposed to any monolithic view point. In fact, it is the need of the hour. *Santhal Family to Mill Re-call* is based on an art installation event. The film takes its cue from it. In my most recent film, *Oh That's Bhanu*, the character Bhanumathi herself demolishes any kind of logic formation and thus creates perspectives of perspectives.

Notes

1 *Ajantrik* (1958) is a Bengali language film directed by Ritwik Ghatak.

2 *Chomana Dudi* (trans. Choma's Drum) (1975) is an Indian film in Kannada language directed by B. V. Karanth.

3 *Pehla Adhyay* (1981) is an experimental film by Vishnu Mathur.

4 M. D. Ramanathan was an Indian musician who is remembered for his unique style of renderings and compositions in Carnatic music, a dominant school of classical music in South India.

5 *Dhrupad* is a documentary film directed by Mani Kaul. The film is on Dhrupad, a form of Indian classical music.

6 *Mati Manas* (1984) is a documentary on ancient Indian pottery directed by Mani Kaul.

7 S. Ramanujan was an internationally known mathematician from India.

8 Chennai is the capital city of Tamil Nadu, a South Indian state.

9 See Paul, Pallavi. (2014), "Interview with R. Ramani," *Wide Screen* 5(1), February. Available online: http://widescreenjournal.org/index.php/journal/article/view/83/12 7 (accessed on September 08, 2019).

Pankaj Rishi Kumar

Figure 24 Image Courtesy: Pankaj Rishi Kumar.

Based in Bombay, Pankaj Rishi Kumar is a graduate from the Film and Television Institute of India (FTII) with a specialization in editing. As a filmmaker who engages with regional themes that have pan-Indian relevance, his films are known for their complex narrative structures and innovative styles. Kumar's first semiautobiographical independent documentary film *Kumar Talkies* is an empirical testimony and a philosophical take on the many meanings of cinema, technology, and viewing practices. *In God's Land*, his critically acclaimed documentary, is an inquiry into the smoldering effects of neoliberalism and Special Economic Zone (SEZ)[1] Act on the poorest farmers and goat herders in Tirunelveli district of southern Tamil Nadu. His films address wide-ranging issues such as agrarian crisis (*Seeds of Dissent*), citizenship and multiple allegiances (*Two Flags*), and honor killings (*Janani's Juliet*). Extremely critical of the existing paradigms of filmmaking practices in India (such as high budget, negligent attitude toward documentary films, and undue importance on specializations in filmmaking), his films make a case for perspectival change in the way filmmaking, screening, and projection happen in India. Although his films integrate live action footage of interviews, cinema vérité images and deals with the themes of political significance, they are rarely agitational. His recent documentary *Janani's Juliet* is India's Oscar entry in 2019.

Selected Filmography

To Die a Frenchman (2020)
Janani's Juliet (2019)
Two Flags (2018)
In God's Land (2013)
Seeds of Dissent (2009)
Three Men and A Bulb (2006)
Pather Chujaeri (trans. The Play Is On) (2001)
Kumar Talkies (1999)

You graduated from a premier film school in India, the Film and Television Institute of India (FTILL), Pune. But in many of your public talks you have been critical of the formal training in filmmaking? Don't you think film schools shape a better filmmaker?

Yes, I agree that film schools make you a better filmmaker. But I am not happy with everything you get from there. I am a filmmaker who does cinema by myself. When I say I do by myself, it doesn't mean camera alone, I do everything related to my film. If you are in this profession for moneymaking, I think it is a disservice to us. If you have Rs. 5 lakhs (half a million), I think of making a film with Rs. 5 lakhs. Film schools are the biggest threats in this aspect. It's so cheap to make films in the present times. But film schools give you a different theory altogether. A cameraman from an institute told me once that a camera alone costs Rs. 2.5 lakhs. I make a full film with that budget. That is the pedagogy I follow. Unless we change this idea of filmmaking, things are not going to change. Even if a documentary is not watched by everyone, I think there is fun in making films. The idea of documentary as documenting is an old nomenclature. Film schools are so specific about nomenclatures. I differ from them. Although I had my training in FTII, the exposure to documentary cinema was very minimal. Focus was more on fiction films. It was all about picking some skills and moving to Bollywood. I don't think film schools should be run in this way. Film schools need to engage with many other aspects of filmmaking.

Comment on the medium and affordances of documentary form and your creative process.

I make documentaries because I do not know anything else to do. I do not have any other skill whatsoever. What I am proud of is my curiosity and lack of inhibition to travel throughout India to make films. My films are not overtly activist but driven by the spirit of engagement and a belief that "the personal is political." I cannot escape the complex nature of human existence which is at once at odds with multiple systems (such as economic, political, and social) and fights the very forces which oppress them. At the ground level, this fight is slow and excruciating. It does not involve shouting and going on a protest march. Sometimes, the fight is alone. The everydayness of the struggle does not produce images which are appealing. In fact, to churn out scenes from the everydayness of life takes a lot of effort. But, once you spend time with a person or a community, patterns of recurrence and fight emerge.

I am interested in the larger picture. Hence, my films are often beyond seventy minutes and made over many years. And, like reality, my images are not always appealing. They are raw, shaky, and sometimes nonsensical. But I want to share what I saw. In fact, I want to make them go through the pain of my patience and perseverance. These become subtexts in the form of "unnecessary" and "boring" scenes. I use them to weave a narrative of the lived reality. In short, my films call for a lot of patience from the audience and empathy too. It has never been easy to make my films. I cut the scene anyway. I retain the moment. The people in the film have experienced horror. One has to bear with the process and watch it.

What made you a documentary filmmaker? Could you share your early influences that shaped you as a filmmaker?

Emotions came first. My grandfather owned a rice mill in Kalpi.[2] Over time it collapsed. In the 1960s, my father turned the defunct mill into a cinema hall. Although not lucrative, I secretly admired his entrepreneurial spirit. In 1992, I completed my course at FTII in editing. I started working at two studios simultaneously to support myself and my family who was dealing with my father's illness. Rishi Kumar, my father, passed away in 1995. The cinema hall was almost taken over by the caretakers. I was dealing with a new city (Mumbai) and the digital studios. My first film was my attempt to come to terms with what was happening around me. I wanted something to hold on to—something to make sense of what was happening to me, my family, the cinema hall, and the surge of nonlinear editing consoles. The documentary form offered me that space. That is how I came to make my first film, *Kumar Talkies*. It turned out to be an ode to my father and cinema in the wake of the onslaught of cable television.

Your film **Kumar Talkies** *details the relationship between a small town (Kalpi in Uttar Pradesh) and the decline of its surviving cinema theater. Revisiting the film after twenty years of its making, is* **Kumar Talkies** *a metaphor for the diminishing traditional filmmaking and viewing practices in India?*

Technology has changed. This change gives rise to different kinds of storytelling. It definitely colors the documentary form itself. I wonder if *Kumar Talkies* would look and have a similar impact if I were to make it now. The meaning of "personal" has changed for me and the meaning of "political" too. Much water has flown under the bridge. As a filmmaker, I think I have adapted. My 2K camera gives me pristine images. I do get overwhelmed when I see it on a big screen. In many ways, the wonderment has remained. The imagination/aura of watching a film in a dark room has remained untouched. There are only interruptions the viewer has on her/his cellphone while watching a film at home or at a busy public space. These are new additions. This does not make me impatient. In fact, I love when people talk during a screening. They are responding, sighing, and discussing with their friend while watching it. I like that moment. I have not been to Kalpi for decades now. Kumar Talkies closed down a few years ago. The dilapidated structure of the cinema hall remains. It rots with each passing day.

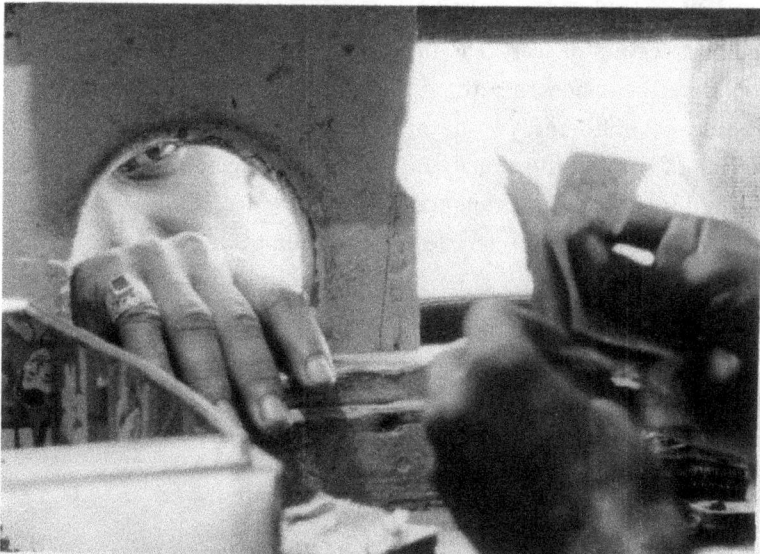

Still 24 A still from the film *Kumar Talkies*. Image Courtesy: Pankaj Rishi Kumar.

There is a reference in **Kumar Talkies** *that women are not usually permitted or welcomed to the talkies. Do you think film watching is a gendered activity in India?*

Let us brutally accept that filmmaking in India is male dominated. The public spaces are still male dominated. And cinema theaters are no different. The women filmgoers to Kumar Talkies are tragically part of a culture that encourages femicide. The presence of them in places where they are not "allowed" result in gossips and then the horror ensues. We need more women filmmakers making more films. I believe they include a gaze; call it female or feminine or feminist. It gives me a good perspective where I stand in the world and what I need to do to correct myself.

Pather Chujaeri *(trans.* **The Play Is On***) was about folk singers who conduct public performances in Kashmir. Unlike other films on Kashmir, your film deals with the art and life-affirming practices as opposed to gunshots. Comment on your creative intention.*

Making *Pather Chujaeri* was a heady experience. I was restless, angry, overwhelmed by what I saw. A journalist friend of mine and I were the first to report from Drass[3] and Kargil[4] before the Indian army's onslaught began in 1999. I experienced FEAR for the first time. On my way back from Kargil, I met the *Bhands* (folk singers) in Srinagar. So, the question is: How does art survive in a regime of fear? The film followed two groups as they prepared for public performances, a rare phenomenon in 2001. I was encouraged by what I found. An illiterate community has sustained a centuries-old tradition in the face of debilitating social and cultural changes. Although perennially intimidated by corruption, violence, and intolerance, the Bhands in Kashmir are still affirming a commitment to their theater, to the critical potential of its form and the liberating joys of performance. Yes, there are no gory images in the film. But the police patrol in Dal Lake,[5] the sunken boats, interrogation by the army, the boat cutting through ice on a winter morning, and, lastly, the Indian state celebrating 26th January in an empty Bakshi Stadium in Kashmir, all these images are very violent. These images were an extension of what I learned from the Bhands.

God's Land *satirizes the exploitation of farmers by religion and its allied apparatus. A lady in the film questions the god performer by asking, "So much* *is happening around us . . . Why do you even exist? With what face have you come here? How can you be so merciless? Aren't you God?" What prompted you to make this film? And why did you use animated images in the film?*

When I began shooting in the village of Inam Alangulam (in the state of Tamil Nadu), I wanted to capture the hopes and aspirations of the villagers with regard to the SEZ (Special Economic Zone). But realities became murkier as I realized that the villagers were not only fighting a court case for land rights but also resisting oppression in the name of God and caste. The politicians also reduced them to mere vote banks by giving them false promises. By the end of the film, I was filled with cynicism toward the SEZ, government, and the temple God. But, like the villagers, I too began seeking solace in the village God (Sudalai Swami), who promises to protect the village, the farm lands and the villager's unique identity. I used animation due to the lack of any material to recreate the history of the village. Its story is driven through oral tradition rather than factual data. As a filmmaker, I felt that it would be a cliché to have an old man narrating the story of the village from his fading memory. Instead, an interesting animation depicting the past will help to go beyond the linearity of the narration. The nomadic villagers did not simply come and settle in this region. They became a part of the complex social structure and the king's rule. They also transformed the dry lands into fertile lands. One cannot underestimate their contribution via an interview or "talking heads" or edited stock footage or voice-over visuals. It is difficult for the audience to get used to the idea of animation as a documentary. It was a new way of thinking. The animated sequences were planned to help the audience make larger connections between the power paradigms.

Your film Two Flags *is an interesting take on national identities, citizenship, and nationalism. These themes are so relevant in contemporary India. Share the politics, aesthetics, and perspective of the film.*

Having begun the work as early as 2007 after reading an *Outlook* (a weekly English magazine) article on the topic, I set out to film in 2012 hoping to cover the French presidential elections in Pondicherry[6] (a former French colony). Elections were the only occasion when the Tamil French people participated in political meetings. It is otherwise a much-closed community. Yet, it was only by the next elections in 2017 that I could make inroads into the film. *Two Flags* lays bare the ambiguity of nationalism very early in the film. While the band plays the French national anthem, the voice-over contends that he identifies with two countries: "India is my heart, I studied here . . . I joined the French Army and worked in it for 22 years. That is my second life and I'm working for my country. I have two countries. First country is France, second country is India." What I found with regard to the angle of nationalism is that because of a tricky historical process, multinationalism in Pondicherry becomes convenient. The only reason why these people are hanging on to their French identity is solely because of economic reasons and not for the country. What I learned from these people is that it's possible to have multicultural and multinational allegiances.

Is there any grammar to being an "activist" filmmaker?

It is a very tricky question. When personal is political, the very act of making a film makes one an activist. In that sense, I am indeed an activist filmmaker. I am also not an "activist filmmaker" in the way I go about shooting, storytelling, editing my films. In many ways, you are making me think. You are asking me if there is any grammar to being an "activist" filmmaker. Maybe there is. I cannot define it. My work is descriptive and observational in approach. I am not interested in the "event" but the "process" or background to the event. Although my films begin with a curiosity, I am emotionally engaged. It need not necessarily translate into a personal voice-over. But I keep confronting myself and my position. Ironically, I turn the camera to myself voluntarily and painfully. It need not be a part of the film. Sometimes, I do take a call and add that. For instance, in *In God's Land*, the circular shots actually are reflective of my inability to understand the world of SEZ and the forces at work.

Notes

1   The Special Economic Zone (SEZ) refers to a geographical area where the economic laws are different from and usually liberal than the rest of the country.
2   Kalpi is a city in Jalaun district in Uttar Pradesh, a Central Indian state.
3   Drass is a hill station in the union territory of Ladakh.
4   Kargil is the joint capital city of Ladakh, a union territory in India.
5   Dal Lake is a lake in Srinagar, also the summer capital of Jammu and Kashmir.
6   Pondicherry is the capital city of Pondicherry, a union territory in South India. Previously, it was a French colony.

Anjali Monteiro | K. P. Jayasankar

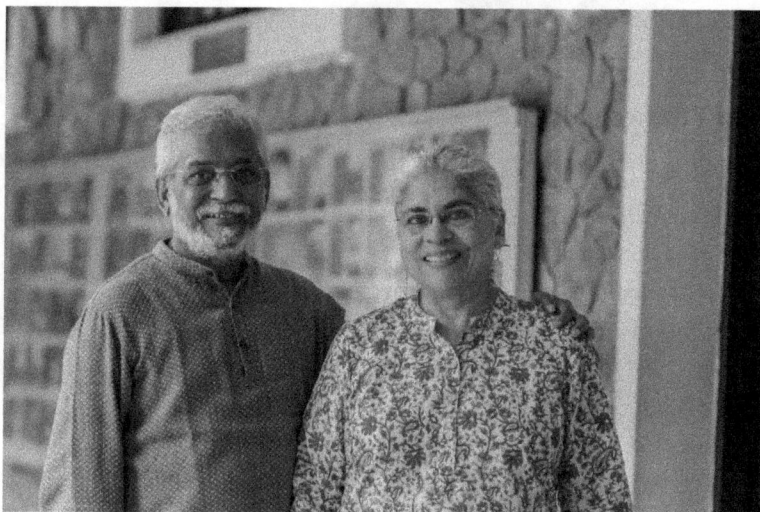

Figure 25 Image Courtesy: Anjali Monteiro | K. P. Jayasankar.

Professors at the School of Media and Cultural Studies (TISS) Mumbai, Anjali Monteiro and K. P. Jayasankar Monteiro are documentary historians, media educationists, filmmakers, and producers based in Mumbai. Besides their involvement in media production and research, they teach courses in documentary and video production at various universities across the world. Using documentary as a medium since 1985, they unearth the subjugated knowledge of the marginalized and represent injustices that plague Indian society. Armed with more than thirty national/international awards, their films deal with fluidity of self and the other, normality and deviance, and the discourses of the local and the global. As such, their films embody a range of perspectives, that is, from the stories and paintings of indigenous people to the poetry of prison inmates. Most significantly, their films constitute alternative meanings and imagine an authentic and secular counter-narrative to outworn religious bigotry and illiberal politics. Some of the major concerns and themes of their films include Bombay riots (*Farooq Versus the State*), traditions of poetry and music (*Do Din ka Mela*), women's writings (*She Write*), and pain and stigma of incarceration (*YCP 1997*). They are also founding members of *Vikalp*, a collective of documentary filmmakers campaigning for freedom of expression. Most recently, they are the authors of *A Fly in the Curry: Independent*

Documentary Film in India (2016), which received a Special Mention in the President's National Awards in the best book on cinema at the National Film Awards.

Selected Filmography

Surshala (2018)
A Delicate Weave (2017)
Farooq Versus the State (2012)
So Heddan So Hoddan (trans. Like Here Like There) (2011)
Do Din ka Mela (trans. A Two Day Fair) (2009)
Our Family (2007)
She Write (2005)
Naata (trans. The Bond) (2003)
YCP 1997 (1997)

Both of you have been involved in making documentary films for more than thirty years as a team. What keeps you motivated as documentary filmmakers? How do you engage with the medium of independent documentary while working within an institutional/academic structure?

We started making documentaries because we felt that it was a medium that offered possibilities for critically exploring our own space and our presuppositions about the world out there. We saw and see it as an art form that allows for an intense engagement with the field as well as with ourselves. Every film is an immersive learning experience that enables us to reach outside ourselves and within ourselves. That some of our films have been selected for festivals or received awards is a bonus. What is more important for us is that the people with whom we have made the film see it as a collaborative project that furthers our collective interests and concerns. It allows us to interact with "subjugated knowledge," as Foucault puts it, local wisdom and little traditions. And also, we enjoy screening our films with various groups as it is an invitation to a dialogue through which we understand how different audiences relate to the work in very different ways. It is always a humbling experience. As far as working within an institutional structure like Tata Institute of Social Sciences (TISS) is concerned, we have been fortunate to have been able to create a space that is relatively open and nurturing. There is often a paucity of resources (which has made us learn and practice multiple roles within the film, from cameraperson, to production manager, to editor, to translator, etc.) but because we have on the whole avoided large sponsored projects and made do with the limited resources available, we feel that we have had more freedom to make the film the way we would like to. Working as a team is a challenging, enjoyable, and enriching process. Like any other team, we have our differences and have had to learn to listen to each other. Over the years, we have been trying to give each other creative space, while at the same time trying to work toward our individual and collective visions of the work at hand.

How did you come to filmmaking? Is documentary making an extension of your academic endeavor?

For both of us, who have academic training in the broad areas of humanities and social sciences, as well as an interest in the arts and activism, it was a pleasant accident when we started making documentary films in the mid-1980s, when VHS (Video Home System) opened up the possibility of making low-cost films. We believe that documentary film offers the possibility of combining many diverse practices, from research to art and from working with communities to advocacy. Our work over the last three decades encompasses documentary production, teaching, and media research. Each of these aspects feeds into the other and allows multiple possibilities for dialogue and critical reflection. In the absence of a formal training in filmmaking, "as self-learning" filmmakers, every film is a challenge and an opportunity to move out of our comfort zones.

Farooq Versus the State *deals with the controversial case of Farooq Mhapkar, one of the key individuals who was wrongly accused in the Hari Masjid case.*[1] *The film revisits the Bombay riots of 1992–3.*[2] *What motivated you to revisit the riot many years after the incident?*

Our experience of living through the turbulent Bombay/Mumbai violence of 1992–3 pushed us to explore how we could handle the themes of identity, secularism, intolerance, and coexistence in times where politics has been increasingly polarized on religious lines. How can we cinematically speak of the politics of hate or resistance to this hate in ways that avoid simplistic polarities and make space for a thoughtful engagement with issues of identity and difference? We have tried to work with this theme, using a range of narrative strategies, from experimental work with found objects (*Identity: The Construction of Selfhood,* 1994), to more narrative-style films that look at peace initiatives (*Naata: The*

Bond, 2003) and little traditions of living with difference (The Kachchh Trilogy: *Do Din ka Mela* 2009, *So Heddan So Hoddan*, 2011, and *A Delicate Weave*, 2017), to working with students to create an online multimedia memorial to the 1992–3 violence in Mumbai mentioned earlier. In all this work, the attempt has been to critically look at the safe secular space from which we speak and to understand that the politics of hate is not just about unfortunate events happening out there but looking at it as a process in which all of us are implicated. In our present times, when Islamophobia and Hindutva are becoming mainstream, it is all the more important to provide counter narratives of various kinds. Ours is a small attempt in this direction, amid a large body of work of many fellow documentary filmmakers.

The Kachchh Trilogy (Do Din ka Mela, So Heddan So Hoddan, *and* A Delicate Weave) *are ethnographic documentaries. Any ethnographic work involves multiple challenges including tension and unequal relationship between the interviewer and the subject, the problem of context and the status of the documentary filmmaker as a foreigner, among others. How do you negotiate these aspects in your film? More importantly, how do you make certain that your films are not voyeuristic?*

In our work, we have often entered worlds that are far removed from ours and engaged with communities within an acute awareness of hierarchies between us and our subjects. An awareness of the politics of representation and of knowledge (how valid knowledge is exclusionary and defined by the dominant social classes) needs to be a part of our practice and also be embedded in the filmic narratives that we produce. We try to take on board "their" view on "our" project in our films and to share the film with them before it is finalized. Though we broadly use ethnographic insights/methods in our work, we do not see ourselves as ethnographers, but more as documentary filmmakers. Our films are shot through with reflexive moments, where the subjects speak to us and express their view of the process of filmmaking and our lifeworld. For instance, in our film *YCP 1997*, Harrison, a poet-prisoner alludes to the prisons we all inhabit. As an answer to a question to us, "Are you free?" he says in the film, that it is a matter of the size—the prisoner occupies a small prison, while we, a larger prison. The film explores the connections between these prisons, trying to make space for the agency of the subjects and their right to negotiate their own representation in the film. As we discuss in *A Fly in the Curry*, "The view from the 'small prison,' the space of the marginalised subjects of the documentary/ ethnographic narrative helps problematise the taken-for-granted codes and conventions of the larger prisons in which we as filmmakers and middle-class audiences are situated" (Jayasankar and Monteiro, 2016).

In *Naata: The Bond*, we chose to insert the strand of our voices more directly, which we felt would move the story beyond a feel-good narrative of the inspiring work being done by our protagonists Bhau Korde and Waqar Khan, as a part of the Dharavi (the largest slum in Asia) *mohalla* committee (neighborhood peace committee). Our stories, which punctuate the film, like a Brechtian alienation effect, use a very different visual register from the rest of the film. In an ironic comment on our middle-class existence, where material possessions are important to our identities, we place commonplace objects of belonging, from toothbrushes to cutlery, within a bare white space. The visual representation of this sanitized space, where we live out our lives, guarding them against messy intrusions from the laboring "others," who live in places like Dharavi, provides a space for critical reflection on our own normal social space.

In our *Kachchh Trilogy*, there are several moments where our subjects discuss the process of filmmaking and the inherent relation of power between us and them. In the film *So Heddan So Hoddan*, where we work with the Fakirani Jatt community and their stories of the medieval Sindhi Sufi poet-saint Shah Abdul Latif Bhitai, we were initially faced with a reluctance from the community to

Still 25 A still from the film *Do Din ka Mela*. Image Courtesy: Anjali Monteiro | K. P. Jayasankar.

allow the recording of women within the film. We understood this as a response to the ways in which the tourism and craft industries have used images of women to promote Kachchh[3] and Kachchhi products, often without their consent. Given this unease, which we were gradually able to overcome, through processes of dialogue and sharing of our material, there were moments when our subjects discussed their feelings about our presence in their lives before the camera, confident that we were not able to understand what they were saying; for instance, the following discussion between Rahimaben and her husband Mustafa took place on our first visit, and we decided to include it within the film:

> Rahima (R): These 4 or 5 people are standing around with the camera that must be worth Rs. 500 thousand. They're shooting the difference between the city and our village? Is it okay to spend so much money?
>
> M: Yes, it's fine.
>
> R: But they're recording and taking it. They may say anything but how do we know what they'll do? We have no way of knowing what they have shot. We will have to go by what they claim. They will make a cassette, a film. People outside will come to know of our traditions, lifestyles, land, and work. If people outside see this, it is alright, isn't it?

There is a sense of "weaving" of filmic elements in your films. How important is form in your films?

We do not believe in a distinction between form and content. The narrative strategies of a particular film emerge out of its context and its relationship with the subjects of the film. We pay a lot of attention to the soundscape and its affective charge, as also to the image, which we often use, nondiegetically. In many cases, the idea is to invite the viewer to the experience of the spaces and life worlds that we engage with in our films. As you rightly point out, we work with the idea of layers that speak to each other, at times colliding with each other, to bring out the complexity of the themes that we document.

What is the future of independent documentary filmmaking in the context of technological advancements, vérité images, and social media networking sites?

The internet and social media have given rise to a plethora of nonfiction genres, from cookery shows and stand-up comedy to political commentary and cat videos. In many ways, the increase in space for nonfiction and the platforms for distribution have expanded the horizon and scope of the idea of documentary. The documentary hence, has to renegotiate its relationship with the "evidentiary" and the "indexical." The growth of digital has made the process of production much easier and accessible to many more people; at the same time, it complicates the relationship of the image with "actuality." The internet allows for the possibility of escaping regimes of control to a limited extent, though the digital divide and difficulties of monetizing and recovering the costs of production still remain under-resolved. In an age where there is a surfeit of images, the documentary film which invites a critical engagement with the image is all the more relevant.

Notes

1 The Hari Masjid case refers to the police firing that happened in a Masjid in suburban Wadala, Mumbai, on January 10, 1993, and which resulted in the killing of seven people.
2 The Bombay riots of 1992–3 refers to the communal riots in Mumbai between December 1992 and January 1993 that resulted in the death of many people.
3 Kachchh is a district in Gujarat, a West Indian state.

Haobam Paban Kumar

Figure 26 Image Credit: Roshan Jose.

An alumnus of Satyajit Ray Film and Television Institute (Kolkata), Haobam Paban Kumar is one of the leading filmmakers from India's northeastern state of Manipur. Before joining the institute, he was assistant to a well-known Manipuri filmmaker, Aribam Syam Sharma.[1] As a documentary filmmaker from a land of insurgency and secessionist movements, his films capture the volatility of Manipur through a realistic style. His early films like *AFSPA 1958* and *A Cry in the Dark* are compelling visual statements in that they record Indian government's excesses and violations of individual rights. As one among the six emerging talents to represent India at the Cannes film festival in 2011, Paban's critically acclaimed documentary, *AFSPA 1958*, offers unique insights into the controversial Armed Forces Special Powers Act (AFSPA), which allows police to shoot on suspicion and to detain anyone without an arrest warrant. Examining wide-ranging issues impinging Manipur, Paban's intense and engaging films address military excess (*AFSPA 1958*), unsustainable development (*Phum Shang*), child rights (*Ruptured Spring*), and HIV/AIDS crisis (*Mr. India*). Although his early documentary films have an urgency of news reportage, they are reflective and nuanced in their critiques of the establishment. Steeped in the aesthetics and politics of Manipur, his films constantly engage the feelings of marginalization and mistrust, dominant ideologies, and political attitudes that shape the northeastern regions of India.

Selected Filmography

Phum Shang (trans. *Floating Life*) (2014)
Ruptured Spring (2012)
Mr. India (2009)
The First Leap (2008)
A Cry in the Dark (2006)
AFSPA 1958 (2005)

How does the local and geopolitical context influence you as a filmmaker?

It is true that growing up in conflict-ridden and insurgency-inflected Manipur had a deep impact on me as a filmmaker. We have grown up hearing stories of conflicts. So, it is quite natural that I made a film like *AFSPA 1958*. There was a general sense of disconnectedness with India during those times. People were against forced incursions of the military and the suspension of basic civil liberties. I have grown up witnessing them. When we went to Delhi or other parts of India, people treated us as if we were not from India. My mother admitted me to a Kendriya Vidyalaya school to learn Hindi so that when we go out of Manipur we could effortlessly get connected to the local public. You need to learn Hindi or come to Delhi to prove that you are an Indian. So, it is quite natural that people from the Northeast feel alienated in India. I had my own politics to tell which won't be so viable in commercial films. In those circumstances, documentary was the right medium. There is a tendency among Indians to homogenize us as someone from the Northeast. It is because of racial prejudice. I always wanted to speak against it. This politics runs through my film irrespective of the format and subtlety of the film.

You grew up during a period of turbulent regional politics and anti-Hindi movements in Manipur. How did you come to filmmaking? Share your early influences that shaped you as a filmmaker.

I was the only child of my parents. Naturally, there was a lot of pressure on me. As a result, I had to pursue my education at the dictates of others. There was also the pressure to get employed and quickly become an earning member of the family. So, I went to Mysore and pursued computer science. By final year, I got fed up with my studies. I realized that my tastes are different. My maternal grandfather, Thiyam Tarun Kumar, was a dance director in Bombay Talkies.[2] He was one of the early people from my family to be associated with films. He worked with Uday Shankar, a known dancer and choreographer. My uncle, Ratan Thiyam, also influenced me. He is known internationally for the kind of spectacular plays which are steeped in traditional mythology and folklore. I have seen how he was respected by others. The kind of respect an artist receives inspired me to choose this field. It is true that I have come to documentary filmmaking not with a political purpose or passion for filmmaking. It was more of an admiration of the work done by my grandfather and uncle.

When I came to filmmaking, documentary was a new medium in Manipur. Although the history of fiction film in Manipur can be traced to the 1970s, documentaries were not so popular then. Only after I joined SRFTI,[3] I started watching documentary films and developed a new sense of the medium. Even now the situation in Manipur hasn't changed much. It was so natural for a first-time filmmaker to start with documentaries in those days. When I told my uncle that I wanted to build a career in filmmaking, he asked me to study in the best institute in the country. He told me that I should do a crash course in cinema to get admission there. After I completed my graduation in 1996, he enrolled me in the Asian Academy of Film and Television in Noida. There I attended a three-month training course on camera. Immediately after completing my training, I started assisting Aribam Syam Sharma, a well-known Manipuri filmmaker for more than five years. By 1999–2000, I had made my first documentary. In 2002, I got admission in SRFTI, where I pursued a postgraduate diploma in direction and screenwriting. That's how I started my filmmaking adventures.

Phum Shang (trans. Floating Life) *is about resistance of a group of fishermen and women who were displaced in the pretext of cleaning. You have deftly used wide-angle shots to capture the land, ecological issues, and its political significance. The film opens with the image of huts in Loktak Lake burning* *down. How did you come to this documentary? And also comment on the women's participation in such a resistance movement.*

I made *Phum Shang* to question the moral authority of the armed forces who audaciously destroy villagers' huts without any orders from the government. I have used images of the amphibian earthmover as a contrasting image to the protesting people there. They are fighting against modernity and brutal state force. I wanted to show the helplessness of the people. You also see the indomitable courage shown by the women there. Irrespective of their helplessness, the courage they show is integral and intrinsic to people here. The unique thing was that they were not ready to leave their land at any cost. That is what I have tried to portray in the film. These people have been living there for a long time. You can't tell them that this place does not belong to you. The burning of the huts occurred in 2011. They were building houses again and again even after the burning of them. It was a forced displacement without any legal backup. The title refers to the situation that they were going through. There is no surety about their life. Their lives were floating just as their houses. They can't claim any right to land because they were floating on the lake. I tried to capture the rhythm of their life: the way they live and catch fish, among other things. Authorities gave a meager compensation for them. Many people left the place. Although their fight was futile since they were not able to defend their place, the indomitable spirit of these people against the military and armed forces is significant. In a sense, they share the repertoire of anger that people feel against the nation and the mainstream culture.

AFSPA 1958 *documents the harsh reality of the Armed Forces Special Powers Act (AFSPA) in Manipur which allows the Indian military to arrest and detain anyone without an arrest warrant. As a filmmaker, how do you engage with human rights violations happening in Manipur as a consequence of such an act?*

The documentary was on the civil disobedience movement in Manipur which happened because of the rape and brutal murder of Ms. Thangjam Manorama Devi, who was picked up from her home in 2004 by the soldiers of the Assam Rifles battalion. The film documents this injustice and brutal murder that provoked waves of protests including the removal of the AFSPA. The film was completed while I was studying in SRFTI (Satyajit Ray Film and Television Institute). My producer narrated the incident. And I quickly understood that it was the first

Still 26 A still from the film *Phum Shang.* Image Courtesy: Haobam Paban Kumar.

time that a lady was killed in police custody in Manipur. This led to massive
protests in Manipur against AFSPA. People demanded the removal of AFSPA.
Women were on the streets. We slowly started documenting these protests. Then
there were no restrictions. We used to go wherever we wanted to shoot the film.
Again, in those days, there were only local cable television networks. Unedited
footage was shown on the TV those times. It was really shocking. I tried to shoot
whatever was possible. I wanted people to watch it and decide for themselves.
Initially, we did not follow any structure or format. But, gradually, I could create
a structure and form. We shot the film for two months. Later, the film was edited
in Kolkata. The extent of protest that happened in 2004 was unprecedented.
Although there were many reported and unreported cases of detention, this was
the incident that shook the state. It was so brutal. And the way women protested
forced even the government to conduct an inquiry into this incident. The whole
state was in havoc and the image of twelve women protesting stark naked in
front of the Kangla Fort,[4] where the Assam Rifles was headquartered, caught
even international attention. I think those images stand even now as symbols of
resistance and protest.

**Mr. India *deals with the resilience of an HIV+ survivor. What forced you to
make this character-oriented film? Where is Khundrakpam Pradip Kumar***

Singh now? Is he still continuing his body building? On a different note, do you follow your characters even after you finish your films? Should a filmmaker follow/engage the subjects of his/her films after the production of films?

The most beautiful thing about documentaries is that you can make many friends. How you connect with your characters really matter in documentary films. I came to know about Pradeep through my editor. I met him and later decided to make a documentary about him. I was waiting for him to win the Mr India title. It was worth waiting. By the time I started shooting, we became very close. There were a few others who were also producing films based on his life. The process of making a documentary was important for me. In that sense it is very difficult to develop a connection with the subject you film. I am still in contact with him. Government has given him a job in the sports department. Documentary is something that teaches you about the importance of connecting with people. It is a very human medium. When I have my rough cut ready, it is my responsibility to show it to them and get their feedback. We are dealing with real people and their lives. It's their story. It is true that you have to switch over to another film after making one. That doesn't mean that you have to completely move away from your early characters.

Unlike fiction films, documentary films are more of an intimate journey into the world of people and subjects. It is almost a necessity to go deep into the issues discussed. At the same time, it is also a medium which journeys into the privacy of the people. How do you maintain the intricate balance between intimacy and distance?

As a documentary filmmaker, it is very difficult to make a film that is distanced from the subject which you depict. Since the film does have a politics to tell, the filmmaker is almost part of it. But such involvement should not make you a voyeur. The approach should be democratic and nonhierarchical. Even the placement of cameras is very important in documentary films. It is extremely important to respect the space of the subjects presented in documentary film. Otherwise, it becomes too exploitative. I am always conscious of this vulnerability of the medium. Before I start rolling the camera, I seek the character's consent. Depending on the type of the film, my approach will change. For example, if you are doing a film like *AFSPA 1958*, you should be a little aggressive. On the other hand, if you are doing a character-oriented film, you should respect people's privacy and space. But it is very important to keep that delicate balance you were referring to.

What is the future of documentary films in India especially in Manipur?

Although you can trace the history of Manipuri films since the 1970s, the contemporary situation of Manipuri cinema is slightly disappointing. I don't see many documentary filmmakers in Manipur. Earlier, I used to do commissioned films and the money thus earned was used for making documentary films. Now I don't do commissioned films. Commissioned films are almost worn out. In the last five years, very few films have been produced from Manipur. The future of films, especially documentary films, is very bleak. Films Division and PSBT (Public Service Broadcasting Trust)[5] have reduced their production. It is very difficult to find producers for documentary films in India. How long can you make films spending your own money? Filmmakers need to sustain. We have television channels for films but not for documentary films. It's a big issue. That doesn't mean that the documentary has no future in Manipur. Documentary films are part of our culture. It's a natural medium for us. I think people will make documentary films because of the situations around them. We can't keep quiet. So, I am very sure that people in Northeast will make more films in future.

Notes

1   Aribam Syam Sharma is an Indian filmmaker from Manipur, a North-Eastern Indian state.
2   Bombay Talkies was a film studio in Mumbai. It was founded by Himanshu Rai and Devika Rani in 1934.
3   Satyajit Ray Film and Television Institute (SRFTI) is a film and television higher educational institution located in Kolkata.
4   The Kangla Fort/the Kangla Palace is an old palace at Imphal in Manipur.
5   Public Service Broadcasting Trust (PSBT) is a nonprofit organization established in partnership with Prasar Bharati (the national public broadcaster) to support the production of independent documentary films in India.

Bilal A. Jan

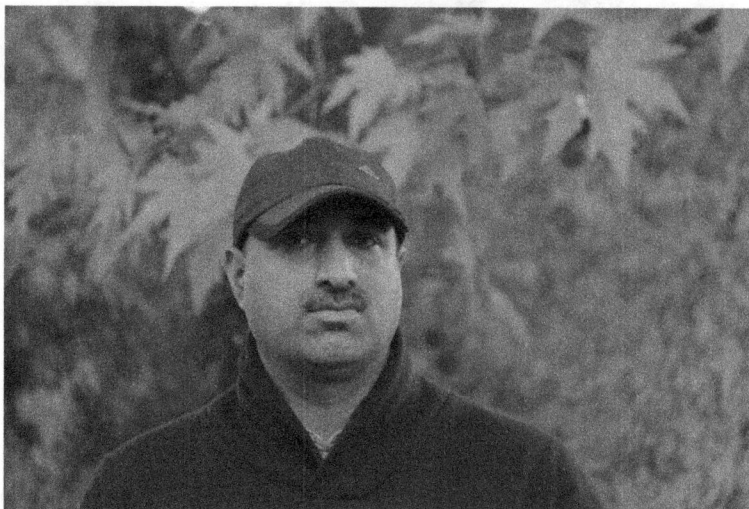

Figure 27 Image Courtesy: Bilal A. Jan.

A native of Kashmir, Bilal A. Jan is a documentary filmmaker whose films encapsulate the experiences of the conflict and combat zones of Kashmir. Rooted in the geopolitics of Kashmir, his films embody the mindscapes of his fellow Kashmiris and the structural violence they encounter. Besides visually transcribing the armed conflicts and territorial disputes in Kashmir, his films also document issues plaguing Kashmiri society such as domestic violence, child labor and dowry violence. Drawing on the multiple aspects of conflicts in Kashmir including the enforced disappearances/militarization (*Ocean of Tears*), domestic violence (*Daughters of Paradise*), and child labor (*The Lost Childhood*), his films offer an insider's perspectives on the national othering and human rights violation of Kashmiris. For instance, his documentary film *The Lost Childhood* is a journey into the agony of young lives in Kashmir who are caught between Indian army and militants. Furthermore, as honest reflections on the politics of the everyday life in Kashmir, Bilal's films are critiques of the establishment and the dominant voices that trivialize Kashmir as a site of terrorism. Again, his *Ocean of Tears* deftly records the impact of conflict on everyday lives of women in the Kashmir Valley. In spite of spirited resistance, it was screened in India and abroad including Aljazeera International Documentary Film Festival, Portuguese International Film Festival, PIBULA Mexico International

Film Festival, among others. Continuing his preoccupation with women and violence's everydayness, Bilal's recent documentary, *Daughters of Kashmir*, delves into the double marginalization suffered by the women of Kashmir both from the patriarchy and from the armed forces.

Selected Filmography

Daughters of Paradise (2018)
Oh! She (2018)
The Poet of Silence (2018)
Ocean of Tears (2012)
The Lost Childhood (2007)

Kashmir is a geopolitical conflict and combat zone. Especially after the 1990s, the situation has worsened. The establishment wants to suppress all the dissenting voices. In that sense, filmmakers as people who show reality to the world are under surveillance. How tough is it to be a filmmaker in Kashmir?

You are right. It is very tough to be a filmmaker in Kashmir if you are critical of the state and the state-sponsored events. Since there is militant occupation and constant surveillance, you are always under scrutiny. Earlier, it was just a joke if someone wants to be a filmmaker in Kashmir. Even now there are no cinema halls in Kashmir. We can't see films here; even the internet is under surveillance and is often cut off. There is no film institute here and the biggest hurdle is how to get trained in film as a craft. Government views the people of Kashmir as potential terrorists/traitors. In fact, there is bare minimum space for the arts here. If you are filming here, your life is at risk. Even with the coming of the internet and other online platforms Kashmiri filmmaker lives in a liminal space. Another threat is Indian censor board. Most films by Kashmiri filmmakers are either banned or refused to issue the Censor Certificate. I think the state is really afraid of the native filmmakers from Kashmir since they visibilize violence and human rights violations that happen here.

What made you a documentary filmmaker? Share your early exposure to film viewing and production.

Frankly speaking, I do not know what exactly prompted me to be a documentary filmmaker. There might be many things. I was born and brought up during the troubled times in Kashmir. Irrespective of the political tensions there, I was interested in whatever cultural activities were available to me then. I used to be part of stage dramas, and radio and TV programs, in whatever possible way. Satyajit Ray winning the first Oscar Award for Lifetime Achievement motivated me to become a filmmaker. Later I started watching his films. Another significant moment is the film appreciation course that I pursued in the Film and Television Institute of India. I am not a formally trained filmmaker. It is my passion for cinema which brought me here. It was very tough for me as a Kashmiri to enter into the world of cinema. We were more easily brought to guns than cameras. I also had a chance to assist Vidhu Vinod Chopra[1] in his film *Mission* Kashmir.[2] Although I was not happy with the narrative of the film, it gave me an opportunity to learn the techniques of cinema. While I was working with Jabbar Patel[3] in his film, he asked me why I can't make my own films. I told him I was from Kashmir. He replied, "Don't you think there are stories? Can't you narrate those stories from your perspective as a Kashmiri?" Those questions provoked me. And that's how I started making films. During this time, I was also fortunate enough to work with Shyam Benegal in his film *Netaji Subhas Chandra Bose: The Forgotten Hero* (2004) as assistant director. In a sense, as a beginner in filmmaking, documentary filmmaking was very close to me in terms of the making style and budget. Moreover, when I watched Anand Patwardhan's *In the Name of God*, I understood how powerful this medium is and felt I could do something with this medium.

Majority of films on/from Kashmir focus on conflicts and combats in the Valley. Although your films reference them, they also delve into the contradictions and discrepancies of Kashmiri society. Your films, in a way, offer insiders' perspective and discuss issues like domestic violence, child labor and dowry violence plaguing the Kashmir Valley. Do you think this is possible because of your insider' status? On a different note, how are your films different from the Bollywood films on Kashmir?

Beyond Kashmir conflict, there are a lot of issues which need to be told in a right perspective. Many subjects were gone under carpet due to the ongoing conflict. Hardly any filmmaker from Kashmir or outside is thinking on such lines. It is tough to be a filmmaker here. Yet I decided to make films on social issues, violence on women, poverty, environmental issues, and human right violations. My film *The Lost Childhood* is on child labor. *Ocean of Tears* was on the violence against women. Regarding the difference between films made by me and filmmakers from outside is quite obvious. Bollywood filmmakers or Indian filmmakers make biased films about Kashmir which are totally impressionistic or sometimes half-truth steeped in the fabrication of things and situations. Majority of the films are totally cliché and made on jingoistic lines. And the reactions and conclusions of such films are most of the time laughable. So, these films rarely represent the politics and ethos of the people of Kashmir. So, it is important for us to make films which offer the other side of the story. I am making films to counter the false narratives built on Kashmir and Kashmir conflict. We need to tell our stories by ourselves which not only represent realities in Kashmir but also film situations that are not biased as well. So, as a filmmaker, I try my level best to do more good movies.

Daughters of Paradise *is about dowry and the ensuing domestic violence that women suffer.* **Ocean of Tears,** *on the other hand, delves into the sufferings of women caused by the violent incursions of the state? Are women at once the definitive victims of domestic and political/state violence?*

In any conflict zone, the worst affected are either children or women. Kashmir is no exception. It was during my research of my first film, *The Lost Childhood*, I found many stories of violence against women. Women are the worst sufferers of the events happening in Kashmir. They undergo domestic violence in terms of dowry and other patriarchal restrictions. As women living in the conflict zone, they are also victims of sexual violence from the Indian army and militants. I came across many brutal cases of rape by the Army here. As a filmmaker, I thought I should bring out both levels of violence that women are going through in Kashmir. They are doubly victimized by soldiers who are supposed to be her protector and by her own family members. I thought I should tell this to the world. And thus was born *Ocean of Tears* and *Daughters of Paradise*.

The Lost Childhood *documents how children lose their serene childhood because of the violence they encounter and suffer every day. Do you have any such personal experience or heard of others in such contexts? Share your vision behind this film.*

It was very shocking for me to make a film on children and the kind of violence they suffer. There are innumerable numbers of exploitation happening in the Kashmir Valley. Many young children are exploited here as child laborers. The law of the land here is unable to stop it. Although child labor is banned in hazardous

Still 27 A still from the film *Daughters of Paradise*. Image Courtesy: Bilal A. Jan.

industries, it winks at the forced labor of children in family and its extended businesses whether in the service sector or in manufacture sector. Since the state is after "terrorists" and Pakistani supporters here, these issues don't catch their attention. I would like to see this as a state-sponsored exploitation since they are either careless or disinterested in ameliorating injustice. I thought I should speak about it in my film. As I was looking for the producer for this film, I met Dr. Nazir Mushtaq, a former Government Medical College pathologist who introduced me to his brother Maqbool, who runs a transport company in Kashmir Valley. He was interested to finance the film because he himself was a victim of child labor. He produced the film with a condition that I should treat the theme in a different way. When we went to shoot the film in Batamaloo area in Kashmir, we were stopped by shopkeepers who were employing children below fourteen in their mechanical and automobile workshops. In fact, some of the automobile shopkeepers manhandled my cameraman, Zefar Iqbal. Irony is that the Labor department of J&K is located in the Batamaloo bus stand. I think the problem of child labor in Kashmir is more of economics. Of course, the political violence of Kashmir has killed thousands of children. But the cause of child labor is more about economics than politics.

Your films are non-status-quoist and consistently interrogate jingoistic expressions of nationalism. Have you ever been intimidated for such a critical stance?

Yes. As a filmmaker, I present things as I see. I present my viewpoints through the characters in the film. I present the "realities" as I see in my place, although I know that there is a subjective element in it. I can only make films as I see the world. The question of objectivity is a big lie in documentary films. How is it possible to be objective in Kashmir when you see your own people are brutally killed and kidnapped? Whatever the establishment is doing there has nothing to do with objectivity and truth. I make films that critique the system and the violence it propagates. Whoever speaks the truth is under surveillance here. While I was making my film *Ocean of Tears*, I was threatened by the authorities for portraying events (human disappearances) happening here. The film took a critical stand against the state and its involvement in these missing cases. There was a serious pressure on me to withdraw the film. I was really afraid in those years. But somehow, I could overcome it. Such threats are so "natural" since I make films in a conflict zone. Although the Censor Board for films in India cleared it, I couldn't screen *Ocean of Tears* in many places. In Kashmir, I was given the permission to screen the film. But on the day of screening the authorities stopped its screening. They didn't give me any reason but said they have reservations about the film. I asked what reservations they have when the film is cleared by the Censor Board of India. They said they can't permit screening. We had to stop its screening and leave the place. The ban was unethical and it was a curtailment of the freedom of expression. As a film, it brings out the administrative, legal, and judicial apathy toward the women of Kashmir who are victims of violence. As a serious critique of the establishment, the film is under an unofficial ban till date. I am not given permission to screen this film in Kashmir till now, although it is available on YouTube. While I was screening the film outside Kashmir, I had many frustrating experiences. The film was prevented from being screened at the Aligarh Muslim University, Uttar Pradesh. My producer also asked me to stop the screening of the film. At VIBGYOR Short and Documentary Film Festival in Kerala,[4] there was opposition from the right-wing forces. The screening was interfered with. Since people and filmmakers supported me to screen the film, I could exhibit the film in Kerala. In India there is a baton charging response to all filmmakers who are critical of the establishment. Our case is extreme. We are seen as potential threats. We know that we are always under scrutiny.

How do you narrate a story you choose? Do you think the way you tell the story is an important part of a documentary film?

I think we need to explore more in terms of the form of the documentary, though content is very important. Both Kashmiris and others had made films on Kashmir. Time has come to explore some nuanced narratives on Kashmiris and Kashmir. It is really tough to make films here now. The whole valley is cut off. Documentary filmmaking has become really tough. The many means and new ways of telling stories of Kashmir is more urgent than ever. Filmmaking in Kashmir has become more sensitive now. We know that we are all tracked and traced. But we need to make films. Form needs to be reworked to reflect and capture what we are going through now. Different styles in filmmaking have come just to echo what is happening around people's lives. Filmmakers will tell about what is happening in Kashmir now through their means.

What draws you to a particular subject? Is it the activist sentiment or the rage at human rights violation that prompts you to make your kind of films?

I am a filmmaker by profession. I love to tell stories. I don't see myself as an activist; but, activism is ingrained as I cannot distance geography and political context from the particular subject of my film. A filmmaker, in a sense, is an intermediate between the art of storytelling and audience. Yes, I have come across many human rights violations in Kashmir. But such violence has happened every day since 1990 till date or may be before. Perhaps this compels and provokes filmmakers like me to work more in the Kashmir Valley.

Notes

1 Vidhu Vinod Chopra is an Indian filmmaker and producer known for films like *1942: A Love Story* (1994) and *Mission Kashmir* (2000).

2 *Mission Kashmir* (2000) is an Indian film directed by Vidhu Vinod Chopra.

3 Jabbar Patel is an acclaimed Indian theater and film director. His major works include *Umbartha* (trans. *The Doorstep*) (1982) and *Dr. Babasaheb Ambedkar* (2000).

4 VIBGYOR Film Festival is an international short and documentary film festival held in Thrissur, Kerala, a South Indian state.

Stanzin Dorjai Gya

Figure 28 Image Courtesy: Stanzin Dorjai Gya.

Born to shepherd-farmer parents and based in Ladakh, Stanzin Dorjai belongs to Gya, a village in the Leh district of Ladakh in India. As the only filmmaker perhaps to seriously address climate change in the Himalayan context, his vision of nature is strikingly original and more relevant to contemporary times. Known for ethnographic and sensitive portrayal of environment and culture, Dorjai's documentaries represent stories unique to the Ladahki region—for instance, if his notable *Jungwa: The Broken Balance* registers the August 2010 flash floods that devastated Leh and Ladakh, then his award-winning *The Shepherdess of the Glaciers* captures the life of his shepherdess sister in the high-altitude Himalayas. His vision of nature is shaped not only by the experiential and empirical realities of the region but also is rooted in the *weltanschauung* of the shepherd community. His oeuvre at once celebrates nature, endorses environmental consciousness, and, at a deeper level, honors the diversity and resilience of the greater Himalayan community.

Selected Filmography[1]

Behind the Mirror (2017)
The Shepherdess of the Glaciers (2016)
Jungwa: The Broken Balance (2012)

Your films are labeled as ethnographic films. How did you realize the potential of ethnographic documentary films?

I did not have much opportunity to watch documentary films during my early years. But when I joined SECMOL[2] (The Students' Educational and Cultural Movement of Ladakh), I could watch a few. It was at SECMOL that I learned more about filmmaking and its possibilities. I never had a formal training in filmmaking. But we had a few filmmakers who frequented Leh for shooting films. There was a filmmaker from Bombay named Lena Tace. There was also another teacher Lars Lidstrom from Sweden. It is from them that I learned how to handle a camera, editing, and every other aspect of filmmaking. The approach was more personal. I wanted to study more filmmaking. I wished to go to Delhi or Mumbai. During that time, I lost my father. It was a bit tough. So I couldn't follow my initial plan. In the meantime, I completed my graduation from the University of Jammu and returned to Ladakh. Everybody wanted me to do some job. But my passion was for filmmaking. My filmmaking friend and teacher, Rahul Ranadive, during this time, guided me to the possibilities of filmmaking. We together made some films too. I wasn't aware of filmmakers like Anand Patwardhan or Rakesh Sharma at that time. When I started filmmaking, I was the kind of person who was after Bollywood films. Although it was entertaining, it left me with so many questions. I found later that Bollywood is a fantasy world. From my experience of watching those films, I felt that it was almost like tasting chocolate. I thought my life was more than tasting chocolate.

We had a great problem in Ladakh because of climate change. But there was no medium to address this. So, I thought visual medium would be an alternative option. So, leaving the candies of popular cinema, I became a documentary filmmaker. I never consciously thought of making films that would be called ethnographic films. I am making films about the world which, I believe, would eventually be called documentary films.

Jungwa: The Broken Balance *registers the August 2010 flash floods that devastated Ladakh. It was later screened at the UN's COP21, Paris Conference (2015). Why do you think climate change needs to be addressed seriously?*

The film was based on a flash flood that distressed Ladakh. Climate change is a reality. Ladakh is in the Himalayas. If climate change is not a reality, how could you even imagine floods in the Himalayas and in Ladakh. When *Jungwa* was made and shown to the people outside Ladakh, they were not even sure where

Ladakh is. When there was a flood, I remember, my first instinct was to take my camera out and shoot the whole thing as it happened. I left my son and wife and started shooting. In our language, *Jungwa* means four elements: air, fire, water, and earth. But those elements are imbalanced now. My intention was to document the floods and its impact. Otherwise, there is a danger that people may forget about it. But it was very difficult to do that as well. Given the delicate geography of the region, it was a bit risky to shoot during floods. Because I was not helping people but filming, many thought I am a photographer having fun. This was emotionally challenging and debilitating. I saw the dead bodies of people and bodies buried in the mud. I kept on shooting, although I felt a bit guilty. Today, people watch my documentary and understand about the things that happened then. *Jungwa* was screened across the world and people came to know about our place and what had happened there. The focus of the film was the flash floods and people's reaction to it. In retrospect, I sometimes feel guilty of leaving my son and my wife to themselves during the flood. Although it was very difficult to shoot, the overall impact of the film was impactful. I could address the issues of climate change convincingly to the people since it was shot from a flood-affected region. Here comes an interesting ethical issue: What should a filmmaker do when one is caught up in a situation like this? Whether you have to stop shooting and help people? Or should you continue shooting the film ignoring the cries of the people? I went for the second. It's a bit tough to take such a call. But my purpose was very clear. I wanted to show the world what we were going through. I want to take the whole world's attention to this climate change which everyone was ignoring. So, I kept on shooting which later resulted in the documentary as you see it today.

The Shepherdess of the Glaciers *is a documentary about your sister. Unlike other documentary films, it is very intense and autobiographical. Share your experience of and motivation behind the making of* The Shepherdess of the Glaciers.

The idea struck me when I was making *Jungwa*. As a part of the screening of the film, I was traveling in France on a train. While I was on the train, I met a few Westerners, and they started a conversation with me. Maybe they felt curious about my appearance. They asked me where I am from and what I do. While explaining to them I felt a strange intuition. I started thinking about my sister and my place. I compared her life to those European women who sat in front of me. Before I finished my journey, I had an idea. When I returned to India, I went to meet my sister in Gya.[3] She was a shepherdess throughout her life. She never went to a school. She felt amazed when I told her that I am planning to make a film about her. I stayed with her in the mountains for a month. It was almost like going back to my childhood days. When I asked her how she could stay all alone in the mountains, she said she never faced loneliness here. She said she is happy with the company of her Pashmina goats and sheep. She said she would often listen to the radio. I really wondered about her knowledge beyond her immediate world. She keeps to herself whatever she hears from the radio. She could even understand Hindi, Urdu, and English words. So the film was about her, her radio, and her life as a shepherdess. It was a sojourn into my memory as well. My sister is one of the few shepherdesses left in our village as the new generation is not much interested in this job. She goes to high-altitude mountains of Leh and Ladakh alone with her sheep and goats. She only carries a radio with her. She easily lives in such a cold place where an experienced mountaineer would require serious training. It took almost three years to complete the film. We followed her daily and shot whatever possible. It was not easy. I think the stay in the mountains made all the difference in the film. Of course, we really had to face challenges. We sometimes shot the film at −36°C when even the batteries do not work. Even charging batteries was a big issue. As a filmmaker, I believe that you should be part of the environment/context that you are filming. That helps you to bring out the best in the film.

Still 28 A still from the film *The Shepherdess of the Glaciers.* Image Courtesy: Stanzin Dorjai Gya.

In **The Shepherdess of the Glaciers,** *there are several shots that focus on radio and how your sister uses it. Sometimes the voice from the radio is used as the background score of the film. Tell us more on the use of radio as a recurring trope.*

Your observation is right. Radio is almost a character in the film. The initial title of the film was *Radio and Shepherdess.* We used to listen to the All India Radio (AIR) channel. Since we were shepherds and moved from place to place, it was easy for us to listen to the radio. Television and the internet facilities are a recent phenomenon here. Earlier, we didn't have electricity. To operate a radio, you need only a few batteries. In those days, radio was also an instrument which connected us to mainland India. But now if we switch on radio, we hear channels from Pakistan. Since we are familiar with Urdu, we listen to those channels too. Radio is almost like my teacher. I have four to five radios.

Filming in inaccessible and harsh weather conditions like Ladakh is challenging and tests one's abilities. Share your filming routine and practices.

It is very difficult to shoot in the mountains. People say that I made films about my family members. Sometimes making films about family members is the most difficult task. Being part of the family, you have to face ethical dilemmas like what you can show and how to shoot your own people and so on. While I was filming my sister, I became a shepherd. Like the way I was in the past. I journeyed 4,500 meters above sea level. There was less oxygen. I had to check my red blood cells. Although I wanted to shoot with all equipment, it was practically impossible. It was too cold. And there was no electricity. I had four to five packs of batteries, and I kept batteries everywhere possible. I could not leave them on the ground. They might not work later. I used to wake up at 2 o'clock in the morning and walk up the hills. I had to carry my heavy equipment. When I would reach there, I wouldn't find my sister. She might have gone to some other valley. During this time, she had around 400 Pashmina goats and sheep. She used to wake up early in the morning when it was too cold (−32°C). From morning through night, she would take care of goats and sheep without having a glass of warm water. She is a strong woman. After experiencing her life, I decided that the film should not merely show the beauty of Ladakh. I wanted to show how people live there. How strong they are irrespective of the conditions in which they live. I wanted to show love, compassion, and the way people live with animals. When I was in the mountains, I used to see snow leopards and wolves.

They were my friends. There weren't many human beings there. If people had seen animals in the documentary, they would have said, "Wow! Snow leopards." In the process, they would forget about my sister's life in the mountains. We wanted our audience to focus on her life. After all, I am primarily a shepherd before I became a documentary filmmaker.

Geographically speaking, Ladakh is hilly and mountainous with less population. Majority of roads and routes are narrow, tortuously hilly, and situated at high altitudes. In such a context, how is cinema as a medium perceived in Ladakh? Share the cinema-going practices and culture at Ladakh.

When I was between six and ten years old, we went to school to learn science and languages. All the art teachers were from Srinagar or Kashmir. So, we had a lot of differences from them. Their language was quite different from us. Mostly, teachers are sent here as a punishment from the mainland Jammu and Kashmir. They don't want to teach here that much. They are worried about why they were sent to this "moon lane." They have a comfortable life in Jammu and Kashmir. But the case is very different in Ladakh. We had a feeling that we were degraded. When we go back home and tell our parents about the lackadaisical attitude of the teachers, they advise us to obey and follow teachers like gods. We thus started disliking our organic food and our traditional dress that we wear because of the teachers. In the last two decades, we have almost lost our culture. Somehow, we are thankful to those filmmakers who come here from India and Europe and make films about Ladakh. With their help, some films are made in Ladakh in our language. Earlier, we had no cinema here. But now people have started watching cinema. Not just Bollywood films but documentary films too. There is a renewed interest in local culture.

What are the challenges in being a filmmaker in a mountainous region such as Ladakh? How are your films received? Comment on the film culture in Ladakh.

Being on the border of China and Pakistan, Ladakh is a sensitive place. Having said that, Ladakh is unlike Kashmir. We are not free as filmmakers ought to be. Since Ladakh is a peaceful place, it is not as difficult as Kashmir. Since Ladakh is a sensitive region, we should take permission from the concerned authorities. When I say I am a documentary filmmaker, people don't take it seriously. People here believe that films mean only Bollywood films. So, when I make films, I make it a point to show them to the people in villages. For instance, when I screened *The Shepherdess in the Glaciers*, people in my village laughed at me and said, "You made a film about your sister." But when I screened in Leh or in other parts of the world, people appreciated it. After receiving many laurels, people now understand and realize the importance of such films. That's a positive change.

Notes

1   Stanzin codirects films with Christiane Mordelet.
2   SECMOL is an alternative school founded in 1988 and based in Ladakh.
3   Gya is a village in the Leh district of Ladakh.

Raja Shabir Khan

Figure 29 Image Courtesy: Raja Shabir Khan.

Raja Shabir Khan is a Kashmir-based independent documentary filmmaker. His documentaries delicately delineate the ideological boundaries of an aspirational Kashmiri caught between the traumatic past and the destructive present as he constantly negotiates the nationalist persuasions, on the one hand, and the separatist moorings, on the other. An alumnus of Satyajit Ray Film and Television Institute (SRFTI), his films deftly portray how the ordinary people are affected by the military conflicts in Kashmir. Subtly critical of the establishment, his films are visual projections of his desire for a peaceful Kashmir. His *Broken, Silence* and *Angels of Troubled Paradise* limns the political in-betweenness of Kashmiris as he showcases the undesirable transformation of paradisiac Kashmir into a conflict zone. His film *Shepherds of Paradise*, which won two National Awards in 2013, studies the nomadic lives of the Gujjar[1] and Bakerwal[2] shepherds of Jammu and Kashmir and specifically deals with the challenges of journeying from the plain land of Jammu to the valley of Kashmir in winter. Cautiously mixing hope with fear, his recent film, *Line of Control*, foregrounds the unending alienation of Kashmiris in their own homeland and its impact on their lives.

Selected Filmography

Line of Control (2018)
Vanishing Glacier (2015)
Shepherds of Paradise (2013)
Angels of Troubled Paradise (2011)
Broken, Silence (2006)

Although Kashmir has been a constant presence in popular cultures, there is very less production/reception of both documentary and feature films in Kashmir. How is cinema as a medium received in an overall cultural space in Kashmir?

Cinema was doing good business before the start of militancy in Kashmir in the 1990s. After the start of the armed freedom struggle, cinema was banned. All the cinema theaters in Kashmir are in ruins now. Some of them are occupied by the security forces and some are even converted into interrogation centers. Nowadays, some artists are trying to introduce films to Kashmir in the way of organizing film festivals and other such events in conference halls or in auditoriums. But there is no dedicated full-time cinema hall in Kashmir.

Is there any difference between films made by the native filmmakers like you and filmmakers from the outside?

I think there is a lot of difference, and it is true for any part of the world. Natives always know the nuances of the place and its people. Unfortunately, a few filmmakers who visit Kashmir and stay here for a few days claim that they know everything about Kashmir. Imagining and treating Kashmir based on reading books and newspapers is entirely different from what you experience while living in a particular place. I made my first documentary (*Angels of Troubled Paradise*) about a kid collecting smoke shells and selling them to a scrap dealer. It isn't just another documentary about the conflict in Kashmir but the way the conflict is taking a toll on the lives of people especially on children. Since documentary filmmaking is an intimate act, it demands more association with people and places.

Angels of Troubled Paradise *is your first documentary. Adil, the protagonist in the film, is a child who lives in fear. The film implies that the very growing up in Kashmir is fraught with anxiety and stress. Is this documentary of any personal significance to you?*

Adil represents almost every child in Kashmir. Not that every kid in Kashmir goes shell collecting, but the trauma and uncertainty applies to every child in Kashmir. Although there are not many autobiographical references in the film, the fact is that both of us grew up in conflict-intense Kashmir and have witnessed violence and bloodshed. The big difference between Adil's generation and my generation is that children of Adil's generation are not as afraid of the warlike situation in Kashmir as they have been witnessing it all through their life. While it was different for us. We witnessed the presence of the military suddenly in our lives. As kids, it was very hard for us in the beginning. I have grown up in Kashmir while there were killings and protests every day. Everyone was terrified by the police and military. When I heard about Adil collecting smoke shells while the police were busy chasing the protesters, I felt intimidated to ask this question to Adil. Because I had many traumatic experiences in my life. I haven't talked about it to anybody so far. It was around 1995 and I was at the intermediate level in a school. As I was returning from school, I was attacked by an ex-militant (*Ikhwanis/naabedh*) who worked for the army and the establishment. He showed me a gun and took me to a strange place and molested me. I never discussed this event with my parents. I lied to them that he took my money away. The event still haunts me. There are many such repressed stories among the people of Kashmir. Such memories haunt us often. It is really an intimidating experience for every Kashmiri to be part of this world.

Your film Broken, Silence *is an intensely personal narrative in terms of your own situation. How does the film deal with themes such as belonging and resistance? And how did the state treat you and your family?*

I am a Kashmiri born and brought up here. So is my family. My father was a government officer. But they imprisoned my father assuming that we are traitors and that we have allegiance to Pakistan. He was a civil servant who served India for a long time. When he went to Delhi, he was arrested by the police. Later he was accused of being an ISI (Inter-Services Intelligence, an intelligence agency of Pakistan) agent and was put in jail for three months. The most ridiculous charge was that he was a Pakistani citizen and an anti-national. It took almost two years in court of law to prove our innocence. Being the eldest son in the family, I had to go to the court and save my father. Further, the fact that you are a Muslim in Kashmir also puts you in a liminal space. Nobody trusts us. You are under constant suspicion. Every minute of my life I am supposed to declare

Still 29 A still from the film *Line of Control*. Image Courtesy: Raja Shabir Khan.

my allegiance to the state. Even if I do, they don't believe me. I think we have suffered enough, and the state has also realized that we were punished for none of our faults. It was a blunder by the state labeling a central government gazette officer as a Pakistani citizen. If this is our situation, you can imagine what will happen to the protesters and people here.

As a Kashmiri filmmaker, how do you see the conflicts in Kashmir? Where does your sympathy lie?

As an individual who was brought up in the most troubled times of Kashmir, I have my political stand. When I was young, my sentiments were with the militants. I had a feeling for them. I think it's quite natural given the fact that I had witnessed militant struggles in Kashmir. Militants at times suspect and treat us as Indian agents. As an Indian, I do feel that I belong to India but the establishment doesn't trust me. Since I am a Kashmiri, they see me as an ISI agent. I was denied a passport many times, and it took several years to get it. Even if I have a passport, I need to declare my allegiance to the state all the time. Imagine what you would feel in these circumstances! The Defense Ministry has denied permission to shoot documentaries in Kashmir. On the other hand, non-Kashmiri filmmakers from Mumbai are given unconditional permission. As a Kashmiri, Pakistan sees me as an agent of RAW (Research and Analysis Wing) and IB (Intelligence Bureau). As I had to shoot my new film, *Line of Control*, in a village close to Pakistan, I had to apply for a Pakistan visa. They gave me only a tourist visa. When I went to the village there, an officer questioned me. He was very rude and accused me that I am an IB agent. I had to stop the shooting of the film. Being a Kashmiri, this is the experience I face. We belong to nowhere. My sentiments are for freedom and peace. I am a Kashmiri. And I want freedom. I am neither with Pakistan nor with India or militants. All I need is freedom.

Although there is a thematic similarity in your films such as* Broken, Silence, Angels of Troubled Paradise, *and* Shepherds of Paradise, *the approach and form of these films are different. Could you comment on the medium of documentary and affordances of form in these films? How important is form in your documentary films?

Although my training was primarily in fiction films, I am a documentary filmmaker. When it comes to documentary filmmaking, I am always curious to know the following: Can we teach documentary filmmaking and how do we learn the art of documentary filmmaking? What I feel is that you cannot teach the art of documentary filmmaking to someone. It is more of a personal adventure into a world of uncertainty. If you look at the background of documentary filmmakers, how many of them are trained in some institutes/universities? Most of the documentaries are either journeys of the filmmaker into the inner world of his/her own or negotiation with the outer selves. My documentary films are in that sense product of my older selves still caught in the world of memory. Being in Kashmir, it is so common for you to make a documentary on the conflicts in Kashmir or the scenic beauty of Kashmir. That is what the popular Bollywood films have done. They have treated Kashmir either as a beauty spot or as a place of terrorism or conflict. As a Kashmiri, I have experienced and lived my life here. Kashmir for me is beyond these binaries. So my approach is more personal. And I feel I should approach Kashmir differently.

I make documentaries about the subjects which I personally feel closer to me. I made my first documentary, *Angels of Troubled Paradise*, about a kid collecting smoke shells and selling them to a scrap dealer. It wasn't just another documentary about the conflict in Kashmir, but the way the conflict is taking a toll on the lives of people especially on children. Although the difference between the filmmaker and the character in the film is differentiated, the film is also a journey into myself. In that sense, form is very significant in this film. The intention was to capture the contrast between the beauty of being in Kashmir and the struggle of being in a conflict zone. If that experience is filmed from the point of view of a child, I thought the impact would be different.

My second documentary, *Shepherds of Paradise*, is very close to my heart. I have been watching these nomadic shepherds since my childhood and always wondered where they come from and where they go. That's why I followed them. Obviously, you don't find any politics in the text. But their life is metaphoric of every Kashmiris' life. Life is a fight for them. They live in the extreme climate. I think there are many similarities between these shepherds and people who live in the Valley. They do fight for their existence. Especially in the context of the recent political developments in Kashmir, the film has become all the more relevant.

There is a crisis for documentary filmmakers in the kind of documentary films they make. Since documentary films are immediate records of the events and situations of a place, there is a chance that these films will look outdated. Although it does have an archival value, the relevance of such documentary films will be for limited audiences like researchers or academicians. But fiction films easily counter the materiality of their context. So, I think it is extremely important to experiment with the form in a documentary. Such approaches will redeem the film from being obsolete or outdated. That doesn't mean that form is everything in documentaries. I think filmmakers and critics should go beyond the conventional binary of form and content while making a film and analyzing a film. For me, it is very tough to draw an exact line of difference between them. I don't follow any particular rule or method while telling a story in documentaries. The subject itself guides me how to narrate a story. I think that is more organic. It is the freedom that only documentary filmmakers enjoy. It is very difficult for such an approach in fiction films. As long as one is honest to the story and the subject, every form or method is justified.

Notes

1   Gujjar is an ethnic pastoral community based in the northwestern region of the Indian subcontinent.
2   Bakarwals/Bakerwals (part of ethnic Gujjars) are mostly a Muslim nomadic tribe based in larger parts of Northern Indian and the Himalayan regions.

Mukul Haloi

Figure 30 Image Courtesy: Mukul Haloi.

Mukul Haloi, an alumnus of Film and Television Institute of India (FTII), is an independent documentary filmmaker from Assam, a northeastern Indian state. His maiden feature-length documentary, *Tales from Our Childhood*, journeys to the years of insurgency in the 1990s Assam. Produced by the School of Media and Cultural Studies at the Tata Institute of Social Sciences in Mumbai and refracted through memories of Haloi's friends and relatives, *Tales from Our Childhood* reconstructs political tension between the Indian army and the ULFA[1] (United Liberation Front of Assam). Mixing personal and political, Haloi's impressionistic films (as opposed to reportage) cogently capture the emotions and psychological states of living in insurgency-inflected and conflict-dominated Assam of the 1990s. Besides documentary films, he has also directed *Days of Autumn* and *Ghormua* (trans. *A Letter to Home*). Known for his nonlinear multiple narratives and an overwhelming sense of bleakness and loss, his films offer new idioms for the visual arts and fresh insights into lives of people in Assam. He was one of the seven Indians who represented the Berlinale Talents 2020 edition.

Selected Filmography

Loralir Sadhukatha (trans. Tales from Our Childhood) (2018)

Share your early influences and exposure to film viewing that shaped you as a filmmaker.

Tales from Our Childhood is my first and only documentary film till now. When I trace the making of this film, I realize that I had been imagining the film even before I joined a film school or even getting introduced to the basics of filmmaking. I was exposed to a handful of world films, among which there were only a few documentaries, during my graduate studies at the University of Delhi. Among those, some were films made of archival materials or newsreel, some propaganda films, and some talking heads. Those films gave me an impression of accessibility to the medium of filmmaking. At the same time, I was discussing with my friends about the possibility of making a film about Assam in the 1990s. All of them shared their experiences. Despite my naivety, I was sure that I would make this film someday and it will be a nonfiction. Maybe it was because of my infantile impression that nonfiction speaks more truth. Fiction did too, but maybe in less believable ways. When my friends narrated their stories of horror, they used to tremble, remain silent, or sigh. And I felt that I wanted to record it as it is. In such contexts, nonfiction would do better. Said differently, my introduction to documentaries was not an accident.

Interestingly and surprisingly, my proposal for the documentary film was awarded a grant by the School of Media and Cultural Studies, TISS, Mumbai. Otherwise, the film would have taken much longer to be made. The learning at the Film and Television Institute of India did help me to understand the multiple possibilities of nonfiction practice. We were initiated into a whole lot of different kinds of nonfictions, from early classics to new experiments of this decade. I remember, in the very first days at the Institute, we were shown Joris Ivens,[2] Agnes Varda,[3] and Dziga Vertov.[4] It was amazing to see different modes of exploration in those films which I hadn't come across before. Gradually, my amazement progressed to an engagement with these films in terms of form and its historical milieu.

It was literature which preceded my interest in cinema. The very first film I saw in 2004 was an Assamese film, played in a tiny black-and-white television, which ran on rechargeable batteries. I saw only six films till I came to Delhi for higher studies in 2008. In fact, it was the study and practice of literature during my childhood and teenage days that led to visual medium such as cinema. During the early decades of the new millennium, poetry as a practice was booming in Assam. Mridul Haloi, my elder brother, who was later awarded *Yuva Puraskar* by *Sahitya* Akademi,[5] used to write and publish poems in newspapers. In a sense, there was a cohort. Poets from different corners of the state used to gather at our house and various poetry summits were held in my district, Nalbari. Inspired by their conversations and camaraderie, I started writing and publishing prose, mainly essays. While answering your question, I feel I was always closer to nonfiction.

Tales from Our Childhood *is a journey into the past that was sandwiched between insurgency and the Indian army. The film is impressionistic and speaks more about a collective self. Do you think your identity as a filmmaker has got to do with the time of conflicts in Assam in the 1990s?*

Tales from Our Childhood is at once an impression of a collective self and an impression of a generation who grew up through the 1990s. It is not just about me growing up at that time but thousands of others like me who had seen the movement and the violence from a close proximity. There is a segment in the film where I read out from Sudakshana's diary. She wrote in her diary about how everyday while returning from school she had to confront either the members of ULFA or the army. She narrated to me an incident (which does not find a place in the film) about how she was on her way to home on her bicycle. The road was through a forest. She was stopped by the army men, and they made her walk along with them. Two days later, the ULFA boys of the neighborhood told her, "Sister, that day it was you who saved the army men. We were all ready for an ambush. We couldn't fire because you were walking with them." In essence, Sudakshana was used as a human shield. So, the title speaks of these impressions which are more or less similar to any traumatic experience.

In the film, I'm as much a teenager growing up during that time and a filmmaker making it now. At certain points in my life, I'm looking at these events from a distance to get a clear view of them. At times, I am part of the narrative as Shakya, Nilim, or my mother. Then where do I place my subjectivity? And what is my ideology? The making of the film has been a journey for me in terms of rethinking concepts such as self-determination, nationalism, nation-state, autonomy of ethnic groups, power structure of state, and so on. If you ask me whether I support ULFA or not, I can't answer a straight yes or no. And it is mostly the same for many people who have personalized understanding of the movement. I had written about the journey of the Assamese society in my proposal titled "Hope to Disillusionment." The short fiction I made after *Tales from Our Childhood* is also based on the same premise. The stories of death and loss do play a role in that film as well. The project I'm working on now is again another impressionistic portrayal. It is about poems about human conflict in a politically charged everyday life.

Part of the atmosphere in your short fiction films or in **Tales from Our Childhood** *is constituted through sound. Conventional wisdom treats film as a medium of images and sound as subsidiary to image. What are the purposes and importance of sound in your film? And what is your take on sound source in relation to image?*

Sound is the "unseen" in a film. I feel it is the most sensorial element in a film. Sound can widen, elongate, or compress an image. It expands the image beyond its limitation of existence on a screen. It gives the much-needed "body" or the "flight" to an image. But that's not just it. For me, sound creates the cosmos of a narrative, of an image or of a scene. Like visuals, sound also initiates an event. And every hearing concretizes the story of that event.

My short fiction movies are heavily dependent on sound because I had to create a landscape of Assam in Maharashtra. Both of my short films, *Days of Autumn* and *A Letter to Home*, were shot in Pune.[6] *Days of Autumn* was completely shot inside the FTII studio. *A Letter to Home* was partially set in the outer regions of Maharashtra which we found to be similar to Assamese landscape. So, how do we create that feeling of atmosphere? Or the life of a space? Or make it authentic? Sound did that job. *Days of Autumn* was set in post-summer. The light was created to give a feeling of elongated days, of humidity and a warm topography. For me, these create a landscape, an atmosphere, and a climate. Even if we don't see the images, these soundscapes do give us a sense of a whole. Yes, sound completes the "whole" in a film. It completes the universe which images try to create. So, it is not about functionality, neither is it about being subsidiary to images. Image and sound are two halves in the process of making a whole.

In *Tales from Our Childhood* too, I kept these thoughts in mind. That is, to knit a world through sounds. The ecology was very important as a setting or

Still 30 A still from the film *Tales from Our Childhood*. Image Courtesy: Mukul Haloi.

as a physical space which contained the events. In the film, sound played the role of a "container." It had to create a sense of a "whole" life. Sounds which consist of sounds of nature such as crickets, frogs, birds, thunder, rain, wind, or other sounds such as spoken words and music created that much-needed space. Sound is a container of events but, at some point, an event in itself.

Before **Tales from Our Childhood,** *you made a few fictional short films. Then you segued to the world of documentaries? Do you believe in the traditional divide between fact and fiction?*

I feel it is not such a watertight demarcation. Filmmakers nowadays use methods of fiction in nonfiction and vice versa. Is there any very specific set of rules that can only be used in nonfiction but not in fiction? I think there is none. My learning at FTII is well divided (though not equally) between fiction and nonfiction. We were practicing nonfiction by making small observational documentaries and through participating in different workshops/talk shows in FTII. It was not a shift from fiction to nonfiction; rather, both were going hand in hand. Particularly about this film, the force was not sudden but a continuous urge to tell the stories of growing up in Assam. There is a lot of literature in Assamese[7] and a few in English about insurgency. But there are almost no films which document or present the collective memory of that period in Assam. For me, the process of making a film was also a process of reengaging with the debates of Assamese sub-nationalism and regional aspirations versus the Indian state.

Tales from Our Childhood *experiments with form to express the personal impressions of a politically charged context. Why was that important to you? And what did you get out of them?*

The narration emerged in a later phase in the process of making this film. I shot extensively across Assam for almost six months to one and a half years. I interviewed families of ULFA members, a filmmaker who made pro-ULFA films, the ULFA leaders who were engaged in peace talks with the center (Government of India) and many youngsters who had lived through that time. The content which got accumulated through this process was huge and there could have been at least five different narratives made out of it. And then there were facts and figures too.

After I edited three different versions, I realized this film can't just be a general representation of events or a specific period of history. It had to be a personalized experience of history, which was the core idea in the whole process of making this film. After consulting my mentors and a few friends, I could recapture the pulse of the film which seemed little lost in the presence of vast materials. I went back to the proposal of the film which helped me to realign my perspective. The first notes I wrote about the film was about an incident in 2011. In 2011, ULFA's many top leaders were released from jail after they were captured in different parts of South-East Asia. One of my friends wrote a very personal essay in a newspaper describing how he along with others went to greet them at the Guwahati Sessions Court[8] and how at their first sight his imagination of a "rebel" changed forever. That was an emotionally charged personal note. But there was a truth in it, a collective truth about the rise and fall of Assam's imagination of the ULFA rebels.

More than the film summing up a specific historical period of Assam, it was about "our" collective memory of growing up in Assam. By "our," I mean, people of my age group. The growing up could've been not unique unless the atmosphere wasn't infused with the political turbulence of the time. That's how and why the personal impressions take the prime seat in the film, often directing the course of the narrative itself. Also, it would have been a misadventure to claim to make a film about ULFA's period of existence in Assam. There are hundreds of narratives through which you can deal with it. It is a complex cosmos and one can't summarize it in one single work. What one can present is an impression of that time through a personalized view or intimate eye.

Also, how do you recollect a past? What are the methods of it? Most importantly, how does one bring that into a film? One important method could be personal recollection in terms of dialogue or interview. Another could be archival materials such as news or photographs and so on. But can they alone create that atmosphere? They may create a believable context but can't touch upon the innermost feelings of the characters involved in a narrative. So, I attempted the film like a personal diary or a travelogue. The whole filming process was a journey from one corner to the other corner of the state. As a viewer, you may experience how the physical journey in the sense of travel is also playing a role in the film, particularly in the way it transfers one space and narrative to the next. The whole act of making the film was also a hectic personal exploration. It helped us to revisit the ideas we had of nationalism, self-determination, and so on. It was also a mourning or a lament for the lives lost in thirty years of the struggle. I feel all of these elements actually constitute the personalized form and impressionistic nature of the film.

Notes

1   United Liberation Front of Assam (ULFA) is a revolutionary militant group that operates for an independent Assam.

2   Joris Ivens was a Dutch documentary filmmaker known for *How Yukong Moved the Mountains* (1976) and *A Tale of the Wind* (1988).

3   Agnes Varda was a French filmmaker known for *Vagabond* (1985) and *The Gleaners and I* (2000).

4   Dziga Vertov was a Russian filmmaker known for his documentary film *Man with a Movie Camera* (1929).

5   Sahitya Akademi is an organization that works for the promotion of literature in Indian languages.

6   Pune is a city in the Indian state of Maharashtra.

7   Assamese is an Indian language spoken in the Indian state of Assam.

8   Guwahati Sessions Court refers to the highest criminal court in Guwahati, the capital city of the state of Assam.

Bibliography

Barucha, Rustom. "Dismantling Men: Crisis of Male Identity in *Father, Son and Holy War*," *Third Text* 9, no. 33 (1995): 3–16.

Basu, Kasturi and Dwaipayan Banerjee, ed. *Towards a People's Cinema: Independent Documentary and Its Audience in India*. Gurgaon: Three Essays Collective, 2018.

Battaglia, Giulia. *Documentary Film in India: An Anthropological History*. New York: Routledge, 2018.

Chadha, A. "Nation and Narration," Art *India: The Art News Magazine of India*, 18, no. 3 (2014): 42–4.

Chakravarti, U. "Autobiography of a Cinephile or the Accidental Birth of a Filmmaker," in K. Basu and D. Banerjee (eds.), *Towards a People's Cinema: Independent Documentary and Its Audience in India*, 61–90. Gurgaon: Three Essays Collective, 2018.

Chatterji, Shoma A. *Filming Reality: The Independent Documentary Movement in India*. New Delhi: Sage, 2015.

Deprez, Camille. "A Space in Between: The Legacy of the Activist Documentary Film in India," in Camille Deprez and Judith Pernin (eds.), *Post-1990 Documentary: Reconfiguring Independence*, 52–67. Edinburgh: Edinburgh University Press, 2015.

Deprez, Camille. "The Documentary Film in India (1948–1975): Independence and the Challenges of National Integration," *Studies in Documentary Film* 11, no. 1 (2017): 64–80.

Fischer, J. "Oppression: Indian Independent Political Documentaries and the Ongoing Struggle for Viewership," *The Columbia Undergraduate Journal of South Asian Studies* 1, no. 1 (2009): 41–53.

Gadihoke, Sabeena. "Secrets and Inner Voices: The Self and Subjectivity in Contemporary Indian Documentary," in Alisa Lebow (ed.), *The Cinema of Me: The Self and Subjectivity in First Person Documentary*, 144–57. New York: Columbia University Press, 2012.

Gangar, A. "A Dreary Desert of Documentaries," in O. Chanana (ed.), *Docu-Scene India*, 35–7. Bombay: Indian Documentary Producers' Association, 1987.

Hughes, Stephen Putnam. "When Film Came to Madras," *Bioscope: South Asian Screen Studies* 1, no. 2 (2010): 147–68.

Jayasankar, K. P. and Anjali Monteiro. *A Fly in the Curry: Independent Documentary Film in India*. New Delhi: Sage Publications, 2016.

Kak, S. "Every Picture has a History," in K. Basu and D. Banerjee (eds.), *Towards a People's Cinema: Independent Documentary and Its Audience in India*, 15–34. Gurgaon: Three Essays Collective, 2018.

Kapur, Geeta. "A Cultural Conjuncture in India: Art into Documentary," in Okwui Enwezor, Nancy Condee, and Terry Smith (eds.), *Antinomies of Art and Culture: Modernity, Postmodernity, Contemporaneity*, 30–59. Durham, NC: Duke University Press, 2008.

Kapur, Jyotsna. "Love in the Midst of Fascism: Gender and Sexuality in the Contemporary Indian Documentary," *Visual Anthropology* 19, no. 3–4 (2006): 335–46.

Karlekar, Tilottama. "Can There Be Another Vikalp? Documentary Film, Censorship Histories, and Film Festival Publics in India," *South Asian History and Culture* 10, no. 4 (2019): 422–42.

Kaushik, Ritika. "'Sun in the Belly': Film Practice at Films Division of India 1965–1975," *BioScope: South Asian Screen Studies* 8, no. 1 (2017): 103–23.

Kishore, Shweta. *Indian Documentary Film and Filmmakers: Independence in Practice.* Edinburgh: Edinburgh University Press, 2018.

Kramer, Max. "Filming Kashmir: Emerging Documentary Practices," in Nadja-Christina Schneider and Carola Richter (eds.), *New Media Configurations and Socio-Cultural Dynamics in Asia and the Arab World*, 345–68. Baden-Baden: Nomos, 2015.

Lal, Vinay. "Travails of the Nation: Some Notes on Indian Documentaries," *Third Text* 19, no. 2 (2005): 175–85.

Majumdar, Rochona. "Debating Radical Cinema: A History of the Film Society Movement in India," *Modern Asian Studies* 46, no. 3 (2012): 731–67.

Mohan, J. *Sukhdev Filmmaker: A Documentary Montage.* Pune: National Film Archive of India, 1984.

Nair, P. K. "A National Cinema Takes Root in a Colonial Regime: Early Cinema in India," in Nick Deocampo (ed.), *Early Cinema in Asia*, 207–20. Bloomington: Indiana University Press, 2017.

Narwekar, Sanjit. *Films Division and the Indian Documentary.* New Delhi: Publications Divisions, Ministry of Information and Broadcasting, Government of India, 1992.

Nichols, Bill. *Introduction to Documentary*, 2nd ed. Bloomington: Indiana University Press, 2010.

Ray, Bibekananda. *Conscience of the Race: India's Offbeat Cinema.* Delhi: Publications Division, Ministry of Information and Broadcasting, Government of India, 2005.

Roy, Srirupa. "Moving Pictures: The Films Division of India and the Visual Practices of the Nation State," in Srirupa Roy (ed.), *Beyond Belief: India and the Politics of Postcolonial Nationalism*, 32–65. Durham and London: Duke University Press, 2007.

Sen, Gargi, and Supriyo Sen. "Indian Documentaries Today: Changing Field, Scope and the Practice of Documentary," in Jane H. C. Yu (ed.), *Asian Documentary Today*, 76–107. Busan: Busan International Film Festival, 2012.

Sharma, Aparna. *Documentary Films in India: Critical Aesthetics at Work.* UK: Palgrave Macmillan, 2015.

Sharma, Aparna. "Documentary as Witness; Documentary as Counter-Narrative: The Cinema of Sanjay Kak," in Ashvin Immanuel Devasundaram (ed.), *Indian Cinema Beyond Bollywood: The New Independent Cinema Revolution*, 117–37. New York: Routledge, 2018.

Sharma, B. D. "From the Raj to the Emergency: A Brief History of the 'Official' Documentary in India," in K. Basu and D. Banerjee (eds.), *Towards a People's Cinema: Independent Documentary and Its Audience in India*, 35–59. Gurgaon: Three Essays Collective, 2018.

Sharma, S. "Reflections on 'The Political' in Indian Documentary," *Marg: A Magazine of the Arts*, September–December 2018: 72–7.

Sutoris, Peter. *Visions of Development: Films Division of India and the Imagination of Progress, 1948–75*. New Delhi: Oxford University Press, 2016.

Sinha, Madhumeeta. "Witness to Violence: Documentary Cinema and the Women's Movement in India," *Indian Journal of Gender Studies* 17, no. 3 (2010): 365–73.

Vasudevan, R. "An Imperfect Public: Cinema and Citizenship in the 'Third World'," *Sarai Reader 01: The Public Domain*, 55–67. Delhi: Sarai, 2001.

Vohra, Paromita. "Dotting the I: The Politics of Self-less-ness in Indian Documentary Practice," *South Asian Popular Culture* 9, no. 1 (2011): 43–53.

Waugh, T. "Why Documentary Filmmakers Keep Trying to Change the World, or Why People Changing the World Keep Making Documentaries," in T. Waugh (ed.), *"Show Us Life": Toward a History and Aesthetic of the Committed Documentary*, xi–xxvii. Metuchen, NJ and London: Scarecrow Press, 1984.

Waugh, T. *The Right to Play Oneself: Looking Back on Documentary Film*. Minneapolis: University of Minnesota Press, 2011.

Wolf, Nicole. "Foundations, Movements and Dissonant Images: Documentary Film and Its Ambivalent Relations to the Nation State," in K. Moti Gokulsing and Wimal Dissanayake (eds.), *Routledge Handbook of Indian Cinemas*, 360–74. Oxon: Routledge, 2013.

Index